DEVELOPMENT AND PLANNING LAW

DEVELOPMENT AND PLANNING LAW

by

BARRY DENYER-GREEN, LL.M., Ph.D., F.R.I.C.S.

of Middle Temple, Barrister
Chartered Surveyor
Reader in Property Law in the School of Law,
Kingston Polytechnic

1987

THE ESTATES GAZETTE LIMITED
151 WARDOUR STREET, LONDON W1V 4BN

First published 1982
2nd edition 1987

ISBN 0 7282 0113 5

© Barry Denyer-Green, 1982, 1987

Printed in Great Britain at The Bath Press, Avon

CONTENTS

	Page
Preface	xi
Table of Cases	xiii
Table of Statutes	xxv
Table of Orders, Regulations and other Statutory Instruments	xxxvii
Table of Circulars	xxxix

Chapter 1   Introduction   1

PART I

THE SCOPE OF DEVELOPMENT CONTROL

Chapter 2   **Development Control and the Carrying Out of Operations**   7
            Introduction   7
            Operations excluded from development control   8
            Building operations   9
            Engineering and mining operations   10
            Other operations   11
            Demolition   12

Chapter 3   **Development Control and Change of Use**   15
            Introduction   15
            Uses excluded from development control   15
            Use Classes Order   17
            Two doubtful cases:
            The division of dwelling-houses, and tipping operations   19
            Meaning of material change of use   20
            Uses that commenced before 1964   32
            Established use certificates   33
            Change of use not requiring planning permission   35

v

Chapter 4   **Permitted Development**   37
             Introduction   37
             Classes of permitted development   38
             Article 4 Directions   46
             Permitted development and compensation   46
             Special development orders   47
             Simplified Planning Zones   47

PART II

THE DECISION-MAKING PROCESS

Chapter 5   **Planning Authorities**   51
             Introduction   51
             The distribution of functions between local
                 planning authorities   52
             The role of the Secretary of State   55
             Delegation to committees and officers   56
             Negligence   57

Chapter 6   **Development Plans**   59
             Introduction   59
             Development Plans—old type   60
             Structure Plans   60
             Local Plans   63
             Unitary Plans   65
             The relationship and legal consequences of
                 development plans   66

Chapter 7   **The Planning Application**   69
             Introduction   69
             The form of the application   69
             Fees   70
             Application for outline planning permission   73
             Notices to Owners and Tenants   75
             Publicity for applications   76
             Development affecting Conservation Areas
                 and Listed Buildings   78
             Development not in accordance with the
                 Development plan   78

Chapter 8   **How the Local Planning Authority determine
             a Planning Application**   81
             Introduction   81

Consultations with other bodies 82
Power of a local highway authority to issue
directions 84
Directions and policy guidance given by the
Secretary of State 85
The effect of the development plan 87
Other material considerations 88
Development in conservation areas, and affect-
ing listed buildings 91
Planning applications in which a local plan-
ning authority has an interest 91
Judicial supervision 92

Chapter 9   **Planning   Permissions,   Conditions   and
Agreements** 93
Introduction 93
Planning Permission 93
Planning Conditions 99
Challenging Planning Conditions 107
Planning Agreements 108

PART III

SPECIAL CONTROLS

Chapter 10   **Listed Buildings, Conservation Areas and
other Special Areas** 117
Introduction 117
Control over Listed Buildings 117
Conservation Areas 123
Ancient   Monuments   and   Archaeological
Areas 125
Protection of the Countryside 126

Chapter 11   **Advertisements, Enterprise Zones and other
Controls** 131
Introduction 131
Advertisement Controls 131
Advertisements excluded from controls 132
Advertisements that may be displayed without
consent 133
Advertisements requiring express consent 136
Advertisements: Areas of Special Control 136

	Enterprise Zones	137
	Pollution and Hazardous materials	141
Chapter 12	**Trees, Minerals and Caravans**	**143**
	Trees: General	143
	Tree Preservation Orders	143
	Trees and Felling Licences	147
	Trees in Conservation Areas	147
	Control over Mineral Workings	148
	Caravans	153

PART IV

POSITIVE PLANNING AND ENFORCEMENT

Chapter 13	**Revocation, Modification and Discontinuance Orders**	**159**
	Revocation or Modification of a planning permission	159
	Discontinuance Orders	161
Chapter 14	**Enforcement**	**163**
	Introduction	163
	Breach of Planning Control	163
	The Enforcement Notice	169
	Appeals against the Enforcement Notice	173
	Prosecution and Enforcement	176
	Enforcement and Listed Buildings	179
Chapter 15	**Development by Public Authorities**	**183**
	Introduction	183
	Land Acquisition and Development Powers	185
	Public Authorities and Planning Permission	187
	New Towns	189
	Urban Development Areas	189
	The Land Authority for Wales	191
	Register of Land held by Public Bodies	192

PART V

RIGHTS AND REMEDIES

Chapter 16	**Appeals and Inquiries**	**197**
	Introduction	197

Appeal to the Secretary of State 198
Public Local Inquiry 199
Written Representations 204
The Decision of the Secretary of State 205
Costs 206

Chapter 17 **Purchase Notices** 209
Introduction 209
The Planning Decisions 209
Land incapable of reasonably beneficial use 211
The Procedure 214

Chapter 18 **Compensation** 217
Introduction 217
Interference to property rights: is there a right
  to compensation? 218
Compensation for refusal of planning per-
  mission 219
Compensation for revocation, modification or
  discontinuance orders 227
Compensation in connection with Listed
  Buildings and Ancient Monuments 229
Compensation in connection with Tree Preser-
  vation Orders, control of advertisements
  and stop notices 231

Chapter 19 **Judicial Supervision** 235
Introduction 235
The Statutory Rights of Appeal to the Courts 236
Common Law Judicial Review 238
Grounds of challenge 239
Private Law Remedies 242
Challenging the validity of Enforcement
  Notices 243

PART VI

SERVICES AND HIGHWAYS

Chapter 20 **Provision and Adoption of Sewers** 249
Introduction 249
Powers of Water Authorities to provide sewers
  and works 251
Right to requisition a public sewer 251

Adoption of sewers   252
Right to connect to a Public Sewer   253

Chapter 21   **Water, Gas and Electricity**   **255**
Supply of Water   255
Supply of Gas   257
Supply of Electricity   258

Chapter 22   **Highways**   **261**
Introduction   261
Obstruction and Interference to highways   263
Adoption of highways   265
Making up private streets   266
Stopping up and diversion of highways   268

PART VII
THE BETTERMENT PROBLEM

Chapter 23   **Betterment and Development Land Tax**   **273**
The Betterment Problem   273

APPENDICES

Appendix A **The Classes Order**   **277**

Appendix B **Classes of Permitted Development—General
Development Order**   **285**

Appendix C **Modifications to the General Development
Order in the special areas**   **317**

Index   321

Preface

This book has been written for students of estate management, surveying, valuation, planning and architecture. It may also be of interest to law students, and to practitioners in these disciplines. I have sought to present a 'development' angle to this subject to assist the many readers who will in due course be involved in the development process, be it a small domestic extension, a change of use of a building, or a large development scheme. The theme is therefore development rather than just planning.

New legislation never ceases in this field, and there is also an ever growing body of case law. I have reflected the law as it is in May 1987. Bearing this date in mind, I hope that most readers will be able to keep abreast of later developments. Thanks to the indulgence of the publishers, it was possible to include something on the Use Classes Order that came into force on 1st June 1987; the new order represents a significant policy shift in development control, and it deserved more comment than I have been able to give at so late a date.

I have taken the opportunity in this edition to reorganise substantially and rewrite the chapter on Judicial Supervision in the light of further developments in this field: I have tried to simplify this topic for the non-lawyer, who requires only an outline explanation. Lawyers will find this branch of the law fully dealt with in other texts. Although it has been possible to delete some material, this edition is longer than its predecessor for two reasons: some 120 cases have been added, most decided in the last five years, and it also has appendices containing the Use Classes Order and the classes of permitted development. Readers may find these useful additions.

Poonam Sood prepared the various tables for the first edition, and much of her valuable work has been used. Abigail Rimmer updated the tables, and prepared the index for this edition: I thank her for this.

B.D-G.
May 1987

Table of Cases

Abbreviations

AC	:	Appeal Cases (Law Reports)
Ch or ChD	:	Chancery (Law Reports)
QB (or KB)	:	Queen's (or King's) Bench (Law Reports)
All ER	:	All England Law Reports
EG	:	Estates Gazette
CSW	:	Chartered Surveyor Weekly
EGD	:	Estates Gazette Digest
EGLR	:	Estates Gazette Law Reports
JP	:	Justice of the Peace Reports
JPL	:	Journal of Planning and Environment Law
LGR	:	Local Government Reports (Knight's)
LT	:	Law Times
P&CR	:	Property and Compensation Reports
Sol Jo (or SJ):		Solicitor's Journal
TLR	:	Times Law Reports
WLR	:	Weekly Law Reports

A

Page

Abbey Homesteads (Developments) Ltd *v.* Northampton CC [1986]
1 EGLR 24; (1986) 278 EG 1249; (1986) JPL 683 111

Adams and Wade Ltd. *v.* Minister of Housing and Local Government (1965)
P&CR 60; [1965] EGD 132 210

A-G *v.* Calderdale B.C. (1983) JPL 310 118

A-G *v.* Howard United Reformed Church, [1975] EGD 871 ....122, 124

A-G *v.* Melville Construction Co. Ltd., (1968) 112 SJ 725 145

Allnatt London Properties *v.* Middlesex C.C., (1964) LGR 304; [1964] RVR
357; 15 P&CR 288; 189 EG 791; [1964] EGD 368 106

Amalgamated Investment and Property Co. Ltd. *v.* John Walker and Sons
Ltd., [1976] 3 All ER 509; [1976] EGD 166; 236 EG 277; 120 SJ 256 ......118, 230

Arlington Securities Ltd *v.* Secretary of State for the Environment 1985 JPL
550 205

Ashbridge Investments Ltd. *v.* Minister of Housing and Local Government,
[1965] 1 WLR 1320; 129 JP 580; 109 SJ 595; [1965] 3 All ER 331; 63
LGR 400; [1965] EGD 146, 215 240

Ashby *v.* Secretary of States for the Environment [1980] 1 All ER 508;
(1979) 40 P&CR 362 ....269, 270

Associated Provincial Picture Houses Ltd. *v.* Wednesbury Corpn. [1948] 1
KB 223; 45 LGR 635 ....86, 101, 240

Atkinson *v.* Secretary of States for the Environment (1983) JPL 599 ....100, 177

Augier *v*. Secretary of State for the Environment, (1978) 38 P&CR 219 105
Avon C.C. *v*. Millard (1986) JPL 211 ....110, 243
Ayr Harbour Trustees *v*. Oswald (1883) 8 AC 623 109

B

Backer and another *v*. Secretary of State, [1981] JPL 357; (1981) 42 P&CR
    48 168
Balco Transport Services *v*. Secretary of State for the Environment, (1981)
    260 EG 709 ....28, 211
Balco Transport Services *v*. Secretary of State for the Environment [1985] 2
    EGLR 187; [1986] 1 All ER 689 211
Barvis Ltd. *v*. Secretary of State for the Environment (1971) 22 P&CR 710;
    Digest Cont. Vol. D 1915 9
Bedford C.C. *v*. CEGB (1985) JPL 43 12
Beecham Group Ltd.'s Application, (1980) 41 P&CR 369; (1980) 256 EG
    829; [1981] JPL 55 111
Belfast Corpn. *v*. O.D. Cars Ltd. [1960] 1 All ER 65; [1960] AC 490; [1960]
    2 WLR 148; 104 Sol Jo 68; [1960] JPL 189; HL 218, 219
Belmont Farm Ltd. *v*. Minister of Housing and Local Government, (1962)
    106 Sol Jo 469; 60 LGR 319; 13 P&CR 417; 183 EG 413; [1962] EGD
    543 17
Bell *v*. Canterbury City Council [1986] 2 EGLR 209 (1986) 279 EG 767 232
Bernard Wheatcroft Ltd. *v*. Secretary of State for the Environment and
    another (1980) 257 EG 934 ....97, 102
Bilboe *v*. Secretary of State for the Environment, [1980] EGD 912; 254 EG
    607; 39 P&CR 495; [1980] JPL 330 ....19, 167, 168
Birmingham Corp. *v*. Minister of Housing and Local Government and
    Habib Ullah; [1964] 1 QB 178; [1963] 3 All ER 668; [1963] 3 WLR
    937; 128 JP 33; 107 Sol Jo 812; 61 LGR 623; 15 P&CR 404; 188 EG
    305; [1963] EGD 629 ....19, 22
Blackpool B.C. *v*. Secretary of State for the Environment, (1980) P&CR
    104; [1980] JPL 527 20
Bolivian and General Tin Trust Ltd. *v*. Secretary of State for the Environ-
    ment, [1972] 1 WLR 1481 34
Bollans *v*. Surrey C.C., (1968) 30 P&CR 745; [1969] JPL 285 232
Brighton B.C. *v*. Secretary of State for the Environment, (1978) 39 P&CR
    46; [1979] JPL 173; (1979) 249 EG 747 89
Bristol City Council *v*. Secretary of State for the Environment (1987) The
    Times 19/3/1987 35
Bristol Stadium Ltd. *v*. Brown, (1980) JPL 107; (1979) EG 803 178
Britannia Ltd. *v*. Secretary of State for the Environment, [1978] JPL 554;
    [1980] JPL 402 103
Brookdene Investments Ltd. *v*. M.H.L.G., (1970) 21 P&CR 545 213
Brooks and Burton *v*. Secretary of State for the Environment, (1978) 120 Sol
    Jo 605; [1977] 1 WLR 1294; [1977] JPL 720; 244 EG 715 23
Broxbourne B.C. *v*. Secretary of State for the Environment, [1979] 2 All ER
    13; [1979] JPL 302 34
Buckinghamshire C.C. *v*. Hall Aggregates Ltd (1985) JPL 634 237
Bullock *v*. Secretary of State, (1980) 40 P&CR 246; 254 EG 1097; [1980]
    JPL 461 144
Burdle *v*. Secretary of State for the Environment [1972] 3 All ER 240 [1972]
    1 WLR 1207; 136 JP 720; 116 Sol Jo 507; 70 LGR 511; 24 P&CR 174;
    [1972] EGD 678 ....24, 25, 31

Burgess *v.* Jarvis, [1952] 1 All ER 592; [1952] 2 QB 41; 116 JP 161; [1952] 1
    TLR 580; 96 Sol Jo 194; 50 LGR 213; 2 P&CR 377; CA 169
Burmah Oil Co. *v.* Lord Advocate, [1965] AC 75; [1964] 2 WLR 1231; 108
    SJ 401; [1964] 2 All ER 348 218
Buxton *v.* Ministry of Housing and Local Government, [1961] 1 QB 278;
    [1960] 3 WLR 866; 124 JP 489; 104 Sol Jo 935; [1960] 3 All ER 408;
    12 P&CR 77 238

C

Calcaria Construction Co. Ltd. *v.* Secretary of State for the Environment,
    (1974) 118 SJ 421; 27 P&CR 435; 74 LGR 398 74
Camden L.B.C. *v.* Peaktop Properties (Hampstead) Ltd. (1983) 45 P&CR
    177; (1983) JPL 669; see Peaktop (Hampstead) Properties Ltd. *v.*
    Camden L. B. C. (1983) 45 P&CR 177 on app. from (1982) 44 P&CR
    233; (1982) 262 EG 239 ....224, 225
Camden, L.B.C. *v.* Secretary of State for the Environment, [1980] JPL 31,
    61 175
Camrose *v.* Basingstoke Corpn. [1966] 3 All ER 161, [1966] 1 WLR 1100,
    (1966) EGD 469 7
Cardigan Timber Co. *v.* Cardiganshire C.C. (1957) P&CR 158 232
Castell-y-Mynach Estate Trustees *v.* Secretary of State for Wales (1985) JPL
    40 ....27, 38
Cawoods Aggregates (Southeast) Ltd. *v.* Southwark L.B.C. (1982) 264 EG
    1087 228
Chalgray Ltd. *v.* Secretary of State for the Environment, (1976) 33 P&CR
    10; [1977] JPL 176 74
Cherwell D.C. *v.* Thames Water Board [1975] 1 WLR 448; 119 SJ 202;
    [1975] 1 All ER 763 256
Cheshire C.C. *v.* Woodward, [1962] 1 All ER 517; [1962] 2 QB 126; [1962]
    2 WLR 636; 126 JP 186; 106 Sol Jo 222; 60 LGR 180; [1962] RVR 148;
    13 P&CR 157; 181 E.G. 635; [1962] JPL 141; [1962] EGD 533 ....9, 153
Church Cottage Investments Ltd. *v.* Hillingdon L.B.C. [1986] 2 EGLR 216 225
City of Bradford *v.* Secretary of State for the Environment, (1986) JPL
    598 .... 104, 105, 110
City of London Corporation *v.* Secretary of State for the Environment,
    (1971) 23 P&CR 169; [1972] EGD 957 ....19, 71, 104
Clyde & Co. *v.* Secretary of State for the Environment, [1977] 1 WLR 926;
    121 SJ 512; [1977] EGD 852; 241 EG 155 and 244 EG 1024 ....90, 91
Coats Patons (Retail) Ltd. *v.* Birmingham Corpn. (1971) 69 LGR 356 57
Coleshill & District Investment Co. Ltd. *v.* Minister of Housing and Local
    Government and another; [1969] 2 All ER 525; [1969] 1 WLR 746;
    133 JP 385; 113 Sol Jo 469; 20 P&CR 679; 211 EG 727; [1969] EGD
    736; HL 10, 11, 12
Collis Radio Ltd. *v.* Secretary of State for the Environment, (1975) 119 Sol
    Jo 302; 73 LGR 211; 29 P&CR 390 90
Colonial Sugar Refining Co. Ltd. *v.* Melborne Harbour Trust Commis-
    sioners [1927] AC 343 101
Company Developments Ltd. *v.* Secretary of State for the Environment,
    [1978] JPL 107 185
Co-operative Retail Service Ltd. *v.* Taff-Ely B.C., (1979) 39 P&CR 223;
    (1980) JPL 232 ....94, 237, 241
Co-operative Retail Service Ltd. *v.* Taff-Ely B.C. (1983) 5 CSW 50 57
Cooper *v.* Wandsworth Board of Works (1863) 14 CDNS 180; [1861–73]
    All ER Rep Ext 1554 239

Copeland B.C. *v.* Secretary of State for the Environment, (1976) 31 P&CR
    403; 239 EG 503; [1976] EGD 791 ....96, 166, 169, 170
Cotswold D.C. *v.* Secretary of State for the Environment, (1985) JPL 407 119
Council of Civil Service Unions *v.* Minister for the Civil Service [1984] 3
    WLR 1174 240
Covent Garden Community Association Ltd. *v.* Greater London Council,
    [1981] JPL 183 ....88, 197, 239, 241
Cox's Application, re, [1985] JPL 564 111
Crabtree & Co. Ltd. *v.* Minister of Housing and Local Government (1965)
    109 Sol JO 927; 17 P&CR 232; 64 LGR 104; [1965] EGD 419 186
Crowborough Parish Council *v.* Secretary of State and Wealden D.C.,
    (1981) JPL 281 16
Cynon Valley B.C. *v.* Secretary for Wales (1986) JPL 283; [1986] 2 EGLR
    191; (1986) 280 EG 195 ....30, 31, 35, 95, 164

D

Davy *v.* Spelthorne B.C. (1983) 3 All ER 278; (1984) AC 262 ....243, 244
Davies *v.* Secretary of State for Wales, [1977] JPL 102, 249 242
Dawson *v.* Secretary of State for the Environment, (1983) JPL 544 39
Day and another *v.* Secretary of State for the Environment, [1979] JPL 538;
    (1980) 78 LGR 30; [1979] 251 EG 163 172
De Mulder *v.* Secretary of State for the Environment, [1974] QB 792; [1974]
    1 All ER 776; [1974] EGD 829 ....25, 172
Debenhams plc *v.* Westminster City Council (1987) JPL 344; [1987] 1 All
    ER 51; [1987] 1 EGLR 248 118
Dover D.C. *v.* McKeen (1985) 50 P&CR 250; [1985] 2 EGLR 191 174
Dymond *v.* Pearce [1972] 1 QB 496 263

E

Ealing B.C. *v.* Ryan, [1965] 1 All ER 137; [1965] 2 QB 486; [1965] 2 WLR
    223; 129 JP 164; 109 Sol Jo 74; 63 LGR 148; 17 P&CR 15 19
East Barnett UDC *v.* British Transport Commission, [1961] 3 All ER 878;
    [1962] 2 QB 484; [1962] 2 WLR 134; 126 JP 1; 106 So Jo 76; 60 LGR
    41; 13 P&CR 27; 180 EG 221; [1962] JPL 262; [1961] EGD
    468 .... 21, 24, 41
Edwin H. Bradley & Son *v.* Secretary of State for the Environment, (1982)
    264 EG 926 237
Eldon Garages Ltd. *v.* Kingston-upon-Hull CBC, [1974] 1 WLR 276; [1974]
    1 All ER 358 169
Enfield L.B.C. *v.* Secretary of State for the Environment, [1975] JPL 155;
    [1974] 233 E. G. 53 ....66, 87, 129
English *v.* Dedham Vale Property Co., [1978] 1 WLR 93; [1978] 1 All ER
    382; [1977] 35 P&CR 148; [1977] 245 EG 745 76
Essex C.C. *v.* Philpott & Sons Ltd. (1987) 125
Etheridge *v.* Secretary of State for the Environment, (1983) 5 CSW 233 74
Ewen Developments Ltd. *v.* Secretary of State for the Environment and
    North Norfolk D.C., [1980] JPL 404 ....11, 166

F

Fairmount Investments Ltd. *v.* Secretary of State for the Environment,
    (1976) 120 SJ 801; [1976] 2 All ER 865; [1976] 1 WLR [1976] JPL 161;
    [1976] EGD 82, 98 ....202, 241

Fawcett Properties Ltd. *v*. Buckingham C.C., [1960] 3 All ER 503; [1961]
    AC 636; [1960] 3 WLR 831; 125 JP 8; 59 LGR 69; 12 P&CR 1; [1960]
    JPL 43: [1960] EGD 215 ....100, 103
Fayrewood Fish Farms *v*. Secretary of State for the Environment, [1984] JPL
    267 ....10, 38, 43, 227
Fourth Investments *v*. Bury M.B.C. (1984) The Times 27/7/1984; (1985)
    JPL 185 ....68, 237
French Kier Developments Ltd. *v*. Secretary of State for the Environment,
    [1977] 1 All ER 296; [1977] JPL 30 205
Fyson *v*. Buckinghamshire C.C., [1958] 1 WLR 634; 122 JP 333; [1959]
    EGD 185 26

G

Garland *v*. Minister of Housing and Local Government, (1968) 112 Sol Jo
    841; 67 LGR 77; 20 P&CR 93; [1969] JPL 275, CA 39, 166, 169, 170
General Estates Co. Ltd. *v*. M. H. L. G. [1965] EGD 98 212
George *v*. Secretary of State for the Environment, (1979) 38 P&CR 609 242
George Wimpey & Co. Ltd. *v*. New Forest D.C. (1979) JPL 100
Gill *v*. Secretary of State for the Environment, (1985) JPL 710 ....103, 104
Givaudon & Co. Ltd. *v*. Minister of Housing and Local Government (1967)
    [1966] 3 All ER 696; [1967] 1 WLR 250; 131 JP 79; 110 Sol Jo 371; 64
    LGR 352; 18 P&CR 88; 198 EG 585 ....205, 242
Grampion R.C. *v*. City of Aberdeen (1984) 47 P&CR 633; (1984) JPL 590 105
Gravesham B.C. *v*. Watson (1984) 47 P&CR 142 268
Great Portland Estate Plc. *v*. Westminster City Council [1984] 3 WLR 1035;
    [1985] AC 661; [1984] 3 All ER 744; (1984) 49 P&CR 34; (1985) JPL
    108 ....68, 237
Green *v*. Secretary of State for the Environment, (1985) JPL 323 164
Grenfell-Baines *v*. Secretary of State for the Environment, (1985) JPL 256 242
Guildford R.D.C. *v*. Fortescue, [1959] 2 All ER 111; [1959] 2 QB 112;
    [1959] 2 WLR 643; 123 JP 286; 103 Sol Jo 350; 57 LGR 169; 10 P&CR
    232; 173 EG 625; [1959] JPL 428; [1959] EGD 184 153
Guildford R.D.C. *v*. Penny, [1959] 2 All ER 111; [1959] 2 QB 112; [1959] 2
    WLR 643; 123 JP 286; 103 Sol Jo 350; 57 LGR 169; 10 P&CR 232;
    173 EG 625; [1959] JPL 428; CA; [1959] EGD 184 ....10, 21, 22

H

Haley *v*. L. E. B. [1965] AC 778; [1964] 3 All ER 185 263
Hall & Co. Ltd. *v*. Shoreham-by-Sea U.D.C., [1964] 1 All ER 1; [1964] 1
    WLR 240; 128 JP 120; 107 Sol Jo 1001; 62 LGR 206; 15 P&CR 119,
    CA 101, 102
Hambledon & Chiddingfold Parish Council *v*. Secretary of State for the
    Environment, [1976] JPL 502 89
Hamilton *v*. West Sussex C.C., [1958] 2 All ER 174; [1958] 2 QB 286;
    [1958] 2 WLR 873; 122 JP 294; 102 Sol Jo 364; 56 LGR 275; 9 P&CR
    279; 171 EG 571; [1958] JPL 441; [1958] EGD 183 75
Hammersmith L.B.C. *v*. Secretary of State for the Environment, (1975) 73
    LGR 288; 30 P&CR 19 ....174, 176
Harding *v*. Secretary of State for the Environment, (1985) JPL 503 42
Harper *v*. Haden & Sons [1933] 1 Ch, 298 263
Hartley *v*. Minister of Housing and Local Government, [1970] 1 QB 413
    [1970] 2 WLR 1; 113 Sol Jo 900; 68 LGR 32; 21 P&CR 1; [1970] EGD
    4 ....26, 28, 29

Hartnell *v*. Minister of Housing and Local Government, [1965] 1 All ER 490; 129 JP 234; 63 LGR 103; 17 P&CR 60, [1965] AC 1134; [1965] 1 WLR 474; 109 Sol Jo 136; [1965] EGD 31, HL 106
Harrison *v*. Duke of Rutland [1893] 1 QB 412 261
Hedley Byrne & Co. Ltd. *v*. Heller & Partners [1964] AC 465; [1963] 3 WLR 101; [1963] 2 All ER 575 57
Heron Corpn. Ltd. *v*. Manchester City Council, [1978] EGD 953, 247 EG 379 ....75, 239
Heron Service Station Ltd. *v*. Coupe, [1973] 1 WLR 502; 117 Sol Jo 305; [1973] EGD 1082 135
Herring *v*. Metropolitan Board of Works (1865) 144 ER 886 263
Hewlett *v*. Secretary of State for the Environment, (1983) JPL 105; (1985) 273 EG 401 8
Hilliard *v*. Secretary of State for the Environment, (1978) 248 EG 226; [1978] JPL 840; [1981] JPL 428 172
Hipsey *v*. Secretary of State for the Environment, (1984) JPL 806 34
Hobbs (Quarries) Ltd. *v*. Somerset C.C., [1975] EGD 466; (1975) 30 P&CR 286 ....152, 228
Howes *v*. Secretary of State for the Environment, (1984) JPL 439 166
Hubbard *v*. Pitt [1975] 1 All ER 1056 261
Hughes (H. T.) & Sons Ltd. *v*. Secretary of State for the Environment, (1985) JPL 486 176
Hutton *v*. Esher U.D.C., [1973] 2 WLR 917; [1973] 2 All ER 1123; [1974] Ch. 167; 117 SJ 417; 26 P&CR 17; [1973] EGD 920 257

I

Iddenden *v*. Secretary of State for the Environment, [1972] 3 All ER 883; [1972] 1 WLR 1437; 137 JP 28; 116 Sol Jo 665; 71 LGR 20; 26 P&CR 553; Digest Cont. Vol. D 931 12
Inverclyde D.C. *v*. Inverkip Building Co. Ltd. (1982) JPL 313 104
Irlam Brick Co. *v*. Warrington B. C., (1982) 5/2/82 The Times 239

J

Jacobs *v*. L.C.C. [1950] AC 361; [1950] 1 All ER 737 263
Jennings Motors Ltd. *v*. Secretary of State for the Environment and another, 28/11/81 The Times CA 30
John *v*. Reveille Newspapers Ltd., (1955) 5 P&CR 95; [1955] JPL 365 132
Jones *v*. Secretary of State for the Environment, [1974] 28 P&CR 362 171
Jones *v*. Secretary of State for Wales, (1974) Local Government Chronicle 596; [1974] JPL 415; [1972] 23 P&CR 125 186

K

Kensington and Chelsea R.B.C. *v*. C.G. Hotels, [1981] JPL 190; [1981] P&CR 40 ....10, 175
Kensington and Chelsea R.B.C. *v*. Secretary of State for the Environment and another, (1981) JPL 50 ....23, 25
Kent C.C. *v*. Kingsway Investments, [1971] AC 72; [1970] 2 WLR 397; 21 P&CR 58; [1970] EGD 44; HL 106
Kent C.C. *v*. Batchelor, [1979] 1 WLR 213; [1977] 33 P&CR 185; [1980] JPL 462 ....144, 178
Kent C.C. *v*. Secretary of State for the Environment, (1976) 33 P&CR 70 97

Kent C.C. *v*. Secretary of State for the Environment, (1977) 34 P&CR 269,
[1980] JPL 118 206
Kerrier D.C. *v*. Secretary of State for the Environment, (1981) JPL 193;
(1980) 41 P&CR 284 ....100, 168
Kingston-upon-Thames L.B.C. *v*. Secretary of State for the Environment,
[1974] 1 All ER 193; [1973] 1 WLR 1549; 138 JP 131; 117 Sol Jo 794;
72 LGR 206; 26 P&CR 480; [1974] EGD 782 ....89, 104
Kwik Save Discount Group Ltd. *v*. Secretary of State for Wales, [1981] JPL
198; (1980) 79 LGR 310, 257 EG 169; (1981) P&CR 166 ....41, 70, 95

L

Lamplugh, Re, (1967) 19 P&CR 125; 66 LGR 6 161
Larkin *v*. Basildon D.C., (1980) 256 EG 389; [1980] JPL 407 ....8, 39
Lavender *v*. Minister of Housing and Local Government, [1970] 1 WLR
1231; 114 SJ 636; [1970] 3 All ER 871; [1970] EGD 215 206
Lenlyn Ltd. *v*. Secretary of State for the Environment, (1985) 82 L. S. Gaz.
358; (1985) JPL 482; (1984) 50 P&CR 129 173
Lever Finance Ltd. *v*. Westminster City Council, [1970] 3 All ER 496;
[1971] 1 QB 222; [1970] 3 WLR 732; 134 JP 692; 114 Sol Jo 651; 21
P&CR 778; [1970] EGD 828 56
London Corpn. *v*. Cussack Smith, [1955] AC 337; [1955] 2 WLR 363; 119
JP 172; 99 Sol Jo 108; [1955] 1 All ER 302; 5 P&CR 65 209
London Docklands Development Corpn. *v*. Rank Harris McDougall Ltd
1985 The Times July 25 191
London Parachuting Ltd. *v*. Secretary of State for the Environment, (1986)
JPL 428 174
Lord Luke of Pavenham *v*. Ministry of Housing and Local Government,
[1968] 1 QB 172; [1967] 2 WLR 801; 131 JP 425; 111 Sol Jo 398;
[1967] 2 All ER 1066; 18 P&CR 333; CA 203
Loromah Ltd. *v*. Haringay L.B.C., [1978] EGD 558; 248 EG 877 229
L.T.S.S. *v*. London Borough of Hackney, [1976] 1 All ER 311; [1976] QB
663; [1976] 2 WLR 253; 119 Sol Jo 886; 74 LGR 210; P&CR 133, CA ...33, 36
Lucas & Sons *v*. Dorking and Horley R.D.C., (1964) 62 LGR 491; 17
P&CR 111; (1964) EGD 382 95

M

Maine *v*. Swansea City Council (1985) JPL 558; (1985) 49 P&CR 26 76
Maidstone B.C. *v*. Mortimer [1980] 3 All ER 552; (1981) JPL 112 144
Malvern Hills D.C. *v*. Secretary of State for the Environment, (1982) JPL
439 98
Manchester City Council *v*. Secretary of State for the Environment, (1987)
The Times 13/4/87; see R. *v*. Secretary of State for the Environment ex.
parte Manchester City Council (1987) The Times 13/4/87 193
Mansi *v*. Elstree R.D.C., (1965) JPL 596; 16 P&CR 153; 189 EG 341 ....171, 172
Marshall *v*. Nottingham C.C. [1960] 1 All ER 659 22
Metallic Protective Ltd. *v*. Secretary of State for the Environment, [1976]
JPL 166 171
Miller *v*. Weymouth and Melcombe Region Corporation, (1974) 118 Sol Jo
421 242
Miller Mead *v*. Minister of Housing and Local Government, [1963] 1 All ER
459; [1963] 2 QB 196; [1963] 2 WLR 225; 127 JP 122; 106 Sol Jo
1052; 61 LGR 152; 14 P&CR 266; 185 EG 835; [1963] JPL 260;
[1963] EGD 572 ....163, 170, 171, 244

Ministry of Agriculture, Fisheries and Food *v.* Henkins, [1963] 2 QB 317;
[1963] 2 WLR 906; 107 Sol Jo 234; [1963] 2 All ER; [1963] EGD 422 187
Mounsdon *v.* Weymouth and Melcombe Regis Corpn., [1960] 1 QB 645;
[1960] 2 WLR 484; 124 JP 231; 104 SJ 332; [1960] 1 All ER 538; 58
LGR 144; 11 P&CR 103; [1960] JPL 692; [1960] EGD 207 96
Murphy & Sons *v.* Secretary of State for the Environment, [1973] 2 All ER
26; [1973] 1 WLR 560; 137 JP 401; 117 Sol Jo 304; 71 LGR 273; 25
P&CR 268 89

N

Nash *v.* Secretary of State for the Environment, [1985] 2 EGLR 186; (1985)
276 EG 1274 ....33, 91, 179
N. Surrey Water Co. *v.* Secretary of State, (1977) 34 P&CR 140 203
Nelsovil *v.* Minister of Housing and Local Government, (1962) 13 P&CR
151 174
Newbury D.C. *v.* Secretary of State for the Environment, [1980] 2 WLR
379, [1980] 1 All ER 731; 40 P&CR 148; HL 30, 99, 101, 102, 168
Niarchos (London) Ltd. *v.* Secretary of State for the Environment, (1977)
LGR 480; (1978) 35 P&CR 259; (1977) EG 847; [1978] JPL 247;
[1978] EGD 927 89
Norfolk C.C. *v.* Secretary of State for the Environment, [1973] 3 All ER
633; [1973] 1 WLR 1400; 137 JP 832; 117 Sol Jo 650; 72 LGR 44; 26
P&CR 273 94
North Warwickshire B.C. *v.* Secretary of State for the Environment, (1984)
JPL 434 16

O

O'Reilly *v.* Mackman [1983] 2 AC 237; [1983] 3 All ER 680 243

P

Parkes *v.* Secretary of State for the Environment, [1979] 1 All ER 211; 36
P&CR 387; 248 EG 595; 77 LGR 39; [1978] EGD 971; CA 10, 161
Peacock Homes Ltd. *v.* Secretary of State for the Environment, (1984) 48
P&CR 20; (1984) JPL 729 167
Peake *v.* Secretary for Wales (1971) 22 P&CR 889 22
Peaktop (Hampstead) Properties Ltd. *v.* Camden L.B.C. (1983) 45 P&CR
177 as app. from (1982) 44 P&CR 233; (1982) 262 EG 239; see
Camden L.B.C. *v.* Peaktop Properties (Hampstead) Ltd. (1983); 45
P&CR 177 on app. from (1982) 44 P&CR 233; (1982) 262 EG
239 .... 224, 225
Penn Central Transport Co. *v.* New York City (1977) 438 US 104 219
Pennine Raceways Ltd *v.* Kirkless M.D.C. [1982] 3 WLR 987; [1982] 3 All
ER 628 ....226, 227, 228
Pennsylvania Coal Co. *v.* Mahon, [1922] 260 US 393. (United States
Supreme Court) 219
Penwith D.C. *v.* Secretary of State for the Environment, (1977) JPL 371 102
Percy Trentham Ltd. *v.* Gloucestershire C.C., [1966] 1 WLR 506; 130 JP
179 ....18, 23
Performance Cars Ltd. *v.* Secretary of State for the Environment, (1977) JPL
587; (1977) P&CR 92 ....201, 241
Perry *v.* Stanborough (Developments) Ltd. (1978) JPL 36; (1977) 244 EG
551 164

Petticoat Lane Rentals Ltd. *v.* Minister of Housing and Local Government and another, [1971] 2 All ER 793; [1971] 1 WLR 1112; 135 JP 410; 115 Sol Jo 487; 69 LGR 504; 22 P&CR 703; 218 EG 707; [1971] EGD 364 ....29, 172
PGM Building Ltd *v.* Kensington Chelsea LBC [1982] RTR 107 264
Philglow Ltd. *v.* Secretary of State for the Environment, (1984) JPL 111; (1984) 270 EG 1192 ....24, 28
Pilkington *v.* Secretary of State for the Environment, [1974] 1 All ER 283; [1973] 1 WLR 1527; 138 JP 191; 117 Sol Jo 894; 72 LGR 303; 28 P&CR 508; [1974] EGD 787 95
Pioneer Aggregates (U.K.) Ltd. *v.* Secretary of State for the Environment and others, [1984] 2 All ER 358 ....28, 30, 95
Plymouth Corpn. *v.* Secretary of State for the Environment, [1972] 1 WLR 1347; 116 SJ 565; [1972] 3 All ER 225; 24 P&CR 88; [1972] EGD 691 211
Preston *v.* British Unions for the Abolition of Vivisection (1985) JPL 132
Prosser *v.* Sharp (1985) JPL 717; [1985] 1 EGLR 175; (1985) 274 EG 1249 .. 16, 179
Prosser *v.* Minister of Housing and Local Government, (1968) LGR 109 ....29, 104
Purbeck D.C. *v.* Secretary of State for the Environment, (1982) JPL 640; (1982) 263 EG 261 211
Pye (Oxford) Estates *v.* West Oxford D. C. (1982) JPL 577; (1982) 264 EG 533 86
Pyrford Properties *v.* Secretary of State for the Environment, [1977] JPL 724; (1977) 244 EG 383 203
Pyx Granite Co. *v.* Ministry of Housing, [1958] 1 All ER 625; [1958] 1 QB 554; [1958] 2 WLR 371; 122 JP 182; 56 LGR 171; 9 P&CR 240; 102 Sol Jo 175; [1958] JPL 442; CA; reversed, [1959] 3 All ER 1; [1960] AC 260; [1959] 3 WLR 346; 123 JP 429; 103 Sol Jo 633; 58 LGR 1; HL 8, 100, 107, 198, 239

R

R *v.* Amber Valley DC ex parte Jackson [1984] 3 All ER 501 92
R *v.* Bournemouth Justices, ex parte Bournemouth Corpn., (1970) 114 SJ 150 144
R *v.* Bradford-on-Avon UDC ex parte Boulton, [1964] 1 WLR 1136; [1964] EGD 370 ....74, 76
R *v.* Camden LBC ex parte Comyn Ching & Co. (1984) JPL 628 ....87, 180
R *v.* Castle Point DC ex parte Brooks (1985) JPL 473 ....74, 239
R *v.* Derbyshire C.C. ex parte N. E. Derbyshire D. C. (1980) JPL 398 150
R *v.* Greenwich LBC ex parte Patel (1985) JPL 851; [1985] 2 EGLR 256 169
R *v.* Hammersmith and Fulham LBC, ex parte Greater London Council (1986) JPL 528 75
R *v.* Hillingdon L.B.C. ex parte Royco Homes Ltd., [1974] 2 All ER 643; [1974] QB 720; [1974] 2 WLR 805; 118 Sol Jo 389; 72 LGR 516; 28 P&CR 231 EG 739; [1974] EGD 811 ....102, 103, 107, 198, 240
R *v.* Jenner [1983] 2 All ER 46 ....178, 243
R *v.* Lambeth LBC ex parte Sharpe (1986) JPL 201 ....78, 91, 123, 188
R *v.* M.H.L.G. ex parte Chichester R.D.C., [1960] 1 WLR 587; 124 JP 322; 104 SJ 449; [1960] 2 All ER 407; [1960] EGD 208 212
R *v.* North Hertfordshire D.C. ex parte Sullivan, [1981] JPL 752 ....121, 197
R *v.* St. Edmundsbury B.C. ex parte Investors in Industry Commercial Properties Ltd [1985] 3 All ER 234 ....79, 85, 92
R *v.* Secretary of State for the Environment, ex parte Hampshire C.C. [1981] JPL 47 180

R *v*. Secretary of State for the Environment ex parte Manchester City
    Council (1987) The Times 13/4/87; see Manchester City Council *v*.
    Secretary of State for the Environment, (1987) The Times 13/4/87 193
R *v*. Secretary of State for the Environment ex parte Ostler, [1976] 3 WLR
    288; 120 SJ 322; [1976] 3 All ER 90; 32 P&CR 166; [1976] JPL 301;
    CA 236
R *v*. Secretary of State for the Environment ex parte Reinisch, (1971) 22
    P&CR 1022, (1971) 70 LGR 126 206
R *v*. Secretary of State for the Environment ex parte Manchester City
    Council 1987 193
R *v*. Secretary of State for the Environment ex parte Southwark LBC (1987)
    JPL 587 65
R *v*. Secretary of State for the Environment ex parte Stewart, (1980) JPL
    175 269
R *v* Sevenoaks DC ex parte Terry (1984) JPL 420 ....92, 112
R *v*. Surrey LC, ex parte Monk (1986) JPL 828 150
R *v*. West Oxfordshire BC ex parte C. H. Pearce Homes Ltd. (1986) JPL 523 94
R *v*. Worthing BC ex parte Burch (1984) JPL 261 87
R *v*. Wells Street Magistrate, ex parte Wesminster City Council, (1986) JPL
    902; [1986] 3 All ER 4 120
R *v*. Yeovil B.C., ex parte Trustees of Elim Pentecostal Church, (1971) LGR
    142; 116 Sol Jo 78; 23 P&CR 39 93
Radstock Co-operative & Industrial Society *v*. North Radstock U.D.C.;
    [1968] Ch 605; [1968] 2 WLR 1214; 132 JP 238; 112 SJ 135; [1968] 2
    All ER 59; [1968] EGD 136 252
Rann *v*. Secretary of State for the Environment, (1980) JPL 109; (1979) 40
    P&CR 113 17
Ransom and Luck Ltd. *v*. Surbiton B.C., [1949] Ch 180; [1949] 1 All ER
    185; 47 LGR 467 109
Ratcliffe *v*. Department of the Environment and Bury M.B.C., [1975] JPL
    728 ....11, 27
Reading B.C. *v*. Secretary of State for the Environment, (1986) JPL 115
    ....67, 88, 206, 242
Rhymney Valley DC *v* Secretary of State for Wales (1985) JPL 27 244
Rhys Williams *v*. Secretary of State for the Environment, (1985) JPL 29 86
Richmond-upon-Thames LBC *v*. Secretary of State for the Environment,
    (1984) JPL 24 ....87, 112
Robert Barnes & Co Ltd *v*. Malvern Hills D.C. [1985] 1 EGLR 189; (1985)
    274 EG 830 233
Robertson *v*. Secretary of State for the Environment, [1976] 1 WLR 371 269
Royco Homes *v*. Eatonwill Construction, [1978] 2 WLR 957; (1977) SJ
    385; [1978] 2 All ER 821 250
Royco Homes *v*. Southern Water Authority, (1979) JPL 249; 78 LGR 56 257
Runnymede BC *v*. Ball[1986] 1 All ER 629 178

S

Salford C.B.C. Re, (1972) JPL 219 11
Saleem *v*. Bradford UBC (1984) 271 EG 119 270
Sample J. (Warkworth) Ltd. *v*. Alnwick D.C. [1984] 271 EG 204; (1984) JPL
    670 233
Scott *v*. Secretary of State for the Environment, (1983) JPL 108 170
Scott Markets Ltd. *v*. Waltham Forest LBC., (1979) 37 P&CR 91; [1979]
    JPL 96; 77 LGR 565; CA 178

Shaddock & Associates Pty Ltd *v.* Parramatta City Council (1981) 55 Australian Law Reports 713 57
Shemara *v.* Luton Corpn., [1967] 18 P&CR 520; [1967] EGD 554 74
Shepherd *v.* Secretary of State for the Environment, (1975) 233 EG 1167; [1975] EGD 837 ....96, 211
Simpson *v.* Edinburgh Corpn., (1960) SC 313 87
Slough Estates Ltd. *v.* Slough B.C. (No. 2), [1969] 2 All ER 988; [1969] 2 Ch. 305; [1969] 2 WLR 1157; 133 JP 479; 113 Sol Jo 307; 20 P&CR 363; 210 EG 337; CA; affirmed, [1970] 2 All ER 216; [1971] AC 573; 68 LGR 699; HL 94, 95
Smith *v.* King, (1970) 21 P&CR 560 ....171, 177
Spackman *v.* Secretary of State for the Environment, [1977] 1 All ER 257; [1977] JPL 174; 33 P&CR 430 98
Square Meals Frozen Foods *v.* Dunstable Corporation, [1974] 1 WLR 59; 117 SJ 875; (1974) 1 All ER 441; [1973] 26 P&CR 560; (1973) 72 LGR 180; [1974] EGD 777 244
Steeples *v.* Derbyshire C.C., [1981] JPL 582 ....92, 112, 188, 239, 241
Stephenson *v.* Secretary of State for the Environment, [1985] 1 EGLR 178; (1985) 274 E.G. 1385 242
Stoke-on-Trent C.C. *v.* B&Q Retail Ltd [1984] 2 WLR 929 178
Street *v.* Essex C.C., (1965) 193 EG 537 8
Stringer *v.* Minister of Housing and Local Government, [1971] 1 All ER 65; [1970] 1 WLR 1281; 114 Sol Jo 753; 65 LGR 788; 22 P&CR 255; 215 EG 1023 ....89, 109, 244
Sunbury-on-Thames U.D.C. *v.* Mann, (1958) 56 LGR 235; 9 P&CR 309; 171 EG 685; [1958] JPL 665; [1958] EGD 187 ....7, 97
Surrey Heath B.C. *v.* Secretary of State (1986) 17 CSW 1010 88
Sykes *v.* Secretary of State for the Environment, (1981) JPL 285 17

T

Tessier *v.* Secretary of State for the Environment, (1975) 120 Sol Jo 8; 74 LGR 279; 31 P&CR 161; 237 EG 117; [1976] EGD 767 18
Texas Home Care Ltd. *v.* Lewes D.C. (1986) 51 P&CR 205; [1986] 1 EGLR 205 233
Thames Water Authority *v.* Blue and White Laundrettes Ltd., [1980] 1 WLR 700; (1979) 124 SJ 100; (1979) 78 LGR 237 254
Thomas David (Porthcawl) Ltd. *v.* Penybont R.D.C., [1972] 1 All ER 733; [1972] 1 WLR 354; 116 Sol Jo 197; 70 LGR 295; 221 EG 1331; affirmed, [1972] 3 All ER 1092; [1972] 1 WLR 1526; 137 JP 85; 116 Sol Jo 765; 71 LGR 89; 24 P&CR 309 ....19, 166
Thrasyroulou *v.* Secretary of State for the Environment, (1984) JPL 732 175
Tidswell *v.* Secretary of State for the Environment, [1977] JPL 104; [1976] 241 EG 83; (1976) 34 P&CR 152 42
Tithe Redemption Commission *v.* Runcorn R.D.C., [1954] 2 WLR 518; [1954] 1 All ER 653; 118 JP 265; 98 SJ 212 ....250, 261
Trevor Warehouses Ltd. *v.* S.S.E. (1972) 23 P&CR 215 171
Turner *v.* Secretary of State for the Environment, (1973) 72 LGR 380; 28 P&CR 123; 228 EG 335; [1973] EGD 1094 238

V

Vale of Glamorgan, BC *v.* Palmer (1984) JPL 334 144
Vickers Armstrong *v.* Central Land Board (1957) 9 P&CR 33 18

W

Wain *v*. Secretary of State for the Environment, [1981] JPL 678; 125 Sol Jo
  791; [1981] 259 EG 857; reversed (1982) 262 EG 337 211
Wakelin *v*. Secretary of State for the Environment, (1978) JPL 769 ....18, 26
Walters *v*. Secretary of State for Wales, (1978) 249 EG 245 89
Ward *v*. Wychavon D.C. [1986] 2 EGLR 205; (1986) 279 EG 77 270
Wealden D.C. *v*. Secretary of State for the Environment, (1983) JPL 234 175
Wealden D.C. *v*. Secretary of State for the Environment, (1986) JPL 753 154
Webb *v*. Secretary of State for the Environment, (1972) 24 EG 869 203
Webber *v*. Minister of Housing and Local Government, [1968] 1 WLR 29;
  132 JP 86; 111 Sol Jo 890; 66 LGR 159; 19 P&CR 1 28
Weitz *v*. Secretary of State for the Environment, (1985) JPL 17 91
Weitz *v*. Secretary of State for the Environment, (1987) CSW 21/5/87, 61,
  on app. from (1983) JPL 811 242
Wells *v*. Minister of Housing and Local Government (1967) 18 P&CR 401;
  [1967] 2 All ER 1041 57
Welsh Aggregates Ltd. *v*. Secretary of State for Wales (1983) 265 EG 43 177
West Bowers Farm Products *v*. Essex C.C. (1985) JPL 857; [1985] 1 EGLR
  271 43
Western Fish Products Ltd. *v*. Penwith D.C., [1980] JPL 2, 331, 419 57
Westminster City Council *v*. British Waterways Board [1984] 3 All ER 737;
  (1984) JPL 507 ....21, 90
Westminster C.C. *v*. Jones, (1981) JPL 750 178
Westminster Renslade Ltd. *v*. Secretary of State for the Environment (1983)
  JPL 454 113
William Leech Ltd. *v*. Severn Trent Water Authority, (1981), [1982] JPL
  110 250
Williams *v*. Minister of Housing and Local Government (1967) 18 P&CR
  514 21
Winchester City Council *v*. Secretary of State for the Environment, [1978]
  JPL 467; 36 P&CR 455 203
Windsor and Maidenhead R.B. *v*. Brandrose Investments Ltd., [1983] 1 All
  ER 818; (1983) 266 EG 1195; (1983) JPL 374 109
Winton *v*. Secretary of State for the Environment, (1984) JPL 188; (1983)
  461 All ER 205 26
Wipperman and another *v*. London Borough of Barking, (1965) 130 JP 103;
  64 LGR 97; 17 P&CR 225; [1965] EGD 349 24
Wivenhoe Port Ltd. *v*. Colchester BC, (1985) JPL 396 94
Wontner-Smith *v*. Secretary of State for the Environment, [1977] JPL 103 205
Wood *v*. Secretary of State for the Environment, [1973] 2 All ER 404;
  [1973] 1 WLR 707; 137 JP 491; 117 Sol Jo 430; 71 LGR 339; 25 P&CR
  303; [1973] EGD 1077 25

Y

Young *v*. Secretary of State for the Environment, (1983) JPL 677; [1983] 3
  WLR 382; [1983] 2 All ER 1105 ....30, 36

Table of Statutes

Page

Acquisition of Land Act 1981 ....268, 270
Alkali Works Regulation Act 1906 141
Ancient Monuments and Archaelogical Areas Act 1979 .... 125, 229, 231
    s. 1 125
       2 ....125, 231
       3 125
       7 231
     12 125
     28 125
     33 126
     35 126
     39 126
     40 126
Agriculture Act 1986 129
Agricultural Holdings Act 1986 76
Caravan Sites and Control of Development Act 1960 153
    s. 1 154
     1(4) 154
     2 154
     3 154
     4 155
     5 155
     5(1) 155
     7 155
     8 155
     9 155
Clean Air Acts 1956–68 141
Community Land Act 1975 ....184, 191, 274
Control of Advertisement Regulations 1984 232
Control of Pollution Act 1974 141
Countryside Act 1968 126
Development Land Tax Act 1976 ....274, 275
Electricity Act 1947 ....258, 259
Electricity Act 1957 258
Electric Lighting (Clauses) Act 1899 ....258, 259
Finance Act 1980 140
Forestry Act 1967 ....143, 147, 232
    s. 9(4) 147
     15(1) 147
Forestry Act 1986 147
Gas Act 1986 257
    s. 10 257
     11 257

    Schedule 3 258
Government of Ireland Act 1920 218
Health and Safety and Work Act 1974 142
Highways Act 1980 .... 262, 263, 266, 268
    s. 35 266
        36 265
        37 265
        38 .... 108, 265, 267
        41 266
        58 266
        116(1) 268
            (3) 268
            (7) 268
        117 268
        118 268
        119 269
        137 263
        139 263
        140 263
        168 264
        169 264
        170 264
        171 264
        172 264
        173 264
        176 264
        177 265
        179 264
        205(1) 266
        208 266
        209 ....266, 269
        210 270
            (1) 270
        211 267
        212 ....267, 270
        214 270
        219(1) 267
            (4) 267
        220 268
        221 268
        222 268
        223 268
        225 268
        228 268
        229 268
        278 108
Housing Act 1985 ....268, 270
Housing and Planning Act 1986 ....18, 47, 48, 142, 207, 211
    s. 41 ....61, 63
       42 207
    Schedule 10 ....61, 63
Land Commission Act 1967 ....184, 274
Land Compensation Act 1961 273
Law of Property Act 1925

s. 84(1) 111
Local Government Act 1972 ....51, 52, 63
s. 101 56
111 108
123 193
222 178
250 .... 190, 206, 207
Sch 16 52
para. 19 83
Local Government Act 1985 ....52, 65
s. 3 55
4 55
5 55
6 55
Local Government (Miscellaneous Provisions) Act 1953
s. 13 254
Local Government (Miscellaneous Provisions) Act 1982
s. 33 108
Local Government and Planning (Amendment) Act 1981 163
Local Government, Planning and Land Act 1980 ....52, 61, 67, 83, 137, 148, 192
s. 86(3) 67, 87
87 70
93 192
94 193
95 193
95(4) 193
96 193
98(1) 193
99 193
102(1) 191
103(1) 191
103(2) 191
103(3) 191
103(5) 191
103(6) 191
103(7) 191
104(1) 192
104(2) 192
105 192
134 189
135(1) 189
136 189
136(3) 190
148(1) 190
148(2) 190
149(1) 190
149(3) 190, 191
150 191
151 191
Sch 14 163
15
para. 7 120
Sch 16 192
Sch 18 191

Sch 20 192
   para. 1 192
        2 192
        3 192
        4 192
        6 192
        6(5) 192
        7 192
        7(4) 192
        9 192
   Schedule 29 ....190, 191
Sch 32 137
   para. 2(1) 137
        2(2) 137, 138
        2(3) 138
        3(1) 138
        3(2) 138
        3(3) 138
        3(7) 138
        4 138
        4(2) 138
        5(1) 139
        5(3) 139
        5(4) 139
        6 139
        17(1) 139
        17(3) 139
        17(4) 140
        17(5) 140
        17(6) 139
        18 140
        22 140
        27(1) 140
        27(3) 140
        28 140
        29 140
   Schedule 32..32
   para. 1 137
Local Land Charges Act 1975
   s. 10 223
London County Council (Tower Bridge Southern Approach) Act 1895 273
National Heritage Act 1983 117
National Parks and Access to the Countryside Act 1949 ....126, 127
   s. 87 127
     88 127
New Towns Act 1946 189
New Towns Act 1981 189
Nuclear Installations Act 1965 142
Public Health Act 1936
   s. 15 ....251, 254
     17 252
     18 ....108, 253
     19 253
     20 249

s. 32 250
34 253
36 253
Redundant Churches and Other Religious Buildings Act 1969 124
Town and Country Planning Act 1932 273
Town and Country Planning Act 1947 ....60, 183, 184, 217, 220, 223
Town and Country Planning Act 1953 274
Town and Country Planning Act 1968 60
Town and Country Planning Act 1971
s. 3A 148
6 61
7 186
7(3) 61
7(5) 61
8 62
9(1) 62
9(3) 62
11 64
11A 63
11B 64
12(2) 64
12(3) 64
12(4) 64
12A 64
12B 64
13 65
14 ....65, 249
14(8) 65
15 66
15B 66
20 66
22(1) 7, 11, 15, 148
22(2) 15, 104
22(2)(a) 8
22(2)(b) 8
22(2)(c) 8
22(2)(d) 16
22(2)(e) 16
22(2)(f) 17, 23
22(3) 11, 17, 19
22(3)(a) 19
22(3)(b) 19
22(5) 221
23 ....28, 32
23(1) 7, 32, 163
23(2) 32
23(3) 32
23(4) 33
23(5) 35
23(8) 31, 35
23(9) 28, 36, 172
24 190
24A–24E 47
26 77

s. 26(2) 77
27(1) 76
27(1)(CC) 149
27(2) 76
27(3) 76
27(5) 76
27(7) 76
28 ....78, 123
29 .... 59, 66, 105, 200, 201
29(1) 81, 87, 88, 99
30 164
30(1)(a) 99, 104, 105
30(1)(b) 100
30A(1) 149
30A(6) 149
30A(7) 149
30A(9) 150
30A(10) 150
30A(11) 150
30A(12) 150
31 85
31A 72
32 98
33 ....28, 97
33(2) 30
34 76
35 ....85, 86
35(5) 86
36 ....107, 198
36(1) 75
36(3) 205
36(4) 199
36(6) 203
37 198
40 189
41 98
42(1) 73
42(2) 75
42(3) 75
42(4) 75
43 98
44 98
44A 150
45 .... 151, 159, 160, 227
45(2) 160
45(3) 160
45(4) 159
46(2) 160
46(3) 160
46(4) 160
46(5) 160
51 .... 151, 210, 227
51(1) 161
51(1A) 151

s. 51(1B) 151
51(1C) 151
51(2) 161
51(3) 161
51(4) 161
51(5) 161
51(6) 162
51(7) 162
51A 151
51B 151
51C 151
51F 151
52 ....128, 186
52(1) 108
52(2) 108
53 .... 7, 20, 27, 57, 198
54 ....118, 229
54(4) 118
54(5) 118
54(6) 118
54(7) 118
54(8) 118
54(9) 118
54A(1) 118
55 ....12, 119
55(2) 120
55(4) 120
55(5) 120
55(6) 120
56(1) 120, 122
56(2) 70
56(3) 91, 121
56(4) 122
56(5) 122
56A 122
56B 122
58 230
58(2) 122
59 143
60 ....147, 231
60(1) 143
60(4) 146
60(5) 145
60(6) 45
60(1A) 143
61 146
61(2) 146
61A 124, 147
61A(3) 147
62 ....145, 146
63 131
63(1) 131
63(4) 131, 136, 137
64 131

s. 87 .... 33, 169, 170
87(1) 163, 164, 171
87(3) 164, 169, 170
87(4) 165
87(5) 165, 170
87(6) 165
87(7) 170
87(8) 170
87(10)(a)(b) 170
87(16) 170
88 .... 173, 243
88(1) 173
88(2) 173
88(5)(d) 175
88(6) 174
88(7) 70, 175
88(8) 175
88A(1) 175
88A(2) 175
88A(3) 176
88B 176
88(10) 174, 177
89 177
90 232
90(1) 177
90(2) 178
90(3) 178
90(4) 178
90(7) 178
91 177
92(1) 179
92A 179
93(1) 179
94(2) 33
94(7) 33
95 35
95(6) 70
96(1) 179
96(1)(b)(ii) 179
96(1)(b)(iii) 180
97 .... 179, 180, 243
98 180
99 180
101 180
101(3) 180
101(4) 180
101(5) 180
101A 180
102(1) 144
102(2) 144
103 145
108 151
108(1) 162
108(2) 162

s. 109 131
112 ....185, 186
112(1) 185
112(1B) 185
112(1C) 185
112(13) 185
113 185
114 181
115 181
117 181
119 186
123 186
123(7) 186
124 186
127 270
127(3) 270
135 221
135(1) 221
136 ....189, 221
136(3) 190
137 221
138 221
139 221
140 221
141 221
142 221
143 221
144 221
146 222
147 222
148 222
148(1) 190
148(2) 190
149 190
149(3) 190
150 191
151 191
152 222
154 222
156 222
157 222
158 223
159 223
160 223
161 223
164 227
164(1) 152
164A 152
165 ....46, 47, 226
169 225
170 229
170(2) 152
170B 153
170B(3) 153

s. 170B(4) 153
171 229
172 230
173 ....119, 230
174 ....146, 231
175 231
176 232
177 ....178, 233
178A 152
178B 152
178C 152
180(1) 210
180(2) 213
181 214
182 214
183 ....214, 215
184 210
188 210
189 210
190 210
191 210
241 236
242 236
242(2) 237
242(3) 237
243 ....243, 244
243(1) 177, 243
244 ....68, 236
245 ....204, 237
246 244
264A 149
264(1A) 148
266(7) 187
270 188
277(1) 123
277(6) 123
277(7) 123
277(8) 123
277(9) 123
277A 12, 124
277B 123
290 ....148, 211, 33
290(1) 9, 16, 148
Sch   5 60
        8 ....213, 221, 223
        9 199
       11 ....101, 121
   para. 5 121
        8 121
Sch   8A 47, 48
Sch 24
   para. 12 32
Town and Country Planning Act 1984 187
   4(2) 173

Town and Country Planning (Amendment) Act 1972 ....61, 63
    s. 3 63
Town and Country Planning (Ammendment) Act 1985 147
Town and Country Planning (Compensation) Act 1985 47
    s. 1 ....225, 226
Town and Country Planning (Minerals) Act 1981 ....148, 160
    s. 7 150
Town and Country Planning (Scotland) Act 1972
    s. 21A–21E 47
    Schedule 6A 47
Tribunals and Inquiries Act 1971
    s. 11 200
Water Act 1945
    s. 27 257
    31 256
    36 256
    37 256
    Schedule 3 ....255, 256
Water Act 1973 ....249, 255
    s. 11 255
    13 255
    14 251
    16 ....251, 252
Water Act 1981 255
Wildlife and Countryside Act 1981
    s. 28 127
    29 128
    29(9) 128
    39(1) 128
    39(2) 128

Table of Orders, Regulations and Other Statutory Instruments

Builders' Skip (Markings) Regulations 1984 264
Notification of Installations Handling Hazardous Substances
    Regulations 1982 18
Order 53 of the Rules of the Supreme Court 238, 243
Town and Country Planning (Agricultural and Forestry Development in National
    Parks, etc) Special Development Order 1986 .... 43, 44, 127
Town and Country Planning Appeals (Determination by Appointed Persons)
    (Inquiries Procedure) Rules 1974 199
Town and Country Planning (Appeals) (Written Representations Procedure) Regula-
    tions 1987 204
Town and Country Planning (Compensation for Restrictions on Mineral Working)
    Regulations 1985 152
Town and Country Planning (Control of Advertisements)
    Regulations 1984 131
    Regulation   3 132
             5 136
             9 .... 133, 136
            12 .... 132, 136
            13 134
            14 .... 134, 136
            15 135
            16 .... 133, 134, 135
            17 136
            19 136
            20 .... 134, 136
            22 136
            23 136
            26 136
            27 136
Town and Country Planning (Determination of Appeals by Appointed Persons)
    (Prescribed Classes) Regulations 1981 199
Town and Country Planning (Determination of Appeals by Appointed Persons)
    Regulations 1986 199
Town and Country Planning (Development Plans) Direction 1981 78
Town and Country Planning (Enforcement) (Inquiries Procedure) Rules
    1981 .... 148, 199
Town and Country Planning (Enforcement Notice and Appeals) Regulations
    1981 .... 169, 173
Town and Country Planning (Fees for Applications and Deemed Applications)
    Regulations 1983 .... 70, 173
    Regulation 4 71
             5 71
             6 71
             7 71

Regulation 8 .... 70, 71, 173
Sch 1 72
    para. 6 73
Town and Country Planning (General) Regulations 1976 .... 91, 188
Town and Country Planning General Development
    Order 1977 .... 37, 81, 125, 198, 220, 226, 285, 317
    Article 3 .... 37, 41
         4 .... 46, 220, 226
         4A 46
         5 73
         6 74
         7 93
         7A 81
         8 77
         10 85
         11 84
         12 84
         14 85
         15 .... 82, 128
         16 83
         17 84
         21 76
    Sch 1 .... 38, 71
Town and Country Planning General Development (Amendment) Order 1981 31
Town and Country Planning (Inquiries Procedure) Rules 1974 199
Town and Country Planning (Listed Buildings and Buildings in Conservation Areas)
    Regulations 1987 .... 121, 124
    Regulation 3 120
         5 121
         6 121
         12 124
Town and Country Planning (National Parks, Areas of Outstanding Natural Beauty
    and Conservation Areas) Special Development Order 1981 .... 38, 124
Town and Country Planning (National Parks, Areas of Outstanding Natural Beauty,
    Conservation Areas etc) Special Development Order 1985 127
Town and Country Planning (Prescription of County Matters)
    Regulations 1980 53
Town and Country Planning (Structure and Local Plans)
    Regulations 1982 .... 62, 64
Town and Country Planning (Tree Preservation Orders) Regulations 1969 as
    amended by the Town and Country Planning (Tree Preservation Order)
    Amendment Regulations 1981 .... 145, 146, 148
    Regulation 4 145
         5 145
         6 145
         8 145
         9 145
Town and Country Planning (Tree Preservation Order) (Amendment) and (Trees in
    Conservation Areas) (Exempted Cases) Regulations 1975 148
Town and Country Planning (Use Classes) Order 1987 .... 17, 23, 40, 277
Town and Country Planning (Use Classes for Third Schedule Purposes) Order 1948
    No. 955 .... 213, 226

Table of Circulars

67/49*	Town and Country Planning (General Development Amendment) Order 1949	20, 21, 24
42/55	Green Belts	129
82/77	Town and Country Planning (Amendment) Act 1977	178
36/78	Trees and Forestry	145
22/80	Development Control-Policy and Practice	86, 164
2/81	Development Control Functions	78, 84, 85
32/81	Wildlife and Countryside Act 1981	128
38/81	Planning and Enforcement Appeals	163
21/82	Mineral Aggregates	148
13/83	Purchase Notices	209, 213
22/83	Planning Gain	86, 112
15/84	Land For Housing	86
16/84	Industrial Development	86
18/84	Public Local Inquiries: Objections	187
23/84	Applications: Conservation Areas	78
1/85	Planning Conditions	101, 107
2/85	Restoration	148
14/85	Development and Employment	86
24/85	Silica Sand	148
11/86	Town and Country Planning (Minerals) Act 1981	148
18/86	Planning Appeals: Written Representations	204
2/87	Statutory Inquiries: Award of Costs	160, 206, 207
4/87	Enforcement Notices: Compensation	178
8/87	Historic Buildings and Conservation Areas	117, 121, 123
11/87	Planning Appeal Regulations	204
16/87	Agricultural Land: Development	86

(The circular marked *, although now withdrawn, still contains useful advice).

Chapter 1

Introduction

This book is divided into seven principal parts to deal with the wide range of topics that fall within the scope of its title. Inevitably development control is one of the most significant matters that concern any person involved in the development of land. Before 1925 the biggest impediment to the full economic realisation of land was the complicated forms of land ownership; today, attention is addressed to development controls, and in particular the use of land or buildings that is lawfully permitted under the planning Acts.

Nowhere outside the countries of the communist world will one find a form of statutory development control as comprehensive and detailed as that of the United Kingdom. The doctrine of supremacy of Parliament means that the Secretary of State for the Environment, the Minister responsible for development control policy and the initiation of legislation, enjoys wider powers in this field than is customary in other countries. The Minister has acquired these powers, including the power to make orders, rules and regulations, by way of delegated legislation, through a gradual process over the last thirty odd years since controls commenced in 1948. This process has been almost imperceptible to the casual observer; the young student of today is conditioned to accept that the State, through its various organs and agencies, exercises wide powers; others are more deeply concerned by this trend.

The growth of Ministerial powers has not gone unhindered by the courts; although it is noticeable that where the Minister loses in the courts, he later seeks legislation to avoid further judicial interference. The courts have been busy considering development control decisions where it is alleged that a decision is *ultra vires* the planning Acts, or there has been some procedural irregularity. The consequence of this judicial activity is a fast growing body of case-law, as the reader will in due course discover. Although most of this case-law is concerned with controlling administrative discretion (within statutory powers) on the part of a local planning authority or the Minister, it is invariably accepted by all concerned with development control in the same way as the precedent of previous cases is accepted in a primarily common law topic such as the law of torts. New concepts have evolved in development control cases,

1

such as the concepts of abandonment, the planning unit, or the planning history, which go further than mere statutory interpretation; they appear to be accepted as law. All these matters concerned with development control are dealt with in Part I.

At the conclusion of Part I, the reader will have some idea of the scope of development control. Part II deals with the decision-making process: the authorities, the development plans and the procedure in relation to planning applications. Some of the special controls that affect the development of land are found in Part III.

Positive planning and the enforcement of development controls are considered in Part IV. In this area the initiative lies with the local planning authorities to take action in respect of activities that are not in conformity with development plans and policies. Additionally, development is carried out in some cases directly or indirectly by public authorities.

Part V deals with the rights and remedies of developers and landowners. Some people regard the development control process as involving the making of political decisions about development, a view that is tenable in the sense that the primary decisions are those of local authorities, and these authorities are part of the political democratic institutions in this country. Other people regard the process as purely administrative decision-making; a technical and objective exercise within powers conferred by Parliament. In fact the truth probably lies somewhere between these two views. As the principal right of the developer or landowner against development control decisions is an appeal to the Secretary of State, his determination of an appeal is therefore partly political and partly objective administrative decision-making. This has not always been recognised by the courts when exercising their powers of judicial supervision. One can foresee that this dichotomy will become increasingly the subject of debate in the future.

Any developer will know that in putting together a development scheme, development control is only one of the matters to be resolved. He may require connections to public sewers or water supplies, or to the other services; and that the inadequacy of some of these facilities may influence the result of an application for planning permission. Sewers and roads may be built by the developer and he will want to be satisfied that these can be taken over by the appropriate authorities on completion of his scheme. The provision, requisition or adoption of these services are set out in Part VI together with the relevant aspects of the law of highways of interest to developers.

Part VII of this book only includes one chapter. Planning the use and development of land causes changes in the underlying land values; this phenomenon has a number of practical and political consequences. This chapter provides an outline of the problem and the way it has been handled.

Inevitably there may be legislative changes that affect some part of this book after it is published. This is a problem which all authors writing on a fast moving subject of a statutory nature have to face. Hopefully the problem has been minimised by concentrating on general principles that seem to possess a certain durability, it cannot be entirely solved so long as Parliament takes the active interest that it does in development and planning law.

The main statute concerned with development control and planning is at present the Town and Country Planning Act 1971, and, unless otherwise indicated, most references are to this Act. It has been much amended over the years so that the text of the amending Acts must also be consulted.

PART I

THE SCOPE OF DEVELOPMENT CONTROL

Chapter 2

Development Control and the Carrying Out of Operations

Introduction	7
Operations excluded from Development Control	8
Building operations	9
Engineering and Mining operations	10
Other operations	11
Demolition	12

2.1 Introduction

One of the most important provisions of the Town and Country Planning Act 1971 (the 1971 Act) is section 23(1), it states: "planning permission is required for the carrying out of any *development* of land." The word development is the key to the scope of development control; it covers two activities: the carrying out of certain operations, (considered in this chapter) and the making of a material change of use (see chapter 3). There is an elaborate enforcement procedure where there has been a breach of development control (see chapter 14). Planning permission for a *use* of land will not authorise the erection of buildings, as this entails the carrying out of *operations* (see *Sunbury-on-Thames UDC* v. *Mann* [1958]). Lord Denning M.R. explained the distinction between *uses* and *operations* in *Camrose* v. *Basingstoke Corpn.* [1966].

Section 22(1) of the 1971 Act defines development as to include "... the carrying out of building, engineering, mining or other operations in, on, over or under land ...". However, in any particular case, the question of what amounts to development is a question of fact, and is decided initially by the local planning authority. They may be asked to determine whether any particular activity is development upon an application for that purpose under section 53 of the Act. They may also make a preliminary determination because they have decided to take enforcement proceedings against an activity that has no planning permission. It is only if the local planning authority, or the Secretary of State upon appeal, make a decision using the wrong criteria, or reach an unreasonable decision in relation to the facts, that a developer will have a case for consideration

7

in the High Court (*Pyx Granite Co.* v. *Ministry of Housing* [1960]). Legal decisions are helpful as to the meaning of development in so far as they indicate the right criteria or the bounds of unreasonableness; they are not conclusive that any particular activity will or will not be development in every case.

2.2 Operations excluded from Development Control

Because the definition of the operations that constitute development is so wide, the 1971 Act excludes certain activities that would otherwise need planning permission. These include "... works for the maintenance, improvement or other alteration of any building, being works which affect only the interior of the building or which do not materially affect the external appearance of the building ..." (section 22(2)(a)); certain maintenance work carried out by a local highway authority within the boundaries of a road (section 22(2)(b)); and, work of inspection, repair or renewal of sewers, mains, pipes, cables or other apparatus by a local authority or statutory undertaker (section 22(2)(c)).

It can be seen that internal building work, of the type described above, is outside development control. But such work may require consent under the building regulations, or, if the building is listed, listed building consent (see chapter 10). Internal building work may be accompanied by a change of use of the building; the change of use may be within development control (see chapter 3).

Work which does not materially alter the external appearance of a building is not always easy to determine. The first question to ask is whether such work is maintenance, improvement or other alteration. In *Street* v. *Essex C.C.* [1965], it was held that the rebuilding of a cottage from damp-proof course up, to comply with housing fitness standards, was not work of maintenance. And, in *Larkin* v. *Basildon D.C.* [1980], where the building owner first pulled down and rebuilt two walls of a dwellinghouse and then subsequently did the same to a further two walls, the Divisional Court upheld the Secretary of State's decision that this was not work of improvement. Lord Parker C.J., in the *Street* case, said "whether works could fairly be said to amount to maintenance or were properly called reconstruction, must be a matter of fact and degree". The same point was made by the Court of Appeal in *Hewlett* v. *Secretary of State for the Environment* [1985] where Sir John Donaldson M.R. said in relation to a series of alterations to a building, that the Secretary of State was entitled to look at the totality of the work, and whether this resulted in a new building: it was not a question of law, but of fact and degree.

Unsatisfactory as it may seem to the developer, questions of fact and degree are first decided by the local planning authority (or the Secretary of State for the Environment upon an appeal). Only if the decision comes within a very narrow category of decisions, can the courts consider a review of the issue (this is more fully explained in chapter 19).

2.3   Building operations

To developers, building operations will be the most important of the operations that constitute development. Building operations are defined as including "... rebuilding operations, structural alterations of or additions to buildings, and other operations normally undertaken by a person carrying on business as a builder ..." (section 290(1) of the 1971 Act). This wide definition is made wider because a building includes "... any structure or erection and any part of a building, but does not include plant or machinery comprised in a building ..." (section 290(1)).

Plant or machinery erected outside a building may be regarded as structures or erections so as to involve building operations:

Barvis Ltd. v. *Secretary of State for the Environment* [1971] D.C.
  Barvis erected in their yard an 89 foot high crane, running on rails 120 feet long. The crane was easily dismantled and re-erected. Bridge J. held that "this enormous crane" could amount to a structure or erection, and the Minister was right in deciding that its erection constituted development.

In an earlier case, Lord Parker C.J. had indicated tests, additional to the language of the statute, to decide the meaning of "operations":

Cheshire C.C. v. *Woodward* [1962] D.C.
  Woodward installed a coal hopper and conveyor in his coalyard without planning permission. It was on wheels, resting on blocks, and 20 feet high. Lord Parker held the Minister was right in deciding the installation of this equipment was not development. Lord Parker said the question was whether the physical character of the land has been changed by operations in or on it; and the problem of determining the sort of operations likely to change the physical characteristics of land is analogous to the problem of deciding whether a fixture passes with the freehold—although one must undoubtedly look at the [1971] Act, the degree of permanency is extremely relevant in determining whether an operation constitutes development.

In *Parkes* v. *Secrtary of State for the Environment* [1979], Lord Denning M.R. applied similar tests in deciding that the storage of scrap was not an operation. He suggested that to be an operation there must be an activity which results in some physical alteration to the land, and which has some degree of permanence to the land itself.

The stationing of reasonably mobile caravans was held in *Guildford R.D.C.* v. *Penny* [1959] not to be an operation, although the stationing of the more permanent form of "mobile" home would seem to come within Lord Parker's test (see chapter 12 for additional controls over caravans).

The installation of external floodlights was held not to be development in *Kensington and Chelsea R.B.C.* v. *C.G. Hotels* [1981]. The work was too minor to be called an operation, and the real environmental consequence was due to the use of electricity in floodlighting. Because external lighting creates environmental problems (that at petrol filling stations is a good example), levels of luminosity may be controlled by planning conditions imposed with a planning permission needed for other building work.

For Ministerial decisions on what constitutes a building operation, reference should be made to the Bulletins of Selected Appeal Decisions (H.M.S.O.—various dates). It would appear that these decisions invariably involve Lord Parker's tests that an operation involves a change in the physical characteristics of the land and a degree of permanence.

2.4   Engineering and Mining operations

Engineering operations are defined to include "the formation or laying out of means of access to highways", otherwise engineering must be given its ordinary meaning, and it will be for the local planning authority (or the Secretary of State on appeal) to decide as a question of fact and degree whether an activity is an engineering operation. In *Fayrewood Fish Farms* v. *Secretary of State for the Environment* [1984], the judge said that an activity would be regarded as an "engineering operation" if the ordinary laymen would so regard it, and not because the activity was supervised by a qualified engineer.

In *Coleshill & District Investment Co. Ltd.* v. *Minister of Housing and Local Government and another* [1969], the House of Lords upheld the Minister's decision that the *demolition* of an embankment surrounding an explosive store was an "engineering operation". The *construction* of an earth embankment was also held to be an "engineering operation" in *Ewen Developments Ltd.* v. *Secretary of State for the Environment and North Norfolk D.C.* [1980].

Work carried out to alter the track of a greyhound racing stadium for stock car racing was held by the Minister to be "engineering operations" in an appeal case (re *Salford C.B.C.* [1972]).

Tipping of refuse or waste material would seem to be an operation: it satisfies both Lord Parker's tests of a change in the physical characteristics of the land and is permanent. In *Ratcliffe* v. *Department of the Environment and Bury M.B.C.* [1975] the Minister had concluded that a particular mode of tipping waste materials amounted to an "engineering operation". Paradoxically, section 22(3) of the 1971 Act provides that the deposit of refuse or waste materials on land involves a *material change of use* if either the superficial area of the deposit is extended or the height of the deposit is extended and exceeds the adjoining ground level. This problem is further considered in chapter 3. The distinction between activities that constitute operations or material changes of use is important for enforcement proceedings: the time limits within which proceedings may be taken can differ. In many cases there will be an overlap between building and engineering operations, as the definition of a building includes a structure or erection.

Although mining operations are within the scope of development control, there are now special provisions which make it more convenient to deal with mining in a later chapter (chapter 12).

2.5   Other Operations

The meaning of "other operations" in section 22(1) is usually interpreted under a rule of statutory interpretation as not adding any further operations to those of building, engineering or mining operations already specified (the *ejusdem generis* rule). Although this was doubted by the House of Lords in *Coleshill & District Investment Co. Ltd.* v. *Minister of Housing and Local Government* [1969] as "building," "engineering," and "mining" operations did not share a common genus; the maxim *noscitur a sociis* probably applied, and an activity must be construed by reference to these operations to be "other operations".

However, in a Ministerial decision ((1985) J.P.L. 129), where the activity in issue was the installation of a protective grill over a shop window, the Minister decided the work was too specialised to be a building operation, and he considered it was an "other operation" and needed planning permission.

One of the issues in *Bedfordshire C.C.* v. *C.E.G.B. and Others* [1985] was whether "Nirex", the Nuclear Industry Radioactive Waste Executive, needed planning permission to carry out site investigations by means of bore holes; the work would only have taken a few days. The judge considered whether such work could be an "other operation", but seemed to reject the idea because the work was so trivial: it did not change the physical appearance of the land, nor was there any degree of permanence.

2.6   Demolition

This activity has presented special problems. The developer is often tempted to demolish a building occupying a suitable site for redevelopment in order to force the hand of the local planning authority, or to avoid a building being listed where it may have a special interest. The local planning authority may not wish to see a building demolished that appears to them to have further use or which makes a contribution to the townscape or landscape.

If a building is listed because of its special interest, listed building consent is then needed for its demolition, and it is a criminal offence to proceed otherwise. In conservation areas, with some exceptions, consent is also required for the demolition of buildings. The exceptions include listed buildings (already protected), ecclesiastical buildings used for ecclesiastical purposes, buildings which are ancient monuments (already protected) and a description of buildings specified in a direction made by the Secretary of State (section 277A of the 1971 Act). It is otherwise an offence to demolish a building without the appropriate consent (section 55 of the 1971 Act—see more generally chapter 10).

Apart from the special provisions just described, the prevailing ministerial and judicial view is that demolition of a building will not usually be development. In *Coleshill & District Investment Co. Ltd.* v. *Minister of Housing and Local Government* [1969], the House of Lords considered the Minister was entitled to find that the demolition of an embankment was an "engineering operation"; this suggests that the scale of the work, and how it is carried out, may be relevant in categorising demolition as development in certain cases. But in *Iddenden* v. *The Secretary of State for the Environment* [1972], the Court of Appeal decided that the demolition of a nizzen hut and an old workshop was not development.

Partial demolition of a building could well involve a building or rebuilding operation, but it seems reasonable to conclude that the total demolition of a building is outside the scope of development control. This conclusion is strengthened by the fact that there is specific statutory provision for buildings in conservation areas which, presumably, would otherwise have been unnecessary (see above).

Chapter 3

Development Control and Change of Use

Introduction   15
Uses excluded from development control   15
Use Classes Order   17
Two doubtful cases: the division of dwelling houses and tipping   19
Meaning of material change of use   20
Uses that commenced before 1964   32
Established use certificates   33
Change of use not requiring planning permission   35

3.1 Introduction

Planning permission is required for development, and development includes:

> "... the making of any material change in the use of any buildings or other land" (section 22(1) of the 1971 Act).

This chapter is largely concerned with the meaning of these words in order to understand the scope of development control over a material change of use. However, some *uses* are specifically excluded from development control; or are *uses* which do not need planning permission because they existed in 1948; or are *uses*, giving rise to what are called "established use rights", which are now immune from enforcement action because they resulted from a material change of use between 1st July 1948 and 31st December 1963.

The Use Classes Order is separately considered: it does not determine whether certain changes of use are development requiring planning permission; its purpose is to exclude certain changes of use from development control.

3.2 Uses excluded from development control

Section 22(2) excludes certain uses from the meaning of development. The effect of this is that in either of the circumstances described below, planning permission is not required for these uses of land or buildings.

1.   Residential use within the curtilage of a dwelling-house

"the use of any buildings or other land within the curtilage
of a dwelling-house for any purpose incidental to the enjoyment
of dwelling-house as such" (section 22(2)(d))

Although the construction or alteration of buildings may be development, the use of buildings within the curtilage for the enjoyment
of the dwelling-house is not. Therefore a loft room above a garage
could be used as an extra bedroom if no building work was involved
that materially affected the external appearance of the building.
A vehicle could be parked on land within the curtilage if it was
there for the enjoyment of the occupiers of the dwelling-house as
such; but this exclusion would not apply if the vehicles were there
for business purposes—it would then become necessary to determine
the substantive point as to whether a material change of use had
occurred (see below).

A hut in *Prosser* v. *Sharp* [1985] was not regarded as a dwelling-
house so that a caravan parked nearby could not be regarded as
"incidental to the enjoyment of the dwelling-house as such".

2.   Agriculture and Forestry Use

"The use of any land for the purposes of agriculture or forestry
(including afforestation) and the use for any of those purposes
of any building occupied together with land so used" (section
22(2)(e))

Any land may be used for agriculture, or for forestry; or agricultural
land may be afforested and forestry land (subject to any tree preservation orders) may be converted into agricultural land, all without
planning permission as such uses are not development. Agriculture
is widely defined and includes horticulture, fruit growing, seed growing, dairy farming, livestock farming, the use of land for grazing,
as meadows, osier land, market gardens, nursery grounds, and the
use of land for woodlands ancillary to farming purposes (section
290(1) of the 1971 Act). In *Crowborough Parish Council* v. *Secretary of State and Wealden D.C.* [1981], the conversion of agricultural land to allotments was held not to involve development as
the use of land for allotments was within the definition of agriculture. In *North Warwickshire B.C.* v. *Secretary of State for the Environment* [1984] the word "land" was said to include buildings, so
that buildings can be used for agriculture, such as the breeding
of animals for their fur.

The use of land or buildings as a stud farm for horses was considered in *Belmont Farm Ltd.* v. *Minister of Housing and Local Government* [1962] to be outside the meaning of agriculture as the keeping and breeding of livestock within that definition was restricted to creatures kept for the production of food, wool, skins or fur, or for the purposes of its use in the farming of land. But in *Sykes* v. *Secretary of State for the Environment* [1981] where land was used for grazing horses, the Secretary of State's decision, that this use was within the definition of agriculture, was upheld by the court. Donaldson L.J. stated that the question in such cases was whether the predominant use of land kept for horses was for grazing—which is not development—or some other purpose which might involve development.

3.3   Use Classes Order

"... in the case of buildings or other land which are used for a purpose of any class specified in an order ... the use of the buildings or other land or, subject to the provisions of the order, of any part thereof for any purpose of the same class [does not involve development] ..." (section 22(2)(f)).

A new order (UCO), the Town and Country Planning (Use Classes) Order 1987, came into effect on 1 June 1987 (see Appendix A). The UCO classifies a number of uses of buildings and other land, and by section 22 of the Act, and article 3 of the order, where a building or other land is used for a purpose within one of the classes, a change of use to another purpose within the same class is not development. It does not follow that a change from one class to another will necessarily amount to development, that depends on general principles: *Rann* v. *Secretary of State for the Environment* [1980]. Certain changes between classes are granted deemed planning permission under the General Development Order (see Chapter 4 below).

The principal classes are reproduced in full in Appendix A, but can be summarised:

Class A1 Shops
Class A2 Financial and professional services
Class A3 Food and drink

Class B1 Business
Class B2 General industrial
Classes B3—B7 Special industrial Groups A—E
Class B8 Storage or distribution

Class C1 Hotels and Hostels
Class C2 Residential institutions
Class C3 Dwellinghouses

Class D1 Non-residential institutions
Class D2 Assembly and leisure

The manufacture, processing, keeping or use of hazardous substances in notifiable quantities is not a purpose within any class (Notification of Installations Handling Hazardous Substances Regulations 1982 (SI1357)). Article 3(6) provides that none of the specified classes includes use as a theatre, amusement arcade, funfair, laundrette or cleaners (where the goods to be cleaned are received direct from the public), petrol filling station, motor vehicle sales, taxi or hire business, scrapyard or breaker's yard.

Article 3(3) of the UCO provides that where a use is ordinarily incidental to any use that falls within one of the classes, it is not excluded from the use to which it is incidental merely because it is specified as a separate class. It is the *primary* use of a building or other land that identifies the class: *Vickers Armstrong* v. *Central Land Board* [1957]. And an incidental use cannot be turned into a primary use in its own right: *G. Percy Trentham Ltd.* v. *Gloucestershire C.C.* [1966]. However, the new business class—B1, which covers offices, research and light industrial, means that an incidental office use may now have independent use rights.

Whether a particular activity falls within a class is determined as a matter of fact and degree. In *Tessier* v. *Secretary of State for the Environment* [1975], it was accepted that the Secretary of State was entitled to decide that a sculptor's use of a building was a use *sui generis* and was not an industrial process falling within the general industrial class. Following amendments introduced by the Housing and Planning Act 1986, where premises are subdivided, and the new units continue to be used for purposes within the use class of the original use, then this will not involve development even if there is an intensification of uses that might on general principles involve a material change of use. This does not authorise any building operations that would otherwise amount to development. Dwellinghouses are excluded from the effect of the 1986 amendment; article 4 of the UCO provides that whenever a dwellinghouse is subdivided, e.g. by the sale of a "granny annex" lodge, nothing in the order has the effect of excluding the subdivision from the meaning of development. The Court of Appeal's decision in *Wakelin* v. *Secretary of State for the Environment* [1978], that the inspector was entitled to decide that the subdivision of a dwellinghouse and a lodge was a material change of use requiring planning permission, is therefore still relevant.

Although a change of use within a class is not development, and does not need planning permission, it was held in *City of London Corporation* v. *Secretary of State for the Environment* [1972] that it was lawful to impose a planning condition (see Chapter 9) restricting a change of use within the same use class.

3.4 Two Doubtful Cases: the division of dwelling-houses and tipping

Section 22(3) of the 1971 Act declares that, for the avoidance of doubt, two matters are to be considered as involving a material change of use:

(i) The use as two or more separate dwelling-houses of any building previously used as a single dwelling (section 22(3)(a)).

The conversion of a house into two flats is therefore a material change of use, and requires planning permission. A building which is in multiple paying occupation, with the tenants and lodgers living separately, although perhaps sharing a communal kitchen, a bathroom and lavatory, is not necessarily a building used as two or more separate dwelling-houses: *Ealing B.C.* v. *Ryan* [1965]. The borough council need not have relied on section 22(3) as a change of use to multiple paying occupation is likely to involve a material change of use: *Birmingham Corpn* v. *Minister of Housing and Local Government and Habib Ullah* [1964] (see also page 22).

(ii) The deposit of refuse or waste materials on land, even if the land is comprised in a site already so used, if either the area of the deposit it extended, or the height of the deposit is extended and exceeds the adjoining ground level (section 22(3)(b)).

This provision may leave in doubt whether tipping that is outside its scope involves a material change of use or is an operation. The Court of Appeal decided that tipping was a material change of use in the case of *Bilboe* v. *Secretary of State for the Environment* [1980]. Paradoxically, the opposite activity, excavation work, is an operation: *Thomas David* v. *Penybont R.D.C.* [1972]. The importance of this distinction has already been noted (page 11).

3.5   The meaning of material change of use

So far we have considered certain uses which are specifically excluded from the meaning of material change of use, and two matters which are stated to involve such a change. Now we must consider the principles for deciding whether there is a material change of use in all other cases.

1.   Question of fact and degree for the planning authority

It must be appreciated that a change of use is only a material change of use, and therefore within development control, when the local planning authority or the Secretary of State so decide. Such a decision will be made when a developer seeks a determination under section 53 of the 1971 Act as to whether a proposal involves development, or when an enforcement notice is served because of an alleged breach of planning control. Developers apply for planning permission to avoid enforcement action and to establish lawful use rights in the interest of the marketability of property.

The role of the law is therefore limited to establishing the matters that planning authorities should or should not take into account in deciding the question on the facts they have before them. Provided they keep within these legal boundaries, whether any particular change of use is development is therefore a factual rather than legal question. In *Blackpool B.C.* v. *Secretary of State for the Environment* [1980], the inspector, in her report to the Secretary of State, stated she was making a practical judgement of the essential nature of an activity and was not laying down any principle of law when deciding that the use of a house for holiday lettings was not a material change of use. The Divisional Court agreed that she was entitled to reach this conclusion as a question of fact and degree.

Early Ministerial guidance as to the intended meaning of material change of use is found in Circular 67/1949, although now withdrawn, it is still a useful starting point to the problem:

> "... in considering whether a change is a material change, comparison with the previous use of the land or building in question is the governing factor and the effect of the proposal on a surrounding neighbourhood is not relevant to the issue."

There are two points here: the effect on the neighbourhood is irrelevant in first deciding whether a change is a material change of use; but if that is answered affirmatively, the effect on the neighbourhood may well be a relevant consideration in deciding whether to *permit* a change of use. The Circular continues:

"The effect of the [word material] is to make clear that a proposed change of use constitutes development only if the new use is substantially different from the old. A change in kind will always be material—e.g., from house to shop. A change in the degree of an existing use may be "material" but only if it is very marked."

This extract identifies two ideas that now need considering: that a material change of use occurs where a new use commences which is substantially different from the old; or, alternatively it may occur where there is an intensification of an existing use.

2. The new use must be substantially different from the old

In *Guildford R.D.C.* v. *Penny* [1959], the Court of Appeal decided that a material change of use depended on whether there was a material change in the character of the use of the property in issue. *East Barnett U.D.C.* v. *British Transport Commission* [1962] was one of the first cases on this problem. Certain land had been used for the storage and distribution of coal; it was then let to Vauxhall Motors Ltd for the storage of boxed motor vehicles. In dealing with the word "material", Lord Parker C.J. said it must refer to material as material for *planning purposes*, and he added:

"What really is to be considered is the character of the use of the land, not the particular purpose of a particular occupier ... the mere fact that the commodity changes does not necessarily mean that the land is being used for a different purpose."

He concluded that the justices had correctly quashed the enforcement notice that alleged material change of use.

Lord Bridge in *Westminster City Council* v. *British Waterways Board* [1984] emphasised that the identity of the occupier was irrelevant; it was the activities carried on at the premises in issue that were relevant in planning law.

In *Williams* v. *Minister of Housing and Local Government* [1967] Widgery J. said that there was a significant difference in the character of a use which involves selling produce of the land itself, and selling goods brought in from elsewhere.

It might be argued that a home occupied by a single family unit and a home in multiple occupation are both in residential use. But Lord Parker C.J. in the *East Barnet* case introduced the idea that it is the *purpose* of the use that is important, and if this is materially different from the previous use from a planning point of view, there is a material change of use:

Birmingham Corp. v. *Minister of Housing and Local Government and Habib Ullah* [1964] D.C.

Three houses had previously been occupied by a single family each. They were then used for multiple paying occupation without planning permission. It was held that such a change of use could be material: the purpose of the new use, letting rooms for gain, is different from the previous use of a house for a private family. (See now Class C3 of 1987 UCO.)

The courts, in construing the meaning of "material change of use", seem to have developed three ideas: a change of use is material if it has planning consequences on the neighbourhood, or there is a change in the character of the use, or the purpose of the use is different from the old.

3.   A change in the degree of an existing use

The suggestion here is that an intensification of an existing use can involve a material change of use. In *Guildford R.D.C.* v. *Penny* [1959] Lord Evershed M.R. said:

> "... increasing intensity of use or occupation may involve a substantial increase in the burden of the services which a local authority has to supply, and that, in truth, might, in some cases at least, be material in considering whether the use of the land had been materially changed."

In other words, if there are planning consequences, there may be a material change of use. In the case, an increase in the number of caravans on a site from eight to twenty-six was not considered to involve a material change of use. In the *Habib Ullah* case, (see above) it was not the increase in the number of occupants of the houses concerned that involved a material change of use, it was the change of the purpose of the use. A material change of the use occurred in *Peake* v. *Secretary of State for Wales* [1971]. The owner of a private garage used it for vehicle repair on a part-time basis. When he lost his job, he then repaired vehicles at the garage on a full-time basis. The change of use from an incidental activity to a use of a more substantial character was material.

In *Marshall* v. *Nottingham C.C.* [1960] an enforcement notice was served alleging intensification of use: the site had been used for the manufacture and sales of wooden buildings, but from 1957, it was used for the selling of caravans and wooden buildings. It was held that there was no material change of use merely because the wooden buildings were no longer made on site, or because caravans were not originally sold. Neither was there a material change of use through intensification as the uses after 1957 were so greatly intensified in comparison with the original uses. The notion that there is some principle of intensification was criticised by the Court of Appeal in *Kensington and Chelsea R.B.C.* v. *Secretary of State for the Environment* [1981]. Donaldson L.J. said that the issue was about a material "change" of use from one condition to another. The problem of intensification of an existing use was clearly stated by Lawton L.J. in *Brooks and Burton* v. *Secretary of State for the Environment* [1978]:

> "... intensification of use can be a material change of use. Whether it is or not depends on the degree of intensification. Matters of degree are for the Secretary of State to decide."

What is also clear from this case is that if a use is within one of the classes of the Use Classes Order, and even if an intensification of the use amounted to a material change of use on the general principles now being discussed, an intensification of such a use does not involve development: changes of use within a class are excluded by section 22(2)(f) of the 1971 Act. Therefore an intensification of any shop use, or an industrial process, can never involve development. Intensification problems are therefore confined to uses outside the Use Classes Order.

4. Ancillary and multiple uses

Where there is a principal use of land or buildings, an ancillary use is regarded as part of the principal use. Therefore if the ancillary use becomes the principal use, a material change of use may be involved. This idea is true whether or not a use is within the Use Classes Order:

> *Percy Trentham Ltd.* v. *Gloucestershire C.C.* [1966] C.A.
> Farm buildings, which had previously been used by the appellant's predecessor for storing farm machinery and equipment in connection with a 75 acre farm, were then used by the appellant for storing building materials. Although both uses were storage, one was incidental to a farming use. The new storage use was for a different principal activity, that of a building contractor, and a material change of use was involved.

In some cases there are mixed uses and no principal use is apparent. Whether the uses are on separate areas, or intermingled, a comparison between the overall use of the land at one time should be made with the overall use at a later time; if that comparison suggests a material change of use, then there is development:

Wipperman and another v. *London Borough of Barking* [1965] D.C.
Prior to 1962 land was used for storage of fence material and for car-breaking. After that date the land was used for storage of materials for the building of conservatories. It was held that the two original uses were not ancillary to each other but dissimilar uses; that the new storage use of the whole area had changed the character of the land as a while and involved a material change of use.

This case also established that the mere cessation of one of a number of uses was not as such a material change of use unless there was some intensification of the remaining use: see also *Philglow Ltd.* v. *Secretary of State for the Environment* [1984].

5.   The Planning Unit

Circular 67 (see page 20) anticipated the problem that occurs where a change of use involves only part of a building:

> "The Minister takes the view that the question whether there is a material change of use should be decided in relation to the whole premises and not merely in relation to the part, i.e., the point at issue is whether the character of the whole existing use will be substantially affected by the change which is proposed in a part of the building. He would not for instance regard as constituting a material change of use the use by a professional man—say a doctor or dentist—of one or two rooms in his private dwelling for the purpose of consultation with his patients so long as this use remained ancillary to the main residential use".

Planning control concerns the change of use of 'any buildings or other land'; that raises the question as to the proper unit for consideration. In *East Barnet U.D.C.* v. *B.T.C.* [1962].
Lord Parker C.J. said it was a matter of common sense. A useful set of guidelines is to be found in:

Burdle v. *Secretary of State for the Environment* [1972] D.C.
An area of land had been used for the business of a scrapyard and car breakers; there was also some evidence of on-site retail sales of car parts; a lean-to had been used as an office in connection with the business. Burdle bought the business. He started to sell new car parts and camping equipment from the lean-to. The local planning authority served an enforcement notice alleging material change of use of the lean-to to a shop. The

Secretary of State's decision that the enforcement notice should only relate to the lean-to and not the whole site was not accepted by the court.

The court had to consider what was the proper planning unit. In other words, had there been a material change of use of the whole site, or of the lean-to? Clearly the answer in each case might be different. This is an important question because if the local planning authority can select some small part of a person's curtilage, it may be easier to show that there has been a material change of use of that small part rather than some larger area. As Lord Widgery L.J. in *De Mulder* v. *Secretary of State for the Environment* [1974] put the matter:

"... a planning authority by an arbitrary division of an area into a number of smaller areas each with its own enforcement notice cannot by that means impose more severe restrictions on the landowner than might have been imposed on him by an enforcement notice applicable to the whole area".

The need for a planning authority to correctly identify the proper planning unit is illustrated by *Kensington and Chelsea R.B.C.* v. *Secretary of State for the Environment* [1981]. The owners of a restaurant extended the seating area into the garden. It was held that the proper planning unit was the whole premises, and not just the garden, so the question was whether there had been a material change of use of the whole premises, and not just the garden area.

Bridge J. in the *Burdle* case propounded some useful tests for determined the proper planning unit:

(a) Where there is a single main purpose of the occupier's use of his land to which secondary activities are incidental or ancillary, the whole unit of occupation should be the planning unit;

(b) Where an occupier carries out a variety of activities and it is not possible to say that one is incidental or ancillary to another, then, again the whole unit of occupation should be the planning unit; and

(c) Where, within a single unit of occupation, there are two or more physically separate and distinct areas occupied for substantially different and unrelated purposes, each area used for a different main purpose (together with its incidental and ancillary activities) is a planning unit.

In relation to two or more uses of one building, Lord Widgery C.J. said in *Wood* v. *Secretary of State for the Environment* [1973]:

"... it can rarely if ever be right to dissect a single dwelling-house and to regard one room in isolation as being an appropriate planning unit ..."

But in *Wakelin* v. *Secretary of State for the Environment* [1978], the Court of Appeal decided that an inspector could, on the facts before him, conclude that the division of a residential property consisting of a house and a lodge (the latter provided at one time accommodation for a relative), into two separate units was a material change of use: planning permission was therefore required for the residential use of the lodge as a separate unit.

This was followed in *Winton* v. *Secretary of State for the Environment* [1984]; it was suggested that the division of a single unit of occupation into two or more units might, if there were planning consequences, amount to a material changed use.

6.   Abandonment of a use

A material change of use suggests a change from use A to use B. Certain problems have arisen where use A has ceased, and, either there has been a period of no use of the land or buildings concerned, to be followed again by use A; or, the change has been use A to use B, and then back to use A. The question in each case is whether a material change of use is involved in reverting to use A. (See part 3.8 of this chapter for certain resumptions of use that do not need planning permission.)

In *Fyson* v. *Buckinghamshire C.C.* [1958], land which had been used for the storage of scrap was unoccupied for a period of seven years. It was held that the resumption of scrap storage use was not a material change of use. But in *Hartley* v. *Minister of Housing and Local Government* [1970], Lord Denning M.R. said:

"I think that when a man ceases to use a site for a particular purpose and lets it remain unused for a considerable time, then the proper inference may be that he has abandoned the former use. Once abandoned, he cannot start to use the site again, unless he gets planning permission: and this is so, even though the new use is the same as the previous one".

And Widgery L.J. (as he then was) said:

"It has been suggested in the courts before, and it seems to me that it is now time to reach a view upon it, that it is perfectly feasible in this context to describe a use as having been abandoned when one means that it has not merely been suspended for a short and determined period, but has ceased with no intention to resume it at anytime. It is perfectly true ... that the word 'abandonment' does not appear in the legislation. We are not concerned with the legislation at this stage, but merely with the facts of the matter."

Lord Denning M.R. then considered a suitable test to determine whether a use has been abandoned:

"Has the cessation of use (followed by non-use) been merely temporary, or did it amount to abandonment? ... Abandonment depends on the circumstances. If the land has remained unused for a considerable time, in such circumstances that a reasonable man might conclude that the previous use had been abandoned, then the [planning authority or the Secretary of State] may hold it to have been abandoned."

The *Hartley* test, if it may be so called, was applied in the following case:

Ratcliffe v. *Department of the Environment and another* [1975] D.C.
A quarry had been used for tipping waste from 1920 until 1961; apart from some minor tipping from trespassers, the site was not used for this purpose thereafter. The appellants made an application under section 53 of the 1971 Act to have determined whether a resumption of tipping needed planning permission. It was held that the Secretary of State was entitled on the evidence, to conclude that the tipping use had been abandoned.

The occupier's intention to abandon or otherwise is more important in the *Hartley* test than the length of time of a cessation of use. If land is not being used merely because a tenant cannot be found for it, it is submitted that the use right is not lost so long as there remains an intention to find a tenant, no matter how abandoned the property may appear physically.

In a Ministerial decision (Ref. APP/5289/G/79/20), reported at 1980 JPL p. 759, the Secretary of State decided that there was no abandonment of a use of certain residential property, that had been vandalised and left empty for 13 years and uninhabitable for 5 years, because the owner had shown an intention not to abandon the use by taking steps to prevent the vandalism.

In *Trustees of Castell-y-Mynach Estate* v. *Secretary of State for Wales* [1985], the following four factors were said to be relevant in deciding whether a use had been abandoned:

  (a) the physical condition of the building;

(b) the period of non-use;
(c) whether there has been any intervening use; and
(d) the evidence, if any, of the owner's intentions.

Seasonal resumptions of use do not involve development:

> *Webber* v. *Minister of Housing and Local Government* [1968]
> C.A.
> A four acre field was used for camping in summer and grazing
> in winter. It was held there was no material change of use
> each summer when the camping use was resumed.

More recently in *Philglow Ltd.* v. *Secretary of State for the Environment* [1984], the Court of Appeal decided that the mere cessation of a use could not itself be a material change of use. Any other decision would mean that a landowner would require planning permission to cease a use. But the resumption of one of a number of uses, after that use has been abandoned for a time, may be a material change of use:

> *Hartley* v. *Minister of Housing and Local Government* [1970]
> C.A.
> A site was used until 1961 as a petrol filling station and for
> the sale of cars. Then for four years the sale of cars ceased.
> It was held that the Minister was entitled on the evidence to
> decide that the resumption of the car sales use in 1965 involved
> a material change of use.

The concept of abandonment was criticised by Glidewell J. in *Balco Transport Services Ltd.* v. *Secretary of State for the Environment* [1983] who pointed out that it was not a concept that is apt to cover a change from one use to another. Indeed section 23(9) of the 1971 Act provides that planning permission is not required to revert to a previous lawful use following an enforcement notice. The House of Lords held in *Pioneer Aggregates (U.K.) Ltd.* v. *Secretary of State for the Environment* [1984] that where the activity of mining operations is authorised by planning permission, a commercial decision to stop those operations for a period of time cannot extinguish the planning permission. Planning permission is granted under statutory powers and ensures for the benefit of the land and successive owners (section 33). In the *Pioneer* case Lord Scarman said:

> "... the introduction into planning law of a doctrine of aban-
> donment by election of the landowner (or occupier) cannot,
> in my judgment, be justified. It would lead to uncertainty and
> confusion in the law, and there is no need for it. There is nothing

in the legislation to encourage the view that the courts should import into the planning law such a rule . . .".

But Lord Scarman did acknowledge that an existing use, such as a use existing before 1 July 1948, and not requiring planning permissions, could be abandoned; he mentioned the *Hartley* case as a good example.

It seems the concept of abandonment will apply to the cessation of an existing use, that is one that could otherwise continue without planning permission: see the *Hartley* case above.

7. A planning permission may extinguish a use

If there is a right to use land or buildings for a particular purpose, is that right lost if planning permission for some other purpose is then obtained?

In *Prosser* v. *Minister of Housing and Local Government* [1968] where planning permission was granted for the rebuilding of a petrol filling station, a condition was attached to prevent retail sales on the site. It was argued for the appellant that if he had a pre-existing right to use the site for sales, he would not need planning permission to display second cars for sale. The Court held that if a planning permission is acted upon, any conditions in it are then binding, and any pre-existing uses are destroyed: planning history recommences with the new building.

The case was applied in *Petticoat Lane Rentals Ltd.* v. *Minister of Housing and Local Government & another* [1971] D.C. A building was constructed on a site previously used for market trading: a condition of the permission restricted the future market trading to Sundays. The building was erected on pillars and market trading continued after the completion of the building on weekdays. In upholding the Secretary of State's decision that the continuance of the weekday market trading involved a material change of use, Lord Widgery C.J. applied *Prosser's* case on the ground that the erection of a building over an area of land creates a new planning unit:

> "The land as such is merged in that new building and a new planning unit with no planning history is achieved. The new planning unit, the new building, starts with a new use, that is to say immediately after it was completed it was used for nothing, and therefore any use to which it is put is a change of use, and if that use is not authorised by the planning permission, that use is a use which can be restrained by planning control."

These cases were considered by the House of Lords in *Newbury D.C.* v. *Secretary of State for the Environment* [1980]. Viscount Dilhorne said that the taking up of planning permission should not prevent an owner relying on existing use rights. He said existing use rights would only be extinguished if the implementation of a planning permission led to the creation of a new planning unit. For example, the complete rebuilding, as in the *Prosser* case, was to be regarded as the creation of a new planning unit. But in the *Newbury* case, the grant of planning permission for a storage use did not create a new planning unit; the buildings in question had existing use rights for storage purposes, and those rights could be relied on in preference to the conditions attached to the planning permission.

Although the *Pioneer Aggregates* case would seem to suggest that a planning permission cannot be abandoned, this requires a qualification in the light of the decision of the Court of Appeal in *Cynon Valley B.C.* v. *Secretary of State for Wales* [1986]. The planning permission in *Pioneer Aggregates* was for mining operations; and that in *Cynon Valley*, was for a change of use. In the latter case, Balcombe L.J. in *Cynon Valley* said that where the development for which planning permission is required is a material change of use, the permission is to change *from* use A *to* use B, and is not merely permission to use the property for use B for the indefinite future. If planning permission is obtained and *implemented* for use C, then the previous planning permission for use B would not survive. He reached this decision after carefully considering the House of Lords case of *Young* v. *Secretary of State for the Environment* [1983]: once a planning permission is implemented, it is then spent, and cannot be revived to authorise the reversion to an earlier permitted use.

If planning permission is granted for the erection of a building, the permission enables the building to be used for the purpose for which it is designed (section 33(2) of the 1971 Act). It is only if the intended use is inconsistent with the permission that the *Prosser* case applies. But, if a building is erected without planning permission, not only is this provision authorising its designed use not available, the erection of the building may extinguish any lawful use previously enjoyed by the site covered by the building, a question considered in the next case:

Jennings Motors Ltd. v. *Secretary of State for the Environment and another* C.A. [1982]
A site was lawfully used for a taxi, car and coach hire business, and for vehicle repairs and car sales. A building was erected

on part of the site without planning permission and was used for the same purpose as the rest of the site. It was held in the Divisional Court that the erection of the building destroyed any previous lawful use of the site now covered by the building so that the building had no lawful use. Any use to which it was put, including the original use of the site, was a material change of use, involving development, and requiring planning permission. But the Court of Appeal allowed an appeal by *Jennings Motors* against this decision. It was said that although some physical alteration to part of a site, such as by the erection of a new building or the alteration of an existing building, is one of the factors to be taken into account in considering whether there has been a break in the planning history of the site, that break had not occurred in this case; the occupiers had continued their existing use right, and were entitled so to do.

The question was formulated by Lord Denning M.R. in this case as to whether there was a "new chapter in planning history": physical alterations to the site or part of it may constitute a break in that planning history only if sufficiently radical. He particularly preferred the theory of a new chapter in planning history to that of a new planning unit in the circumstances of the case. Oliver and Watkins L.JJ. considered that the theory of the planning unit should be preserved for the geographical problems within the guidance given by Bridge J. in the *Burdle* case (see above at page 24). All this is some way from the simple proposition in the 1971 Act that a material change in the use of any buildings or other land constitutes development.

The effect of the General Development Order, and development permitted by the order (see Chapter 4), on a pre-existing planning permission, was considered in:

Cynon Valley B.C. v. *Secretary of State for Wales* C.A. [1986]
Planning permission was granted in 1958 for a fish and chip shop, but a change of use to an antique shop took place in 1978 as development permitted by the General Development Order. It was held that the 1958 permission was spent and did not survive the change to an antique shop. However, section 23(8) of the 1971 Act provides that where development is permitted (subject to limitations) by a development order, permission is not required to revert to the normal use of the land. As the permitted change to an antique shop was subject to the general limitation that excludes certain types of shops from

the general class of shops, the reversion to the previous shop use was permitted and not lost.

3.6 Uses that commenced before 1964

Development control, as we know it today, came into operation on 1st July 1948, and, ever since, planning permission has been required for a material change of use. If planning permission was obtained for a material change of use that commenced before 1964, no more need be said, the continuance of that use is lawful. If the use existed in 1948, statute may have granted an exemption from the need for planning permission for the continuance of that use, thus making its continuance lawful (see 1. below). But if the material change of use occurred after the 1st July 1948 and before 1964 without planning permission, the continuance of that use is unlawful, though it may be immune from enforcement action, a paradoxical distinction we will examine (see 2. below).

1. Uses existing on 1st July 1948—the "appointed day"

The requirements (section 23(1) of the 1971 Act) that planning permission is needed for any development, and this includes a material change of use, does not apply to any development occurring before the appointed day. (Schedule 24, para 12, of the 1971 Act). Thus, any change of use before that date may be continued: it has never needed planning permission.

Section 23 excludes from the need to obtain planning permission, certain uses of a temporary or intermittent nature in 1948:

(a) Where land was used on the appointed day for a temporary use, planning permission is not required to resume the normal use before 6th December 1968 (section 23(2));

(b) Where land was used on the appointed day for one purpose, and also, on occasions, whether at regular intervals or not for another purpose, planning permission is not required for the occasional use before 6th December 1968 nor is it required for the occasional use after that date provided the occasional use took place at least once between the appointed day and the beginning of 1968 (section 23(3)); and

(c) Where land was unoccupied on the appointed day, but had been occupied at some time between 7th January 1937 and the appointed day, planning permission is not required for the resumption of any use of the land begun before 6th December 1968, if the use was for a purpose for which the land was last used before the appointed day (section 23(4)).

Land includes any building (section 290 of the 1971 Act).

2.   Uses that commenced between 1st July 1948 and 31st December 1963 without planning permission

With the minor exception of the making of a change of use of any building to use as a single dwelling house, enforcement action can be taken against any other change of use without planning permission if the breach of planning control occurred after the end of 1963 (section 87 of the 1971 Act). Therefore, a change of use before 1964, without planning permission, is immune from enforcement action in the sense that it is a good ground of appeal against any enforcement notice served to stop the continuance of the use. A use commenced in this way before 1964 is usually referred to as an 'established use', and where the use continues, the owner is advised to apply for a certificate of established use (see below).

However the immunity from enforcement action enjoyed by an established use can be lost if a material change to another use takes place, or an enforcement notice is served in respect of the established use and no appeal is brought. The possibility of losing an established use, in either way, was made clear in *Nash* v. *Secretary of State for the Environment* [1985].

Although a use commencing without planning permission between 1st July 1948 and the end of 1963 is immune from enforcement action, it is not regarded as a lawful use: it is still in contravention of section 23(1) which provides that development requires planning permission. This nice little conundrum arose in *LTSS* v. *London Borough of Hackney* [1976], a case that is more fully considered towards the end of this chapter.

3.7   Established use certificates

The purpose of these certificates is to state the established use of land; this is then conclusive for the purposes of an appeal to the Secretary of State against an enforcement notice (section 94(7) of the 1971 Act). In other words the certificate gives protection against an enforcement notice.

These certificates are available to any person having an interest in land and who can show that a particular use of land has become established (section 94(2)). A use of land is established in the following cases:

(a) Use commenced before 1964 without planning permission and has continued since (this is the circumstance considered on the previous page);

(b) Use commenced before 1964 with planning permission but subject to conditions or limitations that have not been complied with since 1963; or

(c) Use commenced after 1963 as the result of a change of use not requiring planning permission (a change of use may not require planning permission either because it is not a *material* change of use, and is not therefore development, such as a change of use within one of the classes of the use classes order, or because it is a material change of use that is permitted without need of planning permission).

A certificate cannot be granted if the established use is no longer continuing at the time of the application. Nor can it be granted in respect of the use of land as a single dwelling-house. The exclusion of this last change of use seems strange. If, without planning permission, a change of use of any building to use as a single dwelling-house takes place, and an enforcement notice is not served within four years of this breach of planning control, the dwelling-house use is immune from enforcement action and yet it is not a case of established use for which a certificate may be sought.

Where there has been an intensification in the established use by the date of the application for a certificate, the planning authority is entitled to refuse to grant the certificate: *Hipsey* v. *Secretary for the Environment* [1984]. It would seem that a certificate cannot be granted for the lesser use before intensification as this use is no longer *continuing*.

The case of *Bolivian and General Tin Trust Ltd.* v. *Secretary of State for the Environment* [1972] illustrates the relationship between a planning permission and a certificate of established use. If a temporary planning permission is obtained for a use, that would otherwise be in contravention of planning control, the owners will be debarred from applying for a certificate of established use at the termination of the temporary planning permission as during this period the use will not have *continued* in contravention.

In *Broxbourne B.C.* v. *Secretary of State for the Environment* [1979] Goff J. had this to say about a certificate of established use:

> "the purpose of an established use certificate is clear. It does not render a use lawful. To that extent it is unlike a grant of planning permission. Therefore, if, for example, the use specified in an established use certificate is abandoned, it cannot

lawfully be resumed. Its function is to render the specified use, as long as it persists, immune from an enforcement notice."

In the *Broxbourne* case, in respect of a certificate issued in 1972, the specified use was not limited to any part of the site, nor was the intensity of use limited. Use of land and buildings was certified for the storage, sawing, resawing and disposal of timber in the round and this was held not to be so very different from the use at the time of an appeal in 1976: the stacking and storage of planks of timber. An enforcement notice that alleged a considerable increase in the intensity of the use was therefore invalid. It is now the practice of local planning authorities to be particularly precise about the extent and intensity of a use specified on a certificate. There is an appeal to the Secretary of State from a refusal to issue a certificate: section 95.

An established use certificate may be issued for a lesser use than that sought in the application if the local planning authority is only so far satisfied by the evidence: *Bristol City Council* v. *Secretary of State for the Environment* [1987].

The government has considered (1984) abolishing certificates of established use. Whatever the merits of this proposal, there is at least a strong argument, advanced by a joint RICS/Law Society memorandum, that a time limit of, say 12 years, should be introduced within which an enforcement notice for unauthorised changes of use should be issued.

3.8 Change of use not requiring planning permission

Section 23 of the 1971 Act specifies certain changes of use in respect of which planning permission is not required:

(a) planning permission is not required to resume the previous *normal* use of land following the expiration of a planning permission for a temporary use (section 23(5));

(b) where planning permission to develop land has been granted, subject to limitations, by a development order, planning permission is not required for the use of that land which is the previous *normal* use of land following the expiration of a planning permission for a temporary use that is granted by a general development order (see Chapter 4) (section 23(8)). The meaning of permission granted by a development order 'subject to limitations' includes permission to use premises as a shop other than shops excluded from Class I of the old use classes order: *Cynon Valley B.C.* v. *Secretary of State for Wales* [1986].

    (c) planning permission is not required for the resumption of
        a previous *lawful* use of land following an enforcement
        notice (section 23(9)).

In cases (a) and (b) above, a use is not a normal use, if it was
begun in breach of planning control, that is to say without planning
permission where such permission was required. In case (c), the
subsection makes reference to a lawful use rather than a normal
use which is not a contravention of planning control. This distinction
in wording was considered all important in one case:

> *LTSS* v. *Hackney L.B.C.* [1976] C.A.
> A building was used for use 'A' (wholesale warehouse) between
> 1963 and 1969; then use 'B' (display of furniture for retail
> sale) for some time during 1971; and then use 'C' (discount
> sales of furniture) from October 1972. Each change of use took
> place without planning permission. An enforcement notice
> required use 'C' to cease. There could be no reversion to use
> 'B' because this use commenced after 1963 and could still be
> the subject of an enforcement notice. But would section 23(9)
> permit a reversion to use 'A', a use that was immune from
> enforcement action? The Divisional Court considered the differ-
> ence between the wording of section 23(5) and section 23(9)
> and concluded that use 'A' was a lawful use. The Court of
> Appeal disagreed, deciding it was not, thus precluding a right
> to revert to it under section 23(9).

It is submitted that the interpretation of Lord Widgery C.J. in the
Divisional Court is to be preferred. He refers to the wording of
section 23(5)—reverting to a use that had planning permission, and
compares that to the looser wording of section 23(9)—reverting
to a lawful use—commenting that that must include a reversion
to a use immune from enforcement action. However, the House
of Lords in *Young* v. *Secretary of State for the Environment* [1983]
decided that it was not possible to go back in history to find some
earlier use that was lawful; the owner could only revert to the immediately previous use, and then only if that use had been lawful.

Chapter 4

Permitted Development

Introduction	37
The Classes of permitted development	38
Article 4 Directions	46
Permitted development and compensation	46
Special development orders	47
Simplified Planning Zones	47

4.1 Introduction

Planning permission is required for development, and the meaning of development was explained in the preceding two chapters. Although an actual application must be made to the local planning authority for planning permission for most forms of development, there are a number of classes of development of a minor nature for which planning permission is automatically granted in the General Development Order 1977 (as amended). This permitted development can be carried out without any express consent of, or notice to, the local planning authority (section 24 of the 1971 Act).

In special circumstances the automatic planning permission can be withdrawn by what is called an Article 4 Direction. An express application for planning permission is then necessary for any development that would otherwise be permitted but for the Direction.

There would appear to be several interrelated reasons for permitted development. Many of the classes of permitted development concern minor operations such as hard standings to dwelling-houses, or external painting, or temporary uses of land, which although strictly within the meaning of development are not likely to involve planning considerations of any consequence. To require express planning applications for these activities would be an unnecessary burden on owners as well as planning authorities.

There is also an element of Ministerial policy in the classes of permitted development, as the greater their scope, the less control that can be exercised by local planning authorities. These cases include the enlargement of dwelling-houses or industrial buildings, within certain limitations, and the erection of agricultural buildings; by permitting these developments, the Minister is very firmly taking such development out of local control.

The final justification for permitted development concerns the activities of many of the statutory undertakers. Although much of their work will be development, the Minister has decided that certain classes of such development shall be permitted: the statutory under-takers may proceed without need of an express planning permission.

The government introduced Simplified Planning Zones with the Housing and Planning Act 1986. Subject to the designation of such zones, development is permitted in accordance with the schemes for such areas.

4.2   The Classes of permitted development

The classes of permitted development are found in Schedule 1 to the General Development Order 1977. Some of these classes have been amended by the General Development (Amendment) Orders 1981–1985 and the Town and Country Planning (National Parks, Areas of Outstanding Natural Beauty and Conservation Areas) Special Development Order 1985.

Article 3 to the 1977 Order permits the classes of development in Schedule 1, subject to the limitations and conditions imposed in the Schedule. Many of the classes impose some limitations on the dimensions of permitted development. In *Fayrewood Fish Farms* v. *Secretary of State for the Environment* [1984], it was said that if any part of the development exceeded the limitations imposed by the general development order, then the whole of that develop-ment would amount to a breach of planning control, and not simply so much of the development as is beyond the limitations. Nothing in the Order permits development which would be contrary to any planning condition imposed in a planning permission granted after express application to the local planning authority. With minor exceptions, the Order does not permit any development "which requires or involves the formation, laying out or material widening of a means of access to an existing highway which is a trunk or classified road, or creates an obstruction to the view of persons using any highway used by vehicular traffic at or near any bend, corner, junction or intersection so as to be likely to cause danger to such persons."

The classes of permitted development are as follows:

Class I—Development within the curtilage of a dwelling-house Provided a building is still a dwelling-house, and its use has not been abandoned (see *Trustees of Castell-y-Mynach* v. *Secretary of State for Wales* [1985], a dwelling-house may be enlarged, improved or altered provided the cubic content of the original house is not exceeded by 70 cubic metres or fifteen per cent, whichever is greater (50 cubic metres or ten per cent in the case of a terrace house), subject to a maximum of 115 cubic metres.

In the special areas of National Parks, Areas of Outstanding Natural Beauty and Conservation Areas, the lower limits of 50 cubic metres or ten per cent are applied by the Special Development Order 1985.

No building work must go higher than the highest part of the roof of the original dwelling-house; or project in front of any wall of the house fronting on a highway; or exceed the height of four metres if within two metres of any boundary. In *Larkin* v. *Basildon D.C.* [1980] the Secretary of State's decision was that where two walls of a house were rebuilt, followed by the remaining two walls, the work was outside Class I; the Court agreed as the work was beyond simply "improvement or other alteration". The area of the curtilage covered by buildings must not exceed fifty per cent of the total area excluding the dwelling-house.

The erection of a garage is only included in the above calculations if any part of it lies within five metres of the dwelling-house.

The erection of a stable or loose box is always treated as an enlargement of the dwelling-house for the purpose of these calculations. But in the special areas mentioned above, a garage is treated with a stable or loose box as an enlargement of the dwelling-house.

The additional cubic content, by which a dwelling-house may be enlarged under this permission, can be used up by any previous enlargement, improvement or alteration which is expressly allowed by a planning permission granted by the local planning authority, or was carried out as permitted development: see *Dawson* v. *Secretary of State for the Environment* [1983]. It is therefore not possible to enlarge a dwelling-house by, say the fifteen per cent, and then seek to enlarge it again as permitted development. The answer to this is to first obtain an express grant of planning permission, then make use of the permitted development tolerances before implementing the express grant.

If any development is carried out which exceeds the limits imposed by the General Development Order, the whole of the development is unauthorised and in breach of planning control; one cannot argue that only the development in excess of permitted development can be enforced (*Garland* v. *Minister of Housing and Local Government* [1969] C.A.). Although the local planning authority may decide only to take enforcement action against the excess.

Class I also includes permission to erect a porch not exceeding a height of three metres and a floor area of two square metres.

40   Development and Planning Law

The porch must be at least two metres from any boundary fronting onto a highway.

Other buildings may be erected or constructed within the curtilage of a dwelling-house if required for a purpose incidental to the enjoyment of the dwelling-house as such. Such buildings cannot include another dwelling, a stable or loose-box, or in the special areas, a garage, as these are treated as enlargements of the dwelling-house. A garage within five metres of the dwelling-house counts as an enlargement to the house as considered above. No building may exceed a height of three metres, or four metres if it has a ridged roof, or be built in front of a wall of the house that fronts a highway. The area of the curtilage covered by buildings must not exceed fifty per cent of the total area excluding the area of the dwelling-house.

A hardstanding for vehicles, and, within limitations, a tank for domestic heating oil, are also permitted.

One satellite antenna may be installed on or in the curtilage of a dwelling house so long as its measurement does not exceed 90cm, and if placed on the roof, is not higher than the highest part of the roof.

Class II—Sundry minor operations

This class permits the erection, maintenance and alteration of gates, fences walls or other means of enclosure not exceeding one metre in height, where abutting a highway, or two metres elsewhere. It permits the construction of an access to a highway not being a trunk or classified road in connection with any permitted development, and external painting of any building otherwise than for advertisement.

Class III—Changes of use

The following changes of use within the use classes order are permitted:

1. change of use of a building to a use in class A1 (shops) *from* a use in class A3 (food and drink), or *from* a use for the sale of motor vehicles;
2. change of use of a building to:
   (a) a use for any purpose within class B1 (business) *from* any use in class B2 (general industrial) or B8 (storage and distribution);
   (b) a use for any purpose within class B8 (storage and distribution) *from* any use within class B1 (business) or B2 (general industrial).

Where the total amount of floorspace does not exceed 235 square metres.

These amendments were made in 1987, and introduce a fair degree of flexibility between business use and storage and distribution uses, and a change from general industrial use to such uses. It is not possible to change to a general industrial use without express planning permission.

The development permitted by paragraph (1.) above has been the subject of exploitation by some developers. The idea is to obtain planning permission for use, or the erection and use, of a building as a motor showroom. Permission for such use may be more easily available for certain sites than a retail use. After a period of motor showroom use, a change of use to retail use as a shop is then possible under the provision just discussed. This scheme only failed in *Kwik Save Discount Group Ltd.* v. *Secretary of State for the Environment and Oldham B.C.* (C.A.) [1981], because the motor showroom use was too minimal to be regarded as a use in its own right.

Before developers rush off to make use of this device it would be prudent to consider article 3(2) of the G.D.O., which provides that "nothing in this article or in Schedule 1 to this Order shall operate so as to permit any development contrary to a condition imposed in any permission granted or deemed to be granted under Part III of the Act otherwise than by this order". This seems to suggest that a condition could be attached to the first express planning permission to nullify any subsequent change of use which would otherwise be permitted by the G.D.O. This meaning was doubted by Lord Parker C.J. in *East Barnet U.D.C.* v. *B.T.C.* [1962], but if Lord Parker is right, one is left to wonder what is the purpose of article 3(2).

Class IV—Temporary buildings and uses
Temporary buildings, works, plant or machinery are permitted for the duration of any building or engineering operations being carried out under a planning permission.

The temporary use of land (other than a building or the curtilage of a building) is permitted for any purpose or purposes except as a caravan site on not more than 28 days in total in any calendar year (of which not more than 14 days in total may be devoted for the purpose of motor car or motor-cycle racing or for the purpose of the holding of markets), and the erection or placing of moveable structures on the land for the purpose of that use. This permitted development has been the subject of several cases. The problem for the local planning authority is to decide whether the commencement of a use without express planning permission is a temporary use within this class, which will cease after 28 or 14 days, as the case may be, or a permanent change of use. If the latter, the authority may immediately commence enforcement proceedings. In *Tidswell* v. *Secretary of State for Environment* [1977], this distinction was considered, it was decided that the local planning authority could commence enforcement action against a Sunday market after only nine Sundays, and leave the issue as to whether the owner could bring himself within the permitted development (a maximum of 14 days in any year) to be decided at the appeal. This is a little unfortunate to the owner who may have to appeal just to prove he is acting within the G.D.O. permission.

Class V—Uses by members of recreational organisations
An organisation (such as the Scouts Association) with a section 269 Public Health Act 1936 certificate of exemption may use land for recreation and instruction, and erect tents for the purpose of this use.

Class VI—Agricultural buildings, works and uses
This class permits building and engineering operations on agricultural land exceeding one acre, and part of an agricultural unit, that are requisite for the use of the land for the purposes of agriculture. The meaning of agriculture has already been dealt with in chapter 3, and is relevant for the purpose of this class. In *Jones* v. *Stockport M.B.C.* [1984] it was decided that this case only applies if the land is actually being used for agriculture, and the proposed buildings do not have to be ancillary to the existing agricultural use of the land. Where an extension is added to a dwelling-house for use as a sterilising room and farm office, and deliberately designed to look like part of the house, it was said in *Harding* v. *Secretary of State for the Environment* [1985], that the question as to whether the extension is permitted by Class VI depends on the words "requisite", which has a functional connotation, and "designed", which has to do with the appearance of the building. Thus, the inspector was correct when he decided that as the extension did not have the appearance of having been designed for agricultural purposes, it was not permitted by Class VI.

The ground area covered by buildings to be erected under this class, together with any other buildings erected within the previous two years, and within 90 metres of the proposed buildings, must not exceed 465 square metres. If any part of the building or engineering operations are within 25 metres of such a road, then the whole work is unauthorised, and not just the offending part: *Fayrewood Fish Farms* v. *Secretary of State for the Environment* [1984]. The height of such buildings must not exceed three metres if within three kilometres of an aerodrome, or twelve metres in other cases; the buildings must not be within 25 metres of a trunk or classified road. A dwelling-house is not permitted or included as building within this class.

In the National Parks and certain areas of natural beauty, development consisting of the erection, alteration or extension of any building and the making of private roads within the scope of this Class must first be notified to the local planning authority (Town and Country Planning (Agricultural and Forestry Development in National Parks, etc.) Special Development Order 1986. The authority have 28 days within which they may then require that their approval is necessary for the design or external appearance of the proposed development.

The erection of a roadside milk-churn stand is also within this class, as well as the working and winning of minerals for fertilisation or for the maintenance, improvement or alteration of any buildings or works used for agriculture. In *West Bowers Farm Products* v. *Essex C.C.* [1985], it was decided that any operations which might coincidentally involve excavation of minerals for sale would not be permitted development even if the excavated site could be used for agricultural purposes. This has now been reinforced by the 1985 amendments: any extracted minerals shall not be moved off the land, similarly, the deposit of refuse or waste materials is not permitted if the material is brought onto the land from elsewhere.

The construction of fishponds became permitted development in 1985 subject to the area of the site not exceeding 2 hectares, nor any part being within 25 metres of a trunk or classified road. Minerals can be extracted for this purpose so long as the excavation does not exceed a depth of 2.5 metres, and the area excavated (together with other excavations within the preceding two years) does not exceed 0.2 hectares.

Class VII—Forestry buildings and works

Building and other operations (with the exception of the erection of a dwelling-house) may be carried out on forestry land provided any buildings or works do not exceed 3 metres in height if within 3 kilometres of an aerodrome, or are erected within 25 metres of a trunk or classified road. The formation, alteration and maintenance of private ways are permitted. The provisions of the Town and Country Planning (Agricultural and Forestry Development in National Parks, etc.) Special Development Order 1986 applies in the special areas. Notification is required, as described above under agricultural buildings, to enable the local authority to control the design and external appearance of any buildings or private roads.

Class VIII—Development for industrial purposes

If an industrial undertaker uses land or buildings for any industrial process for which he has planning permission, or which is not in contravention of any previous planning control, the following development is permitted:

(i) the provision, rearrangement or replacement of private ways, railways, sidings or conveyors;

(ii) the provision or rearrangement of sewers, mains, pipes, cables or other apparatus;

(iii) the installation or erection, by way of addition or replacement, of plant or machinery, or structures or erections, not exceeding 15 metres in height, or the height of the item replaced;

(iv) the extension or alteration of buildings so long as the height of the original building is not exceeded, nor the cubic content of the original building (measured externally) is not exceeded by more than twenty-five per cent nor the aggregate floor space by more than 1,000 square metres (in the special areas mentioned on page 39 the limits are ten per cent and 500 square metres respectively).

The external appearance of the premises must not be materially affected by any work carried out under (iii) or (iv); and in the case of (iv), no part of a building must be within five metres of the boundary.

The erection of an additional building counts as an enlargement for the purpose of the calculations. Two or more buildings are aggregated to ascertain the cubic content and floor space if used together as one unit for the purpose of the undertaking. If they can be treated as separate units, then each building may be enlarged within the scope of this permitted development. The Secretary of State takes the view that the increase in cubic content and floor space is related to the original building, and a building does not become a new original building after each enlargement, to which further enlargement is possible (see APP/5143/G/80/61—reported in the Estates Gazette, February 20, 1982 at page 664).

Class IX to XXI—Miscellaneous

These classes will not be separately described, but they include: repairs to unadopted streets and private ways; repairs to services; rebuilding and restoration of war damaged buildings, works and plant; development under local or private Acts; development by local authorities (such as street furniture); development by local highway authorities, drainage or water authorities (largely maintenance work); development for sewerage and sewage disposal (below ground); development by statutory undertakers (in connection with railways, docks, water transport, lighthouses); development by mineral undertakers and British Coal; and the uses of aerodrome buildings by the British Airports Authority. The permitted development in the foregoing classes is limited in scope, in some cases, and frequently subject to imposed conditions.

Classes XXII and XXIII refer to certain limited caravan uses, and to development required by a caravan site licence (see chapter 12).

Classes XXIV and XXV permit communication development. Class XXIV authorises British Telecom and other telecommunications operators to instal, alter or replace telecommunications apparatus with specified limitations. Class XXV permits the installation of up to two microwave antenna on non-residential buildings or structures exceeding 15 metres, subject to terrestrial microwave antennae not exceeding 1.3 metres measured in any direction, and no higher than 3 metres higher than the building or structure; and in the case of satellite antenna, the size does not exceed 90 cm, measured in any direction.

Article 4 directions cannot be made in respect of the permitted telecommunications development in Classes XXVI.2 and XXVII.2 unless the direction contains a specific provision to that effect.

Classes XXVI and XXVII permit temporary operations for mineral exploration and the removal of material from mineral-working deposits.

Class XXVIII permits the extension or alteration of a building which is lawfully used as a warehouse so long as the cubic content is not increased by more than 25 per cent and the aggregate to floor space by more than 1,000 square metres. No part of the building may be within 5 metres of the boundary after the work; the external appearance must not be materially altered; and there must be no loss of carparking.

Class XXIX permits limited development on land lawfully used as an amusement park.

Class XXX permits certain development by or on behalf of the Historic Buildings and Monuments Commission for the purpose of securing the preservation of the buildings or monuments.

4.3   Article 4 Directions

Under Article 4 to the General Development Order 1977, either
the local planning authority or the Secretary of State may issue
a direction which requires that an express planning application must
be made for any development that would otherwise be permitted
by the Order. The effect of this is that the automatic planning permission is not available for all or any of the classes of development
for any area, or any particular development, specified in the direction
(Article 4(1)).

The approval of the Secretary of State is necessary for any Article
4 direction issued by a local planning authority with the following
exceptions:

(a) directions relating to listed buildings or buildings notified
     by the Secretary of State as of architectural or historic inter-
     est or development within the curtilage of a listed building;
     and
(b) directions relating to any development within classes I to
     IV of the 1977 Order (development within the curtilage
     of a dwelling-house, sundry minor operations, changes of
     use and temporary buildings and uses).

In the case of a direction within (b) above, it will only remain in
force six months unless approved by the Secretary of State; it will
cease to have effect if disallowed by him within that period.

Where a direction is made, notice shall be served on all owners
and occupiers of the affected land unless the area covered by the
direction is so large that individual service would be impractical.
In that event, the direction shall be advertised locally and in the
London Gazette.

Article 4A was introduced in 1985 to provide for a direction
withdrawing planning permissions granted by Classes XXVI.2
(mineral exploration) and XXVII.2 (extraction from mineral working deposits) by a special and speedier procedure.

4.4   Permitted development and compensation

The general philosophy of planning legislation since 1948 has been
that with very few exceptions no compensation is payable for a
refusal of planning permission: the right to develop land is no longer
a right belonging to the landowner. However, under section 165
of the 1971 Act, if permission has been granted for development

by a development order, and that permission is withdrawn by the revocation or amendment of the order, or by an article 4 direction, and a subsequent planning application is refused, or granted subject to conditions, compensation is payable. The compensation is payable for any expenditure in carrying out work which is then rendered abortive, or for any other direct loss or damage attributable to the withdrawal of the planning permission in the Order (section 164).

The Town and Country Planning (Compensation) Act 1985 was passed to restrict the circumstances in which compensation is payable under section 165 of the 1971 Act. Where planning permission granted by a development order is withdrawn by revocation or amendment, the right to claim compensation only applies if a planning application is made within 12 months of the revocation or amendment, and the application is subsequently refused or granted subject to conditions (see further Chapter 18).

4.5 Special development orders

Under a special development order, the Secretary of State can grant planning permission for any development specified by such an order. These have been restricted in the past to special areas such as National Parks, Areas of Outstanding Natural Beauty, Conservation Areas, and to specific public development such as the extension of the Windscale processing plant.

The Secretary of State has considered the use of special development orders to permit development in particular areas for industrial or housing development. The effect of such an order would be to override the power of the local planning authorities in relation to the grant of planning permissions. If the orders were not related to the development plans, the efficacy of these plans would need to be considered.

4.6 Simplified Planning Zones

Part II of the Housing and Planning Act 1986 makes provision for Simplified Planning Zones. It introduces sections 24A–24E and new Schedule 8A to the Town and Country Planning Act 1971 and sections 21A to 21E and new Schedule 6A to the Town and Country Planning (Scotland) Act 1972. Where a SPZ scheme is adopted or approved, the effect is that planning permission is deemed granted for development specified in the scheme or for any development of any class that they be specified. Planning permission may be unconditional or subject to such conditions, limitations or exceptions as may be specified in the scheme.

Every planning authority is required to consider the desirability of making SPZ's for any parts of their area, and to keep the question under review. A planning authority shall prepare a scheme for any part of their area they think desirable for such a purpose. Nothing in a SPZ scheme shall affect the right of a person to carry out something that is not development, or is development which either has planning permission, or does not need it. Development permitted by the SPZ scheme shall prevail over any limitation or restriction imposed under a planning permission outside of the scheme.

A SPZ scheme shall last ten years from the date of its adoption or approval. It may be altered by adding or excluding land; adding or withdrawing development for which planning permission is granted; or for adding or deleting limitations or restrictions.

Land in the following areas may not be included in a SPZ: National Parks, conservation areas, areas of outstanding natural beauty, green belt and sites of special scientific interest. Further areas may be added by order of the Secretary of State.

Schedule 8A sets out the details of a SPZ, and how it is to be adopted or approved. A SPZ is to consist of a map and written statement, and such diagrams, illustrations and descriptions as thought appropriate. It shall specify:

(a) the development or classes of development permitted by the scheme;

(b) the land in relation to which permission is given; and

(c) any conditions, limitations or exceptions subject to which it is granted.

Any person may request a local planning authority to make a SPZ, and if it fails to do so, or to decide to do so within three months, the person concerned may refer the request to the Secretary of State. He will pass details of the request to the LPA who have 28 days to make representations. He may give the LPA a SPZ direction. The direction is a request to make a SPZ scheme.

Where a local planning authority is considering a proposal to make or alter a SPZ scheme, publicity must be given and representations considered. Copies of the appropriate documents go to the Secretary of State. The LPA may hold a public local inquiry, and shall do so unless objectors have agreed in writing that they will not be appearing. The Secretary of State may call in proposals for a SPZ, and then the proposals will not take effect unless approved by him. He also has default powers to make SPZ schemes where he thinks the LPA are not taking the necessary steps.

When these provisions of the 1986 Act are brought into effect, regulations may be made to make further provision for SPZ schemes.

PART II

THE DECISION-MAKING PROCESS

Chapter 5

Planning Authorities

Introduction   51
The distribution of functions between local
planning authorities   52
The role of the Secretary of State   55
Delegation to committees and officers   56
Negligence   57

5.1 Introduction

By now the reader will have understood the scope of development control, and will know whether a proposal constitutes "development" needing planning permission. This chapter explains the planning authorities, their power and functions. Although planning and development control are essentially matters for local government, the Secretary of State for the Environment possesses very wide powers. Another feature of the administration of planning is the division of responsibilities between upper and lower tiers of local government; this is a consequence of the Local Government Act 1972 and the subsequent reorganisation of local government in 1974; planning functions were, unhappily, divided between upper and lower tier authorities. There are also certain authorities, without planning functions, that have a right to be consulted, and, in some cases may sometimes issue directions which may affect the processing of development plans or planning applications; examples include parish and community councils, highway and water authorities.

Unhappy with the discharge of planning functions by some local planning authorities, the government in recent years has increasingly altered the balance of power away from local government. The powers of the Secretary of State to decide planning appeals, to widen the scope of the general development order, and to initiate policy circulars and new legislation, has given central government a considerable say in planning matters.

5.2   The distribution of functions between local planning authorities

1.   Outside London

Following the reorganisation of local government in 1974, and the abolition of the six metropolitan county councils under the Local Government Act 1985, we now have an arrangement in England and Wales outside London that looks like this:

County Councils
There are 53 counties. A county council is a local planning authority for its area.

District Councils
There are 369 districts, of which 36 are in the former metropolitan counties and are called metropolitan district councils. Some districts are entitled to be described as boroughs. A district council is a local planning authority for its area.

Parish Councils
All areas that had parish councils before April 1, 1974 continue to have parish councils, but other areas may now also have parish councils. Sometimes a parish council is called a town council. In Wales a parish council is called a community council. Parish councils are not local planning authorities, but are entitled to be consulted on certain planning and development control matters.

The Local Government Act 1972 makes both counties and districts local planning authorities; the powers and duties of local planning authorities are found in the Town and Country Planning Act 1971; and the distribution of these functions is found in Schedule 16 to the Local Government Act 1972, as amended by the Local Government, Planning and Land Act 1980. Following the abolition of the six metropolitan county councils in 1986, their functions are now largely discharged by the metropolitan district councils. The functions conferred are as follows:

COUNTY PLANNING AUTHORITY	DISTRICT PLANNING AUTHORITY
Planning:	*Planning:*
Preparation of survey and structure plans.	Preparation of local plans within the local plan scheme.
Preparation of a local plan scheme and any local plans allocated to the county within that scheme.	

Development control:
The functions opposite are only exercised by the county planning authority in what is called a "county matter"—or in a National Park—see below.
Tree preservation orders (power to make an order is restricted— see chapter 12).

Development control:
Receiving, processing and deciding planning applications, applications under section 53 and for established use certificates.
Completion notices, revocation, modification or discontinuance orders; enforcement notices and stop notices.
Building preservation notices: listed buildings consent application and enforcement notices; control of advertisements.
Tree preservation orders.

Conservation areas:
(A *power* to determine and designate.)
Acquisition and disposal of land.

Conservation areas
(A *duty* to determine and designate.)
Acquisition and disposal of land.

County matters
Applications for the following classes of development will be dealt with as county matters (see also the Town and Country Planning (Prescription of County Matters) Regulations 1980):

1. *Minerals*

    (a) Mineral workings;
    (b) The erection of buildings, plant or machinery to be used for mineral working, or for the treatment or disposal of minerals on land adjoining mineral workings;
    (c) The erection of buildings, plant or machinery (or the use of land) for any process of preparing or adapting a mineral for sale or manufacturing a product from it where—
       (i) the development is on or adjoining the mineral workings, or
       (ii) the mineral is to be brought from the mineral workings by pipeline, conveyor belt, aerial ropeway or similar plant or machinery, or by private road, private waterway or private railway;
    (d) The erection of buildings, plant or machinery which a mineral operator proposes to use for grading, washing,

grinding or crushing of minerals (no matter where they are sited);

(e) The use of land for any purposes required in connection with rail or water transport for aggregates (including artificial aggregates) and the erection of associated buildings, plant and machinery;

(f) The erection of buildings, plant or machinery for use for coating roadstone, producing concrete or concrete products or artificial aggregates where—

   (i) the development is on land forming part of or adjoining mineral workings, or

   (ii) the development is on land forming part of or adjoining land used in connection with rail or water transport or aggregates;

(g) Searches and tests for mineral deposits (and the erection of associated buildings, plant and machinery);

(h) Disposal of mineral waste;

(i) Cement works;

(j) Any development, on a current or disused mineral working site, which would conflict with or prejudice compliance with a restoration condition imposed in respect of the mineral working;

2. *Others*

(k) Waste disposal sites, including waste transfer stations and similar facilities for treating, storing, processing or disposing of refuse or waste materials, in England only;

(l) Development straddling the boundaries of a National Park.

Although a county planning authority has development control functions only in respect of these matters, there is a code of practice for consultation between district and county planning authorities in respect of certain other development control functions (Circular 2/81). This is dealt with further in chapter 8.

   National Parks

In National Parks most of the planning and development control functions are exercised by the county planning authority or, where a park is in more than one county, a joint planning board of the authorities affected.

2. In Greater London

The arrangement in London now results from the London Government Act 1985:

London borough councils	*City of London*	*The Temples*
There are 32 boroughs	The Corporation has the planning functions of a borough council	Although Middle and Inner Temples are separate areas of local government for certain purposes, they are under the City of London for planning and development control.

The Greater London Council was abolished as from 1 April 1986. The London boroughs are local planning authorities for their areas with responsibility for local plans and development control (Local Government Act 1985, section 3) The two-tier system of development plans (see chapter 6) is replaced in London by a single system of "unitary plans": Local Government Act 1985, section 4. The 1985 Act (section 5) also provides for a joint planning authority for London to:

(a) consider and advise the London borough councils on matters of common interest relating to the planning and development of Greater London;

(b) inform the Secretary of State of the views of those authorities, and other matters he has requested their advice on; and

(c) inform local planning authorities and other bodies in the vicinity of London of the views of the London borough councils on planning matters.

The functions of the now abolished Greater London Council in respect of listed buildings, conservation areas and ancient monuments have been largely transferred to the Historical Buildings and Monuments Commission (Local Government Act 1985, section 6).

3.   New Town and Urban Development Corporations

New Town development corporations, and urban development corporations such as those in Liverpool (South Docks) and in London (Docklands), possess certain planning and development control functions (see chapter 15).

5.3   The Role of the Secretary of State

The responsibilities and functions of the Secretary of State are so numerous that they cannot all be outlined in this chapter. His powers to influence planning policies and planning decisions should not be underestimated. He initiates planning legislation and, increasingly reserves to himself, powers to make directions, orders or regulations. General development orders and special development orders are examples of orders made by the Secretary of State which grant planning permission independent of local planning authorities for classes of development chosen by him. The approval of the Secretary of State is required for the structure plans prepared by county planning authorities; he has the power to call in any planning application; he (or inspectors appointed by him) decides appeals against certain decisions made by local planning authorities; and, he may issue guidance to local authorities in what are called circulars. A circular is not an item of legislation, although it may contain a direction having legal effect; its purpose is to explain government policy or legislation. A circular can be a "material consideration" which a local planning authority is required to have regard to in the exercise of many of its powers (see chapter 8).

The sum total of these responsibilities and functions is to place in the hands of the Secretary of State enormous powers. Whether Parliament has been wise in so doing is certainly questionable.

5.4   Delegation to committees and officers

There is a wide power in section 101 of the Local Government Act 1972 for a local authority to delegate the discharge of any of its functions to a committee, a sub-committee or an officer of the authority. In practice many planning functions are delegated to the planning committee of an authority. Where delegation has properly taken place, the council is then bound by the decisions of its committee or officer acting within the delegated powers.

Circumstances may sometimes arise where an officer, without any express authority, but acting within the scope of his ostensible authority, makes a representation or statement upon which another person acts. This occurred in *Lever Finance Ltd.* v. *Westminster City Council* [1970] where a planning officer told a developer that he did not need planning permission for a variation to an already approved scheme. The Court of Appeal decided, that as the developer had acted upon the officer's representation by completing a house, the Council was bound by that officer's representation, and "estopped" from taking enforcement proceedings against the developer. The word "estopped" comes from the doctrine of estoppel. This can be applied in a situation where party A believes in what is represented by party B, and then acts to his detriment; estoppel then prevents party B from denying the truth or effect of his representation.

The application of the doctrine of estoppel in planning cases was considered to be limited in *Western Fish Products Ltd.* v. *Penwith D.C.* [1980] where a differently constituted Court of Appeal considered that before estoppel arose, the mere fact that the officer making the representation was a planning officer was not sufficient to assume he was acting within the scope of his ostensible authority; there must be some evidence that the authority had been delegated to the officer; in any event estoppel cannot prevent a council from exercising its statutory discretion or performing its statutory duty. In the case, it was held that the council were entitled to refuse planning permission for development which the planning officer had represented was within an existing use right if the extent of that use was established.

The limited application of the doctrine of estoppel in *Western Fish* is, it is submitted, to be preferred; the practice of consultation with planning staff is valuable, and is not discouraged by this case.

In *Wells* v. *Minister of Housing and Local Government* [1967], it was said that a letter from a planning officer stating that planning permission was not required for a certain activity could be regarded as a determination of the position under section 53 of the Town and Country Planning Act 1971 (see page 7).

5.5 Negligence

The principle in *Hedley Byrne & Co. Ltd.* v. *Heller & Partners* [1964], that there can be liability for negligent mis-statements, would seem applicable to planning authorities and their officers. Local authorities owe a duty of care in statements and representations they may make in connection with planning matters. There was liability in *Coats Patons (Retail) Ltd.* v. *Birmingham Corpn* [1971] where a local authority clerk gave an incorrect answer to a question put to him about his council's proposals to build a subway. In the Australian case of *Shaddock & Associates Pty Ltd.* v. *Parramatta City Council* [1981] the *Hedley Byrne* principle was said to apply to public authorities which follow a practice of supplying information, even where the official supplying the information did not know of the precise use to which the information would be put.

In *Co-operative Retail Services Ltd.* v. *Taff-Ely B.C.* [1983], where the town clerk issued a planning consent neither he nor his authority had power to issue, the judge said:

"a careful and prudent chief executive in such circumstances would have realised that to issue a notice of consent which

might be invalid could cause loss or damage even to the person
to whom it is issued ... it would clearly be foreseeable that
some damage might result even to the applicant himself if a
notice of planning consent was issued which was of doubtful
validity. So viewed, I have no doubt that the action of [the
clerk] would be regarded as negligent."

The judge continued by saying that had an invalid planning consent come into the hands of a bona fide purchaser for value of
the affected property, without notice of the circumstances, the local
authority would have been liable if the purchaser relied upon it
and suffered damage. In fact the claim failed as the party seeking
damages knew, or was deemed to know that the planning consent
was invalid.

Chapter 6

Development Plans

Introduction   59
Development Plans—Old-Type   60
Structure Plans   60
Local Plans   63
Unitary Development Plans   65
The relationships and legal consequences of
   Development Plans   66

6.1 Introduction

Land use planning involves two tasks, planning, and development control. The developer is mainly concerned with development control, for that affects his decision-making in the most direct way. The landowner will be concerned with both; planning may affect his land, beneficially or injuriously, and development control may be the final confirmation of those effects. In exercising development control, the local planning authority is required to have regard to the contents of the development plan (section 29 of the 1971 Act), the development plan being the document which describes the culmination of the planning task. So planning and development control are interrelated; simply put, planning eventually allocates land uses, and development control is the detailed day-to-day implementation of the planning task. Although this book concentrates on development control, some attention must be given to the planning process and the legal consequence of development plans as they impinge on development activities.

Planning throws up a number of contradictions which the reader may care to think about. Although the right to develop was nationalised in 1948, the initiative to develop was left with the private landowner and developer to a very large extent. The inclinations and decisions of these parties are clearly crucial to development. However, it is a very different group of people that decide, through the planning process, where and what sort of development should take place. This group, the planning authorities, the Secretary of State, their technical advisers, and the members of the public who are interested, make technical and political decisions about land use, and decisions about land not in their ownership. The landowner will usually make economic decisions with regard to his land, and it is therefore not surprising that these economic decisions are so often in conflict with the technical and political decisions of others. This conflict is reduced if planning and landownership is combined in one party either in the state, or in the individual in co-operation with the state (see D. Denman Co-operative Planning 1974). The former is not universally favoured, the latter, although accepted in some countries, has never been tried here.

In recent years new tensions have been introduced into the role of development plans for development control purposes. Ministerial circulars containing policies favoured by central government may be in sharp conflict with policies found in development plans. That conflict occasionally gets an airing in the courts, and the decisions of the courts show no easy resolution. Although the logic of present government philosophy (1987) points to the almost complete abolition of development plans, even national planning policies require local articulation, and such matters as green belts need some formulation.

6.2 Development Plans—Old-Type

Under the Town and Country Planning Act 1947, local planning authorities were required to prepare a development plan "indicating the manner in which a local planning authority propose that land in their area should be used, whether by the carrying out thereon of development or otherwise, and the stages by which such development should be carried out" (see now 1971 Act, Sched. 5). The plans included maps and statements which defined the sites of roads, buildings, etc.; and allocated areas for agriculture, residential and industrial or other purposes.

These plans were detailed, took a long time to prepare and amend, and were often out of date. Accordingly, following a report of the Planning Advisory Group set up by the Minister of Housing and Local Government, the Town and Country Planning Act 1968 was enacted to provide for a new type of development plan consisting of a structure plan and local plans. Most areas are covered by structure plans, and local plans.

6.3 Structure Plans

The new arrangement for development plans, introduced in 1968, envisages a structure plan containing policies and statements of a strategic large scale nature generally on a county level, and a more detailed treatment of these matters in local plans, at a district level, or on a subject by subject basis. The legal requirements for the preparation of these plans are found in Part II of the 1971 Act; with certain amendments to these in the Town and Country Planning (Amendment) Act 1972 and the Local Government, Planning and Land Act 1980. Further amendments were made by the Housing and Planning Act 1986, section 41 and schedule 10.

1. Survey

Preliminary to the preparation of the new plans, the local planning authority may institute a survey of their area to examine certain matters and thereafter keep them under review. The matters to be examined are:

(a) the principal physical and economic characteristics of the area;
(b) the size, composition and distribution of the population;
(c) the communications, transport system and traffic; and
(d) any other relevant or prescribed matters as well as projected changes in any of the matters so far listed (section 6 of 1971 Act).

The purpose of the survey is to provide the data and technical background to subsequent planning. It will seek to discover how people live in the area, and their age, structure, birthrates, employment, shopping characteristics etc.

2. The Preparation of the Structure Plan

This is a written statement "formulating the local planning authority's policy and general proposals in respect of the development and other use of the land in [the] area ... stating the relationships of those proposals to general proposals for the development and other use of land in neighbouring areas ... and containing other prescribed matters" (section 7(3) of the 1971 Act).

The county planning authority may indicate any part of their area as an *action area*. Such an area is selected for comprehensive treatment in a local plan for development, redevelopment or improvement (section 7(5) of the 1971 Act). In relation to structure plans approved after November 13, 1980, action areas will no longer be identified in a structure plan, but within the context of the local plans (Sched. 14 Local Government, Planning and Land Act 1980).

In form and content, the structure plan must comply with the Town and Country Planning (Structure and Local Plans) Regulations 1982. A written document, it may be illustrated by diagrams that are not map based. The policy formulated by the county planning authority is to relate to such of the following as is appropriate: distribution of population and employment; housing; industry and commerce; transportation; shopping; education; other social and community services; recreation and leisure; conservation; townscape and landscape; utility services and any other relevant matter. The written statement must also cover the existing structure of the area; projected changes and opportunities for change; population trends; regional and social policies; the resources available to the local planning authority; broad criteria for development control; relationship between formulated policies; inter-county consideration; and other relevant matters.

The county planning authority must consult with, and take into consideration the views of, the appropriate district planning authorities.

The developer and landowner may be interested in taking advantage of the procedure for the making and approving of a structure plan, as this gives an opportunity for any member of the public to make his views known. The county planning authority is required to give publicity to their survey, and to the proposals to be contained in the structure plan before it is finally drafted (section 8 of the 1971 Act). Accordingly, the authority must take steps to enable persons who may wish to make representation to do so. The experience of this exercise in the different counties suggests little public interest in structure plan making; and because these are not map based, it is difficult for any interested person to formulate specific representations in respect of any particular area.

When the structure plan has been approved by the county planning authority itself, it is submitted to the Secretary of State for his formal approval before it becomes a valid and effective document. At the same time copies are made available for public inspection, and objections to the plan may be made within a specified period of not less than 6 weeks to the Secretary of State (section 8 of the 1971 Act).

After considering the submitted structure plan, the Secretary of State has discretion to approve it, in part or in whole, and with or without any modifications, or he may reject it (section 9(1) of the 1971 Act).

Unless the Secretary of State decides to reject the plan, he must consider any objections that have been received by him. The procedure is for the Secretary of State to appoint, usually three, persons to form a panel and who will hold an examination in public of a selection of the issues raised by the objections (section 9(3) of the 1971 Act as amended by section 3 of the Town and Country Planning (Amendment) Act 1972).

Individual objectors do not have a right to present their objections at the examination in public, but may be invited to do so. Experience indicates that the broad statements of strategy in a structure plan, the planning jargon used, and the general issues selected for the examination in public, do not encourage the average member of the public, landowner, or developer to attend these lengthy and costly affairs.

The procedure just described will also generally apply to the alteration, repeal or replacement of a structure plan, but the Secretary of State may dispense with the examination in public (Sched. 14, Local Government, Planning and Land Act 1980).

6.4 Local Plans

If the object of the structure plans is to provide a broad strategic statement of planning policies for an area, that of the local plans is to implement the detail at a district or subject level. Some simplification of procedures was introduced by the Housing and Planning Act 1986, section 41 and schedule 10.

1. The Local Plan Scheme

The Local Government Act 1972 divided the planning functions between the county and district planning authorities, and amended the 1971 Act to require the county to prepare a development plan scheme which would be an agreed programme and statement of the local plans to be prepared (section 11A of the 1971 Act). This is now known as a local plan scheme and must include a programme for the making, altering, repealing or replacement of local plans; district planning authorities are to keep under review the need for and adequacy of local plans (see the Housing and Planning Act 1986, schedule 10). Although certain local plans may be prepared by the county, such as mineral subject plans, the preparation of most local plans is allocated to the districts.

2. Preparing and altering Local Plans

A local plan consists of a written statement "formulating in such detail as the local planning authority think appropriate their proposals for the development or other use of land in their area, or for any description of development or other use of such land, including such measures as the authority think fit for the improvement of the physical environment and the management of traffic". The plan must also include a map showing their proposals, and such diagrams, illustrations or other descriptive matter as seems appropriate (section 11, 1971 Act).

The Town and Country Planning (Structure and Local Plans) Regulations 1982 provide that where a local plan is based on a comprehensive consideration of matters affecting the development and other use of land in the area to which it relates, it shall be called a district plan; a local plan for an action area shall be called an action area plan; and a local plan which deals with a particular form of development or use of land shall be called by the name of the subject to which it relates. A district plan may be concerned with one town, or part of a town. A subject plan may be concerned with roads, or with recreation, to take but two examples.

The matters upon which policies should be formulated, in a local plan, are specified in the 1982 Regulations, and are almost the same as those for structure plans (see page 62).

After consultation, the Secretary of State has power to direct a local planning authority to make, alter, repeal or replace a local plan (section 11B, 1971 Act).

Similar to the preparation of a structure plan, the preparation or altering of a local plan also involves two stages to encourage public participation. The local planning authority must give adequate publicity to the proposals to be contained in a local plan to enable persons who may be expected to have an interest to make representations. The authority is then expected to take those representations into account (section 12(2) of the 1971 Act). The local planning authority must consult the county planning authority, and give them a reasonable opportunity to express their views which have to be taken into consideration (section 12(3) of the 1971 Act).

The local planning authority will then prepare the proposed plan, or its alteration, obtain a certificate that it conforms with the structure plan, and make copies available for public inspection. Copies are also sent to the county planning authority and the Secretary of State (section 12(4) of the 1971 Act). Objections to the plan may be made within a specified period of not less than 6 weeks to the local planning authority itself.

There is a slightly shorter procedure to deal with alterations which do not warrant the full procedure. The authority proceeds directly to the draft alteration without need of prior consultation (section 12A of the 1971 Act).

If the Secretary of State is not satisfied about the publicity and consultations, he may serve directions on the local planning authority (section 12B of the 1971 Act).

Where objections are made to a draft plan, an inspector must be appointed to hold a public local inquiry, unless the objectors confirm in writing that they do not intend to appear. In other cases, the local planning authority may hold such an inquiry (section 13 of the 1971 Act). The inspector is ordinarily appointed by the Secretary of State. The conduct of an inquiry is more fully described in chapter 16. But, unlike the examination in public of the structure plan, every objector has a right to appear.

Before finally adopting the local plan, the local planning authority must take into consideration the report of the inspector at the public local inquiry, and whether or not to take any action as respects the plan in the light of that report. They must also take into account the objections made during the specified period and "any other objections made to the plan" and "of any other considerations which appear to the authority to be material" (section 14 of the 1971 Act). They must not adopt any proposals which do not conform generally to the structure plan. If the Minister of Agriculture, Fisheries and Food makes an objection, and the local planning authority do not modify the plan to take his objection into account, the authority shall not adopt the plan until the Secretary of State authorises.

Before formally adopting the local plan, the local planning authority shall notify the objectors, whose objections have not been withdrawn, and any other interested persons, and serve a certificate on the Secretary of State to that effect. A copy of the local plan will have been sent to the Secretary of State at the commencement of the period for making objections. The Secretary of State may direct that the proposals for the preparation or alteration of a local plan shall be submitted to him for his approval. The Secretary of State called in the North Southwark local plan, and rejected it in 1986. In R. v. *The Secretary of State for the Environment ex parte Southwark LBC* [1987] it was said that the Secretary of State was under no obligation to consult before calling in a plan.

6.5 Unitary Development Plans

The abolition of the Greater London Council and the metropolitan county councils in 1986 removed a number of strategic planning authorities responsible for structure plans. In these special areas, the Local Government Act 1985 contains provisions for unitary development plans to replace the system of structure and local plans. Unitary development plans will be similar to local plans but will take into account strategic guidelines to be issued by the Secretary of State. The procedure for the making and preparation of unitary plans is very similar to that for local plans elsewhere.

6.6   The relationship and legal consequences of Development Plans

1.   Conformity

Section 20 of the 1971 Act explains that in relation to planning, compensation and highway enactments, the term "development plan" for any area is to mean the following documents: the structure plan, and the Secretary of State's formal approval; alterations to the structure plan, and the Secretary of State's formal approval; the local plan, and the local planning authority's resolution of adoption (or, if applicable, the Secretary of State's formal approval); and any alterations to the local plan together with the appropriate resolution of adoption (or formal approval).

To ensure conformity of local plans with the structure plan, there is a procedure for the issue of a certificate by the county planning authority of conformity, and where that certificate cannot be issued, the matter is referred to the Secretary of State (section 15 of the 1971 Act).

If there is a conflict between any of the provisions of a local plan and the provisions of the structure plan, the provisions of the local plan shall prevail for all purposes (section 15B of the 1971 Act). The local plan will not, however, prevail if it is the structure plan that has meanwhile been altered.

2.   The Role of Plans

The development plan is not the definitive statement as to whether planning permission will or will not be given for development. Although section 29 of the 1971 Act requires a local planning authority to "have regard to the provisions of the development plan, so far as material to the application, and to any other material considerations", a provision that is repeated elsewhere in the Act in relation to the exercise of several of the discretionary powers, this has been held to mean that the development plan need not be followed implicitly, but it is one of the considerations to be taken into account, (*Enfield L.B.C.* v. *Secretary of State for the Environment* [1975]. The publication of government policy on planning issues in circulars has, perhaps, reduced the significance of development plans. A circular can be a "material consideration" to which the local planning authority, or the Secretary of State on appeal, must have regard. But it is wrong for the Secretary of State to prefer his own policies; he must give proper consideration to the provisions of the development plan: *Reading BC* v. *Secretary of State for the Environment* [1986]. Section 86(3) of the Local Government, Planning and Land Act 1980 states that it is the *duty* of a local planning authority, when determining a planning application, "to seek the achievement of the general objectives of the structure plan for the time being in force for their area". Doubtless there may be applications to the High Court alleging breach of this duty, with extraordinary results if the local plan is not in conformity with the structure plan!

The Local Government, Planning and Land Act 1980 also requires that a structure plan shall be accompanied by an explanatory memorandum "summarising the reasons which in the opinion of the local planning authority justify each and every policy and general proposal formulated in the plan, stating the relationship thereof to expected development and other use of land in neighbouring areas where relevant and containing such other matters as may be prescribed". This memorandum is not part of the structure plan, but is clearly going to contain some important statements justifying the contents of the plan: it will be one of the "material considerations" to which reference must be made in exercising the discretion in deciding a planning application (see further in chapter 8). This will give the explanatory memorandum a legal significance.

3.   Blight and Compulsory Purchase

One of the less attractive consequences of the development plan is the blighting it can cause to properties affected by the possibility of unattractive public authority schemes. The provisions of the development plan that directly cause blight—making property difficult to sell, except at a depressed price—may enable certain owner-occupiers to serve blight notices to compel the appropriate authorities to acquire the property concerned.

The provisions of a development plan are important in the assessment of compensation for a compulsory purchase of land. Certain assumptions as to planning permission, based upon the development plan, may be made by a claimant to establish the value of his land had no compulsory purchase taken place (see Compulsory Purchase and Compensation by Barry Denyer-Green (Estates Gazette) 1985).

4. Challenging a Plan

Any person aggrieved by a plan, or its alteration, repeal or replacement, may bring proceedings in the High Court (section 244 of the 1971 Act).

> *Great Portland Estates Plc.* v. *Westminster City Council* [1984]
> The district plan stipulated that office development would not normally be permitted outside the central activities zone of the city. The circumstances when office development might be permitted outside that zone were set out in a guide which was not part of the district plan. This part of the plan was quashed as it did not set out the local planning authority's "proposals of the use and development" of the land—these were partly in the guide.

In *Fourth Investments* v. *Bury MBC* [1984], part of a local plan was quashed as the inspector should not have included certain land as part of the green belt had he properly considered the housing needs envisaged by the structure plan.

Chapter 7

The Planning Application

Introduction   69
The form of the application   69
Fees   70
Application for Outline Planning Permission   73
Notices to Owners and Tenants   75
Publicity for applications   76
Development affecting Conservation Areas and Listed
    Buildings   78
Development not in accordance with the Development
    Plan   78

7.1 Introduction

The scope of development control was set out in chapters 2 and 3; in chapter 4 certain development for which planning permission is automatically granted was outlined; this chapter considers the planning application for development that needs the express consent of the local planning authority.

7.2 The form of the application

It is important to the applicant for planning permission that he uses the correct form, completes it satisfactorily, informs the parties entitled to be told of an application, and sends the form, appropriate certificates, plans and fee to the right authority. If he is successful thus far, he may be excused any impatience he may later experience in the processing of his application.

Most application forms ask for brief particulars of the proposed development including the purpose for which the land and or buildings are to be used. These should be provided as fully and as accurately as is possible. This is because a planning permission may be granted "... in accordance with the plan and application submitted ...". The description, particularly of the proposed use, that is contained in the application form, may therefore be the only form of words available for an inspector or court to consider if an enforcement notice is served alleging development without planning permission. In *Kwik Save Discount Group Ltd.* v. *Secretary of State for Wales* [1981], the Court of Appeal decided that the description "retail showroom including new display windows", in the application form, had to be construed within the context of the whole application, which was for alterations and extensions to a service station, and could not be isolated out to enable a supermarket use to take place. This point is further considered in chapter 9.

It is no longer possible for planning permission to operate as a listed building consent, accordingly, any work to a listed building must be the subject of a separate listed building consent application (section 56(2) of the 1971 Act).

7.3   Fees

Section 87 of the Local Government, Planning and Land Act 1980 empowers the Secretary of State to make regulations providing for the payment of fees to local planning authorities in respect of any application for planning permission, consent, approval, determination or certificate under the planning Acts. Provision is also made for the payment of a fee to the Secretary of State where he decides a deemed planning application in connection with an appeal against enforcement proceedings (see chapter 14).

The present regulations are the Town and Country Planning (Fees for Applications and Deemed Applications) Regulations 1983. The fees are increased from time to time.

The fees are payable upon an application for planning permission; for the approval of reserved matters; for the consent for the display of advertisements; and for deemed applications for planning permission (under sections 88(7) and 95(6) of the 1971 Act). In the case of deemed applications there are exemptions (Regulation 8).

The fee must be paid at the time of the application, which will otherwise be invalid. There is no refund if the application is not consented to!

No fee payable

A fee is not payable in a number of circumstances.

No fee is payable if the local planning authority is satisfied that the application relates "solely to the carrying out of operations for the alteration or extension of an existing dwelling house or the carrying out of operations (other than the erection of a dwelling house) in the curtilage of an existing dwelling for the purpose, in either case, of providing means of access to or within the dwelling-house for a disabled person who is resident or proposes to reside in that dwelling-house, or of providing facilities designed to secure his greater safety, health or comfort" (Regulation 4). This regulation now includes alterations to public buildings.

No fee is payable where an application is made solely for development within Schedule 1 to the General Development Order 1977 (development for which planning permission is normally automatically available without application) and express planning permission is necessary for such development (Regulation 5). This may happen where an Article 4 direction is in force withdrawing such atomatic consent (see Chapter 4), or because of the requirements of a condition limiting the permitted development (see chapter 9; particularly *City of London Corporation* v. *Secretary of State for the Environment* [19783]). Regulation 5 includes applications for the retention of a building or the continuance of a use without complying with a condition that limits development otherwise permitted by the GDO. The purpose of Regulation 5 is to recognise that, in the ordinary case, development specified by the General Development Order needs no application, and therefore no fee would ordinarily become payable.

No fee is payable where an application is made for planning permission, or the approval of reserved matters for a *modified proposal* within twelve months of the grant of planning permission to the same applicant (Regulation 6).

A fee is not payable in a number of circumstances where a new application is made within twelve months of the withdrawal, before a notice of decision was issued, of a previous application; or, within twelve months of the refusal of consent by the local planning authority or the Secretary of State (upon appeal or after reference to him). The applications within this exemption are those for planning permission, or the approval of reserved matters (see below). The second application must be made by or on behalf of the same applicant; relate to the same site as that of the earlier application, or to part of that site (and to no other land); and relate to development of the same character or description as the development in the earlier application (and to no other development). Additional land for a new access may be included. Only one such further application may be made without payment of the fee (Regulation 7).

A fee paid in connection with an enforcement notice—a deemed planning application—is refunded if the appeal succeeds (Regulation 8).

Provision was made in 1986 for the refund of fees where an invalid planning application is made, or an invalid enforcement notice has been issued. Applications to consolidate existing planning permissions for mineral operations are now exempt, and so too are applications for advertisements following the withdrawal of deemed consent.

Reduced fees

Schedule I, to the Regulations, makes provision for reduced fees in the following circumstances.

One quarter of the full fee is payable upon a second application for planning permission or for approval of reserved matters, if made within 28 days of the earlier application for planning permission, or application for approval of reserved matters, in respect of which the full fee was paid. The second application must be made by or on behalf of the same applicant; relate to the same site; and relate to the same development or same reserved matters, as the first application. This sensible concession acknowledges the common practice of submitting more than one application for a development proposal, or for approval of reserved matters, each with some variation.

There is a reduced fee payable where an application is made for planning permission by a club, society or other organisation for a material change of use of land to a playing field or to carry out operations (not including the erection of a building) for purposes connected with a playing field. The club, society or organisation mut be non-profit making and have, as its object, the provision of facilities for sport or recreation; the proposed development must be intended for the club, society or organisation to fulfil these objects.

There is a reduced fee for an application for the approval of reserved matters other than matters concerning design and external appearance of the building authorised by the outline planning permission, i.e., siting, means of access or landscaping. There is also a reduced fee for an application for a change of conditions under section 31A of the 1971 Act.

For an application for the approval of the design and external appearance of a building, the full fee in accordance with the scale is payable. Although once the full fee has been paid, any further applications for approval of reserved matters are at a reduced fee.

Special fees

There is a special fee category for applications associated with oil and gas exploration.

Calculation of the fee

It will be seen from the scale that certain fees are calculated with reference to the area of the site, or area of the building or proposed building. Paragraph 6 of the 1st Schedule to the Regulations provides that the calculations are to be made to the next whole unit for fee purposes. Bearing in mind both this point and the various fee maxima, careful calculation should always be made to maximise the areas for any given fee.

Where the proposed development is for a building to be used partly for residential purposes and partly for other purposes a fee is payable, according to the scale of fees, for each dwelling-house created, together with the appropriate fee for the non-residential floorspace. Where the building is to contain common parts for the use of residential and non-residential occupiers alike, the appropriate proportion of that space, as the non-residential use bears to the gross floor space of the building is added to the non-residential area for fee calculation purposes.

Where the proposed development relates to more than one of the categories of development in the table of fees, the fee for each category of development is first calculated, and the highest of the amounts so calculated shall represent the fee payable in respect of all the development.

7.4 Application for Outline Planning Permission

Outline planning permission is defined in the 1971 Act as "... planning permission granted ... with the reservation for subsequent approval by the local planning authority ... of matters (referred to ... as "reserved matters") not particularised in the application" (section 42(1)). Such an application may only be made in respect of the erection of a building (Article 5 of the General Development Order).

Outline planning permissions are not otherwise separately considered or provided for in the 1971 Act (other than in relation to a time limit for the application for approval of reserved matters). An outline permission is in all senses and for all purposes *the* planning permission; the only difference from a planning permission, that is not outline, is that it is granted subject to conditions that require the approval of the local planning authority to certain matters that commonly include: design and external appearance of the building or buildings, their siting, means of access and the landscaping of the site. For other conditions that may be imposed, see chapter 9.

Although an application for outline can therefore save design time and costs, the local planning authority may notify the applicant within one month of the application that further details must be submitted before it can be considered (see Article 5 of the General Development Order 1977).

When submitting an application for the approval of the reserved matters, it is important that a planning application form is not used, as otherwise the authority may be entitled to consider the application de novo. However in *Etheridge* v. *Secretary of State for the Environment* [1983] it was said that an application for full planning permission is at the same time an application for the approval of reserved matters: what matters is not the form of the application, but the objective effect. Article 6 of the General Development Order specifies that an application for the approval of reserved matters should be in writing, identify the outline planning permission, and include such particulars, plans and drawings as are necessary to deal with the reserved matters. The further certificates as to ownership are not therefore required (*R.* v. *Bradford-on-Avon U.D.C. ex parte Boulton* [1964]).

The application for the approval of reserved matters should not radically differ from the development proposed by the outline. If it does, the local planning authority will be entitled to consider the application as one for planning permission, and refuse it (see *Shemara* v. *Luton Corpn.* [1967]). In *Calcaria Construction Co. Ltd.* v. *Secretary of State for the Environment* [1974], where outline planning permission had been granted for a warehouse of 55,000 square feet for wholesale and retail distribution, it was decided that the local planning authority, and the Secretary of State, had rightly refused consent to the detailed application which showed a supermarket and ancillary storage and parking space; a warehouse for wholesale and retail distribution could not mean a supermarket.

Matters took a different course in *Chalgray Ltd.* v. *Secretary of State for the Environment* [1976], where the application for approval of the reserved matters included a new access which was not intended in the outline. Following the refusal of consent by the local planning authority, the Secretary of State actually declined to decide the appeal as he said the details submitted were *ultra vires* the original planning permission. An appeal against his decision was dismissed. In *R.* v. *Castle Point D.C. ex parte Brooks* [1985] outline planning permission was granted for a bungalow, but the plans and details approved as the "reserved matters" were of a house; a neighbour was successful in having the decision quashed by the procedure known as judicial review (see Chapter 19).

Where outline planning permission is granted for the carrying out of building or other operations, it shall be granted subject to conditions that the application for approval of the reserved matters is made within 3 years of the grant of the outline planning permission, and that the development itself must be begun within 5 years of the grant of the outline planning permission, or within 2 years of the approval of the reserved matters, whichever is the later date. Any outline planning permission not containing these conditions is deemed to contain them. The local planning authority may substitute for these periods of time such other periods as they consider appropriate (section 41(2)–(4) of the 1971 Act).

These conditions can cause problems if the local planning authority refuse consent to an application for approval of the reserved matters and the time limit has expired for making a further application. In practice it is advisable to submit more than one such application, each slightly different in detail, and all in good time. A right of appeal against a refusal to approve the reserved matters required by a planning condition was introduced by an amendment to section 36(1) of the 1971 Act in 1980.

The planning authority cannot, in considering the application for the approval of the reserved matters, decide that no approval shall be given because the original outline planning permission would no longer be so decided (*Hamilton* v. *West Sussex C.C.* [1958]). But, if they have already given approval to the reserved matters, can they refuse to consider a further application for the approval of reserved matters? The Court of Appeal decided in *Heron Corpn Ltd.* v. *Manchester City Council* [1978], where the first approved detailed scheme was rendered abortive by the subsequent listing of certain buildings, that the second application for the reserved matters was within the scope of the original outline planning permission and must be considered by the local planning authority. In *R.* v. *Hammersmith and Fulham LBC ex parte Greater London Council* [1986] the Court of Appeal applied the *Heron* case, and decided that where an application for the approval of reserved matters omitted a bus garage and public library from a large scheme of development that had an outline planning permission, approval could be validly given: the development approved was not something different from that in the outline.

7.5 Notices to Owners and Tenants

The applicant for planning permission is required to sign a certificate that:

(a) he is owner of the land concerned; or

(b) he had notified the owner, or other owners, as the case
    may be; or
(c) he had notified the owners of whom he has names and
    addresses and taken steps to trace the other owners; or
(d) he does not know the names and addresses of any of the
    owners (section 27(1) of the 1971 Act).

In respect of certificates under (c) and (d), the applicant must first
advertise for the owners in a local newspaper (section 27(2)).

The term "owner" means the freeholder and the owner of a lease
of which not less than 7 years remain unexpired (section 27(7)).
This means that tenants with lesser interests are not entitled to be
notified of a planning application affecting their property. To this
there is an exception in the case of an agricultural holding within
the meaning of the Agricultural Holdings Act 1986; the applicant
must certify that he has notified any tenant of the agricultural holding. This exception exists because an agricultural tenant may lose
security of tenure if planning permission is granted (section 27(3)).

It is a criminal offence to sign a certificate under this section
which is false or misleading (section 27(5)). If no certificate is issued,
the local planning authority will have no jurisdiction to consider
the application. Even if a certificate is issued that is incorrect, the
decision of the authority will remain valid (*R.* v. *Bradford-on-Avon
U.D.C. ex parte Boulton* [1964] where the applicant mistakenly
certified that he owned all the land). In *Maine* v. *Swansea City
Council* (CA [1985], the certificate was wrong as part of the land
the subject of the application was owned by someone who had
not been given notice. This omission did not render the subsequent
grant of planning permission a complete nullity as the court had
a discretion, which it exercised, to refuse to quash the permission
because of the lapse of time (three years). Where an applicant completes an application, and the appropriate certificate, purporting
to do so as agent of the true owner, he will be required to account
for any profits he may obtain if he later acquires the land from
an unsuspecting owner at a price below market value (*English* v.
Dedham Vale Property Co. [1978]).

The date for determining whether a person is an owner is the
date 21 days before the date of the application.

7.6 Publicity for Applications

Every planning application must be entered on a register (section
34 of the 1971 Act). The General Development Order makes
detailed provision for these registers, and for the details they must
contain (article 21).

They are kept at the offices of the local planning authority, and are available for public inspection. They contain not only new applications yet to be decided but also a permanent record of all applications and decisions.

Apart from the register, applications for certain forms of unneighbourly development must be given wider publicity (section 26 of the 1971 Act). The classes of development are designated in the General Development Order (article 8) as follows:

(a) construction of buildings for use as public conveniences;
(b) construction of buildings or other operations, or use of land, for the disposal of refuse or waste materials or as a scrap yard or coal yard or for the winning or working of minerals;
(c) construction of buildings or other operations (other than the laying of sewers, the construction of pumphouses in a line of sewers, the construction of septic tanks and cesspools serving single dwelling-houses or single buildings in which not more than ten people will normally reside, work or congregate, and works ancillary thereto) or use of land, for the purpose of the retention, treatment or disposal of sewage, trade waste or sludge;
(d) construction of buildings to a height exceeding 20 metres;
(e) construction of buildings or use of land for the purposes of a slaughterhouse or knacker's yard; or for killing or plucking poultry;
(f) construction of buildings and use of buildings for any of the following purposes, namely, as a casino, funfair, or a bingo hall, a theatre, a cinema, a music hall, a dance hall, a skating rink, a swimming bath or gymnasium (not forming part of a school, college or university), or a Turkish or other vapour or foam bath;
(g) construction of buildings and use of buildings or land as a zoo or for the business of boarding or breeding cats or dogs;
(h) construction of buildings and use of land for motor car or motorcycle racing;
(i) use of land as a cemetery.

To comply with the publicity requirements, the applicant must advertise his intended application in a local newspaper and by affixing a site notice on the land concerned (section 26(2)). The forms are specified in the General Development Order. The forms of advertisement and site notice invite any person to make a representation

to the local planning authority. If the applicant has no right to
fix a site notice, he will have to certify accordingly.

What has just been described are the minimum legal requirements
for giving publicity to a planning application. It is the practice of
many planning authorities to take further steps, and to inform neighbours or a wider public of an application. Where an authority has
such a policy, it may be guilty of maladministration if it fails in
any case to give publicity (see reports of the Local Government
Commissioner).

7.7   Development affecting Conservation Areas and Listed Buildings

Conservation areas and listed buildings are considered more fully
in chapter 10. However, any application for development which
would, in the opinion of the local planning authority, affect the
character or appearance of a conservation area, or affect the setting
of a listed building must be given publicity by the authority (section
28). The publicity consists of a newspaper advertisement and site
notice inviting any person to make representations to the authority.
The application must not then be determined within 21 days of
the notices appearing. The difficulty for the developer that arises
from this publicity requirement is that it concerns not simply development in a conservation area, or of a listed building, but development that merely affects such an area or building.

A notice that fails to state the date by which objections and representations are to be made is not a proper notice, and a subsequent
planning permission may be invalid: *R*. v. *Lambeth LBC ex parte
Sharp* [1986]. Strict compliance with these requirements is expected
where a local planning authority is exercising a power to grant
planning permission to itelf and is not exercising a duty.

Applications affecting the character or appearance of a conservation area must also be referred to the Historic Buildings and Monuments Commission if they are listed for the purpose in Circular
23/84.

7.8   Development not in accordance with the Development Plan

Where the local planning authority propose to grant permission
for development that is not in accordance with the development
plan, it must comply with the Town and Country Planning (Development Plans) Direction 1981. This sets out a procedure for advertising
what is called a "departure application", and in cases where the
application would materially conflict with or prejudice the imple-
mentations of the structure plan, or a modification to a local plan

introduced by the Secretary of State, the Secretary of State must be informed. In *R*. v. *St Edmundsbury BC ex parte Investors in Industry Commercial Properties Ltd.* [1985], it was said that the omission to advertise was breach of a directory rather than a mandatory requirement. In the circumstances there had been widespread publicity in local newspapers.

Chapter 8

How the Local Planning Authority determine a Planning Application

Introduction   81
Consultations with other bodies   82
Power of a local highway authority to issue directions   84
Directions and Policy guidance given by the Secretary of State   85
The effect of the development plan   87
Other material considerations   88
Development affecting Conservation Areas and Listed
    Buildings   91
Planning applications in which a local planning authority
    has an interest   91
Judicial supervision   92

8.1   Introduction

It may be thought that a local planning authority, as an element in the democratic processes of local government, has a fair degree of discretion in deciding a planning application. But, not only are there a number of statutory directions and procedures to be followed; and other authorities and bodies to be consulted; there is also a considerable number of legal decisions which have circumscribed the limits of discretion available to the authority. A local authority is of statutory creation exercising statutory powers and duties: it is subject to judicial control and some degree of Ministerial supervision.

Much of the detailed guidance to local planning authorities is found in the General Development Order 1977 (GDO). One important provision is that, unless the applicant agrees, a decision on an application must be made within 8 weeks (article 7A). In recent years Ministerial Circulars have been more direct and specific in giving guidance to local planning authorities.

The local planning authority makes its decision on an application by virtue of section 29(1) of the 1971 Act: it may grant planning permission unconditionally, or subject to such conditions as it thinks fit; or it may refuse planning permission. The Secretary of State is similarly bound when determining an appeal.

8.2   Consultations with other bodies

Before planning permission can be granted by the local planning authority, in the circumstances mentioned below, the authorities or persons indicated must be consulted (article 15 of the GDO):

Circumstances	*Authorities or persons to be consulted*
(a) Where it appears to the LPA that the development is likely to affect land in another LPA area	the district planning authority; London Borough Council (or City of London); or county planning authority in a National Park.
(b) Where it appears that the development is likely to create or attract traffic resulting in volume entering or leaving a trunk road or affecting a railway level crossing.	the regional office of the Department of the Environment (Department of Transport)
(c) Where development involves the formation, laying out or alteration of any access to a highway (not a trunk road)	the local highway authority (usually the county council).
(d) Erection of a building in a coal mining area notified by British Coal	British Coal
(e) Development within 3 kilometres of Windsor Castle, Great Park or Home Park; or 800 metres of any other Royal palace or park	the Department of the Environment.
(f) Development consisting of or including: works to the bed or or banks of a river or stream; building or other operations for refining or storing mineral oils and their derivatives; use of land for refuse tipping; work or the use of land for certain specified sewerage	the water authority for the area.

treatment or disposal facilities; and use of land as a cemetery.	the water authority for the area.
(g) Development of land specified as of special interest by the Nature Conservancy Council (Sites of Special Scientific Interest)	Nature Conservancy Council.
(h) Development on land on which there is a theatre	Theatres Trust.
(i) Non-agricultural development which is not in accordance with the development plan involving the loss of more than 10 acres (or less than 10 acres if this is likely to lead to a further loss of agricultural land)	Ministry of Agriculture, Fisheries and Food. (see below)

The government has (1987) proposed amending the consultation requirement where the loss of more than 10 acres of agricultural land is involved. It is proposed that consultation would only be required for the loss of 20 hectares or more of Grades 1 or 2 agricultural land and which, in the opinion of the authority, would materially conflict with or prejudice the implementation of the policies and proposals of the development plan. The Secretary of State may, by a direction, add further consultation requirements. At least 14 days must be allowed for these consultations, and the local planning authority must take into account any representations they receive.

Certain development is specified as being a county matter (see chapter 5), and if an application is received that appears to the district planning authority to relate to such a matter, the county planning authority decides the application. The county planning authority are required to afford an opportunity to the district planning authority to make recommendations; and are bound to take these into account (article 16 of the GDO).

Paragraph 19 of Schedule 16 to the Local Government Act 1972 (as amended by the Local Government, Planning and Land Act 1980) requires a district planning authority to consult the county planning authority before determining certain planning applications. The applications concerned relate to development of land which:

   (a) would materially conflict with or prejudice the implementation of policies or general proposals in an approved or submitted structure plan, or a matter to be included in such a plan, an old development plan, or a local plan prepared by the county;

(b) by reason of its scale or nature of the location of the land, would be of major importance for the implementation of an approved structure plan;

(c) will affect or be affected by the winning or working of minerals, being an area notified by the county;

(d) the county have notified to the district that they intend to develop, or which would prejudice such development; and

(e) is land notified by the county to be used for waste disposal or which would prejudice such use.

The county may direct that these consultations be dispensed with in relation to a particular application or class of application. There is a Code of Practice for consultations in circular 2/81.

Parish and community councils are entitled to require the district planning authority to notify them of planning applications (either all or as specified). In these cases, the parish and community councils will have an opportunity to make representations to the district planning authority (article 17 of the GDO).

8.3   Power of a highway authority to issue directions

Where an application is for development consisting of the making or altering of an access to a trunk road with a 40 m.p.h. speed limit, or to a special road; or other development within 67 metres of an existing or proposed trunk road, the Secretary of State must be consulted. The application cannot be determined except in accordance with a direction. However, the application can be determined if a direction is not received within 28 days (article 11 of the GDO).

A local highway authority may issue a direction to the local planning authority restricting the latter's power to grant planning permission except in accordance with the direction (article 12 of the GDO). This applies where development consists of (a) the formation, laying out or alteration of any means of access to a classified road or a proposed road the route of which has been notified; and (b) other operations or use of land which appear to the local highway authority to be likely to result in a material increase in the volume of traffic entering or leaving the road, to prejudice the improvement or construction of the road, or result in a material change in the character of the traffic so entering, leaving or using the road.

The local planning authority may determine the application if no direction is received within 28 days, or they have been notified that no direction will be issued.

8.4 Directions and Policy guidance given by the Secretary of State

Sections 31 and 35 of the 1971 Act contain wide powers for the Secretary of State to issue directions in relation to planning applications.

1. The general power of direction

The Secretary of State may give directions restricting the grant of planning permission by a local planning authority, either indefinitely or during such period as may be specified, in respect of a particular development or any specified class of development. The local planning authority must then comply with such a direction (article 10 of the GDO).

2. Development not in accordance with the development plan for the area

Subject to the significance of the development plan in all planning determinations, and considered more fully below, the Secretary of State may issue directions governing the grant of planning permission that is not in accordance with the development plan (article 14 of the GDO).

The present direction for England outside Greater London is the Town and Country Planning (Development Plans) (England) Direction 1981 (in circular 2/81). A failure to comply with the Development Plans Direction does not render the planning permission null and void; the directive is not mandatory: see *R. v. St Edmundsbury BC ex parte Investors in Industry Commercial Properties Ltd.* [1985]. Where county matters are concerned, county planning authorities decide if an application involves a departure from the development plan. Otherwise it is for the district planning authorities to make the decision. If a departure application is so identified, and the respective planning authorities are not going to refuse it, it must be advertised locally. This gives an opportunity for representations to be made; the planning authority, when making their decision, must take these representations into account. A departure application which would materially conflict with or prejudice the implementation of the policies and general proposals of the structure plan must be referred to the Secretary of State if the authority do not intend to refuse it. The same applies to a conflict with a provision of a local plan introduced by way of modification by the Secretary of State. In either case the Secretary of State may issue a direction within 21 days.

3. The call-in procedure

The Secretary of State may give directions requiring planning applications or applications for the approval of reserved matters to be referred to him for decision. A direction may be given to a local planning authority, or to all such authorities; it may relate to a particular application or to a class of applications as specified (section 35 of the 1971 Act). This power appears to confer on the Secretary of State an unqualified direction which is subject only to the *Wednesbury* principle of judicial review (see chapter 19). The Secretary of State, in deciding to call in applications, can only be challenged if his decision is perverse or totally unreasonable; his decision is one of policy or value judgment for him: *Rhys Williams* v. *Secretary of State for Wales* [1985].

As there is no right of appeal from a decision of the Secretary of State, he will, if requested by either the applicant or the local planning authority, appoint an inspector before whom the parties may appear (section 35(5)).

4. Policy guidance

The Secretary of State for the Environment issues policy guidance to local planning authorities in several ways. Through the Development Control Policy Notes, which contain advice in respect of specific development problems from development in residential areas to out of town shopping centres; Department of the Environment Circulars; and, occasionally a government white paper. The Development Control Policy Notes contain durable technical guidance on the planning of development. They are plainly written by planners for planners. Circulars very often contain advice which is less durable in that it may reflect the policies of a particular Secretary of State. Circular 22 of 1980—Development Control—Policy and Practice is a current example of this. Particularly important circulars include: Planning Gain (22/1983); Land for Housing (15/1984); Industrial Development (16/1984); and Development and Employment (14/1985).

Circulars have been held to be "material considerations", and therefore regard may have to be paid to any relevant policies they contain: see *Pye (Oxford) Estates* v. *West Oxford D.C.* [1982].

But, provided the local planning authority has considered the policy in a relevant circular, it may depart from the policy if it has reasons for doing so: see *R. v. Camden L.B.C. ex parte Comyn Ching & Co.* [1984].

It would be wrong for a local planning authority to allow a circular to decide an application without the full exercise of its own proper discretion: see *R. v. Worthing B.C. ex parte Burch* [1985].

8.5 The effect of the development plan

There is a significant administrative, democratic and public participation effort behind the preparation or amendment of the development plans. It might be assumed that the provisions of these plans actually dictate the development control decisions in relation to the consideration of a planning application. This may be the position in many cases, if the development plans are reasonably up to date, but the legal provisions to ensure this are somewhat weak.

Because most development control decisions are in the hands of district planning authorities, there may be insufficient regard to the structure plans prepared by the county planning authorities. It is now the duty of a local planning authority (and this includes the Secretary of State) "to seek the achievement of the general objectives of the structure plan ..." (section 86(3) of the Local Government, Planning and Land Act 1980). This rather nebulous provision awaits baptism in a court of law.

The main provision concerning development plans is found in the 1971 Act: "... in dealing with the application [the local planning authority] shall have regard to the provisions of the development plan, so far as material to the application ..." (section 29(1)). The words 'shall have regard to' did not mean 'to follow implicitly' in the Scottish case of *Simpson v. Edinburgh Corpn* [1960]. This case was followed in England in *Enfield L.B.C. v. Secretary of State for the Environment* [1975]. The local planning authority do not therefore have to slavishly adhere to the provisions of the local plan; they may follow some different policy; but they must give consideration to the plan and the merits of the application before following that policy.

The Secretary of State is in no different position with regard to the effect of the development plan when deciding appeals. In *Richmond-upon-Thames L.B.C. v. Secretary of State for the Environment* [1983], the inspector was held to be wrong to give preference to a report critical of planning gain over a clear policy on the subject in the development. Similarly a decision of the Secretary of State in *Reading B.C.* v. *Secretary of State for the Environment* [1986] was quashed as it was materially defective in its reasoning and conflicted with the development plan. These cases do not decide that planning decisions cannot be made that are inconsistent with the development plan; such decisions can only be made if supported with full and proper reasons, and, according to *Surrey Heath B.C.* v. *Secretary of State for the Environment* [1986], adequate evidence upon which the reasons are founded.

If a local planning authority do decide to grant planning permission that is not in accordance with the development plan, they must follow the departure procedure outlined above at section 8.4, and take into account any representations they receive. If this occurs, the policy that contradicts a provision of a development plan is not subject to the public participation process that applies to the making or modification of the local or structure plans. This occurred in *Covent Garden Community Association Ltd.* v. *Greater London Council* [1981] where the G.L.C. granted planning permission to itself that was contrary to the local action area plan. But because they had followed the statutory procedures, and were not regarded as having been in breach of the rules of natural justice (see chapter 19), the Community Association were left without any legal remedy to compel the G.L.C. to submit the new policy to an inquiry.

8.6   Other material considerations

The 1971 Act provides that a local planning authority, in dealing with a planning application, must not only have regard to the development plan but additionally "... shall have regard ... to any other material considerations" (section 29(1)). This also applies to the Secretary of State or an inspector when a planning appeal is being determined. Although it must be assumed that, where the decision is made by the Secretary of State, he does have regard to his own circulars even if he does not specifically refer to these in terms: see *Hewlett* v. *Secretary of State for the Environment* [1985].

There are a number of cases on this provision: the issue is usually either that some matter is alleged to be a material consideration, and was not considered; or, particular regard was paid to some matter which it is alleged was not a material consideration. It has already been mentioned that circulars containing relevant policies may be material considerations.

The view of the Secretary of State as to the meaning of other material considerations is found in Development Control Policy Note No. 1 (1969):

"... [they] cover a wide field—the effect of a proposal on road safety or the beauty of the surroundings, the effect on public services such as drainage and water supply, conflict with public proposals for the same land, ... and many other factors. They must be genuine planning considerations i.e. they must be related to the purpose of planning legislation, which is to regulate the development and use of land and not some extraneous purpose."

In *Stringer* v. *Minister of Housing and Local Government* [1970], Cooke J. said: "In principle ... any consideration which relates to the use and development of land is capable of being a planning consideration. Whether a particular consideration ... is material in any given case will depend on the circumstances".

Economic considerations

Can economic questions be material considerations? Ackner J. in *J. Murphy & Sons* v. *Secretary of State for the Environment* [1973] considered this problem and said:

"I have never heard it suggested before that a planning application involves a valuation exercise ... I hold that as a matter of law the Minister [or the local planning authority] is not entitled to have regard to the cost of developing a site in determining whether planning permission ... should be granted".

Later he was to say that he had stated the proposition too widely (*Hambledon & Chiddingfold Parish Councils* v. *Secretary of State for the Environment* [1976]). In *Brighton B.C.* v. *Secretary of State for the Environment* [1978], Sir Douglas Frank upheld the Secretary of State's decision that by granting planning permission to the applicants, certain school trustees, this would generate funds to enable the maintenance and refurbishment of a listed building nearby: a distinct planning benefit. The same judge, in *Walters* v. *Secretary of State for Wales* [1978], decided that it would be wrong if a planning authority justified their refusal of planning permission for development on the ground that it would be uneconomic.

He said:

"... the grant of planning permission cannot depend on the resources and intention of the applicant. It is for the developer to make the economic decision whether to carry out the development and not the local planning authority".

It seems that economic matters can, in appropriate cases, be material considerations: although the unprofitability of any particular development proposal should not be a reason for refusal. In *Niarchos*

(London) Ltd. v. *Secretary of State for the Environment* [1978], it was held that the planning authority should consider the costs of adaptation of premises to residential use notwithstanding a policy in the development plan in favour of residential use, rather than a continuance of office use under a temporary planning permission: economic viability was considered by the judge to be an important consideration in deciding the applicability of that policy.

The cases present no very clear pattern as to whether economic considerations can be taken into account. It is submitted that the economic viability of a proposed development should never be considered by a planning authority as a ground for refusing planning permission. On the other hand, it would be wrong for a planning authority to ignore economic matters that are obvious and relevant, or which will become consequential to their decision.

Effect on future decisions

In *Collis Radio Ltd.* v. *Secretary of State for the Environment* [1975], it was held that if planning permission were granted for the development sought, the fact that it would make applications for similar development in the locality difficult to refuse could be a material consideration. The local planning authority may therefore rely on this argument to refuse permission even if they have no other objection to the actual application before them.

Preserving or encouraging uses

The desirability of preserving existing uses of land and buildings is a material consideration even if there is no other objection to an application for change of use. This was upheld in *Clyde & Co.* v. *Secretary of State for the Environment* [1977] where the local planning authority desired to retain residential accommodation in an area of housing shortage. Although an authority has no powers to compel an occupier to use his land for a permitted use, it is a perfectly proper planning consideration to encourage that use by refusing permission for other uses. But if planning permission is refused for, say, offices, on the ground that another use such as residential would be preferred, consideration must be given to whether the residential use was a realistic expectation: *Finn & Co.* v. *Secretary of State for the Environment* [1984].

The matter was considered further by the House of Lords in *Westminster City Council* v. *British Waterways Board* [1984]. It was accepted that planning permission could be refused if the ground of refusal was the desirability of protecting the existing use of premises, but that planning permission could not be refused if the ground of refusal was to protect the occupation of the present occupier of the premises.

Non-Statutory Policies

The *Clyde & Co.* case is also important for another aspect of this problem. It had been argued that a planning consideration could only be such, and therefore a material consideration, if set out as a policy in the development plan. This was rejected in the Court of Appeal. Planning authorities are entitled to have regard to other policies than those formally within the development plans.

Other material considerations

The list of material considerations is never closed, as any relevant fact or issue of a planning nature may be pertinent. In *Nash* v. *Secretary of State for the Environment* [1985], where existing use rights had been lost because the landowner had failed to appeal against an enforcement notice, it was said that the existing rights were a factor, although not conclusive, to be considered. A similar point arose in *Weitz* v. *Secretary of State for the Environment* [1985] where it was said that an existing unlawful use, to which there had been no objections, was a minor consideration.

8.7   Development affecting Conservation Areas and Listed Buildings

In considering whether to grant planning permission for development which *affects* a Listed Building or its setting, or a building in a Conservation Area or its setting, the local planning authority, or the Secretary of State, shall have special regard to the desirability of preserving the building or its setting or any features of special architectural or historic interest which it possesses (section 56(3) of the 1971 Act).

The further controls that apply to Conservation Areas and Listed Buildings are considered in Chapter 10.

8.8   Planning applications in which a local planning authority has an interest

The General Regulations 1976 make special provisions for applications made by the local planning authority itself. If the requirements as to the procedure are not followed, the decision may be quashed:

R. v. *Lambeth L.B.C. ex parte Sharp* [1986]
The local planning authority granted itself planning permission for some athletics facilities in a Conservation Area. The decision

was quashed because the authority had failed to display proper notices and failed to give proper consideration to the Conservation Area at the appropriate stage.

In *Steeples* v. *Derbyshire C.C.* [1981], where the local planning authority was said to have a financial interest in granting planning permission for a large project it had an interest in, the permission was quashed on the ground of a breach of the rules of natural justice. The case was distinguished in *R.* v. *Amber Valley D.C. ex parte Jackson* [1984], where the majority of the councillors were predisposed towards the proposed development. Because the authority had no contractual or financial interest, unlike in the *Steeples* case, there was said to be no reason why they could not make a fair decision.

This problem was considered further in *R.* v. *St Edmundsbury B.C. ex parte Investors in Industry Commercial Properties Ltd.* [1985]. It was acknowledged that there are many cases where a local Planning authority will have an interest in the outcome of its own planning decisions. There is no presumption that because it has an interest there must be bias. The test, considered in *Steeples*, whether the reasonable man, knowing all the facts, would conclude that the planning decision was fairly reached, is more suited to judicial rather than administrative decisions. The test today is probably whether the authority took into account what was relevant, and disregarded the irrelevant: see *R.* v. *Sevenoaks D.C. ex parte Terry* [1985].

8.9 Judicial supervision

When a planning authority is exercising its statutory discretion in determining a planning application, it is subject to the judicial supervision exercised by the Divisional Court of the Queens Bench Division. The purpose of this supervision is, in simple terms, to ensure fairness. But because this supervision is applicable to more circumstances than a planning application, the matter is separately considered in chapter 19.

Chapter 9

Planning Permissions, Conditions and Agreements

Introduction   93
Planning permission   93
Planning conditions   99
Challenging planning conditions   107
Planning agreements   108

9.1 Introduction

In the preceding chapter a number of matters relevant to the submission of a planning application were considered. We now move forward to the decisions a local planning authority may make on an application. This chapter is concerned with the nature and effect of a planning permission, and of the conditions that may be attached to a permission. It also considers planning agreements between landowner and local planning authority that may be involved with a planning decision. If a decision involves refusal of planning permission, the reader should turn on to chapter 16. The reader should bear in mind that what is said here in relation to a local planning authority also applies in those cases where the Secretary of State grants or deems to grant planning permission.

9.2 Planning permission

1. What is the planning permission?

This important question has arisen on a number of occasions where there has been a disparity between the decision of the planning committee and the formal notification; or the committee redecide an earlier decision.

Under article 7 of the General Development Order 1977, every decision of the local planning authority, on an application for planning permission, shall be given to the applicant by a notice in writing. In *R. v. Yeovil B.C., ex parte Trustees of Elim Pentecostal Church* [1971], the planning committee resolved that their town clerk be authorised to approve the application for planning permission subject to certain conditions. At a later meeting, the committee decided to refuse planning permission. The applicants appealed to the Divisional Court, contending that the committee had granted a conditional permission at their first meeting. The court decided that there existed no planning permission, as no notice in writing had been issued as is required by the General Development Order. In this decision Lord Widgery C.J. relied on dicta of Lord Denning M.R. in *Slough Estates Ltd.* v. *Slough B.C. (No. 2)* [1969] C.A. where he said that the grant of a planning permission has to be in writing.

However, the statutory requirement that the grant of permission should be in writing, in the *Slough* case, was worded differently from the present requirement that the *notice* of the decision should be in writing.

Lord Widgery C.J. himself came to a different conclusion in *Norfolk C.C.* v. *Secretary of State for the Environment* [1973] where it was decided that the decision of a planning committee to refuse an application was *the* decision, and the written notification, which incorrectly granted planning permission, could not be regarded as having any validity.

The *Norfolk* case was followed in *Co-operative Retail Services Ltd.* v. *Taff-Ely B.C.* [1979]. Here a resolution of the district planning authority favoured the grant of planning permission, but subject to a consultation procedure with the county planning authority as it involved a county matter: the Court of Appeal decided the resolution was not a grant of planning permission. The later issue by the Clerk, of the district planning authority, of a planning consent was held to be void and of no legal effect. In *R* v. *West Oxfordshire B.C. ex parte C.H. Pearce Homes Ltd.* [1986], Woolf J. fully reviewed the case law and decided that the decision of the planning committee could not by itself be the planning permission.

These cases suggest that the written planning consent cannot always be relied upon if there has been a mistake in its issue, a forged signature, or it is issued without authority. A purchaser paid £500,000 for certain land in the *Co-operative Retail Services*' case on the sight of the written planning consent that turned out to be of no legal effect. A justification for declaring the permission void in that case was given by Lord Denning M.R.: a wrong planning permission may result in damage to the public interest and this must prevail over any harm to the private interest of individuals who may be able to resort to private remedies.

Reference has already been made in chapter 7 to the importance of the planning application. The details it contains may be considered in construing the meaning of the planning permission where that permission expressly refers to the application and therefore incorporates it into the permission (see *Slough Estates Ltd.* v. *Slough B.C.* (no. 2) [1969] H.L.

There was no such express reference in *Kwik Save Discount Group Ltd.* v. *Secretary of State for Wales* [1981], where the Court of Appeal concluded that an application for planning permission, taken as a whole, was impliedly limited to the use of the subject premises for the sale of motorcars; the planning permission could not be construed as including a supermarket.

2.   The effect of planning permission

Unless a planning permission otherwise provides, any grant of planning permission lasts for the benefit of the land and of all persons with an interest in land (section 33 of the 1971 Act). Planning permission for mining operations is therefore not abandoned during a period when the operations are suspended: *Pioneer Aggregates* v. *Secretary of State* [1984]. But where planning permission has been granted for a material change of use, it is "spent" once the authorised change has taken place and cannot be used to revert to the same use on a second occasion: *Cynon Valley B.C.* v. *Secretary of State for Wales* [1986]. Where land has the benefit of more than one planning permission, can any permission, or any part of a permission, be utilised?

> *Lucas & Sons* v. *Dorking and Horley R.D.C.* [1964], planning permission was granted in 1952 to erect 28 houses on a plot of land. A further permission was granted in 1957 to erect 6 detached houses on the same plot. Lucas built two detached houses, under the 1957 permission, and 14 houses under the 1952 permission. Winn J. decided that, in the case where a planning permission covered a scheme of development, there could not be a breach of planning control by the completion of only some of the houses within the scheme, because of the obvious injustice to the purchasers of those houses were the law otherwise. Accordingly the 1952 permission was valid as to the 14 houses built, and so also was that of 1957.

The problem may arise rather differently where a subsequent planning permission is inconsistent with an earlier:

> *Pilkington* v. *Secretary State for the Environment* [1973] D.C. In 1953 permission was granted to erect a bungalow in the northern part of a plot of land, with the rest of the plot to

be used for a smallholding. In 1954 permission was granted
to build a bungalow in the middle of the plot, and a further
permission was granted to build another bungalow in the southern part of the plot. The two bungalows authorised by the
later two permissions were erected. It was held that the permission of 1953 could then no longer be implemented as intended,
as it was inconsistent with the later permissions which now
prevented the use of the plot as a smallholding.

Planning permission may authorise a number of separate buildings,
as in the *Lucas* case, or just one. And whilst not all the development
need be carried out in the circumstances that arose in the *Lucas*
case, is there a breach of the planning permission if part only of
one building is not completed, or not completed in accordance with
the permission? The following case deals with this point in the context of enforcement. But the same question could arise under section
44 of the 1971 Act where, following a completion notice, planning
permission may cease to have effect if the development authorised
by the planning permission is not completed. This section is dealt
with below.

Copeland B.C. v. *Secretary of State for the Environment* [1976]
D.C.
A house was built in accordance with a planning permission
with the exception that the roof tiles were different in colour
from those specified. It was held that there was a breach of
that planning permission, notwithstanding that most of what
it authorised was carried out, the part not so authorised or
carried out meant that the development was not as authorised.

Obvious difficulties still remain. What if a planning permission is
for development consisting of a house and detached garage, and
that garage is not built. Is the development that is carried out, in
this case only the house, development authorised by the planning
permission? In *Shepherd* v. *Secretary of State for the Environment*
[1975], Willis J. divided a complex planning permission which in
part related to a change of use that was not, in the end, carried
out. Certain conditions in the planning permission were not complied with, but by dividing the planning permission, the conditions
were found to relate to the change of use and therefore no breach
of these conditions occurred by carrying out the development that
did not involve the change of use. Conditions are not binding if
the permission to which they relate is not exercised: *Mounsdon*
v. *Weymouth and Melcombe Regis Corpn.*, [1960].

3.   Planning Permissions differs from application

Questions have arisen as to whether the local planning authority may grant permission for part of the development sought in the application. For example, if an application is for the erection of ten separate houses on ten separately identifiable plots, can the authority grant permission for only five of the houses? Sir Douglas Frank thought so in *Kent C.C.* v. *Secretary of State for the Environment* [1976] provided the application contained separate and divisible elements; it was then lawful to deal with each separately.

A different view was taken in *Bernard Wheatcroft Ltd.* v. *Secretary of State for the Environment* [1980] where permission had been sought for the residential development of some 35 acres. Forbes J. considered that it would be unlawful to grant planning permission for development which was substantially different from that sought in the application, as to do so would deprive those entitled to be consulted of their consultation rights. He thought that a test of substantial difference was to be preferred to the test of severability; but if the latter test was used, it should only be in connection with the test of substantial difference. The correct test, in his view, was whether the development to be permitted was substantially different from that in the application, and the difference in substance was to be determined in relation to the rights of those to be consulted. Forbes J. considered that a planning condition which had the effect of reducing the permitted development to 25 acres was therefore valid; residential development on 25 acres was not substantially different from residential development on 35 acres. This planning condition is considered further on page 102.

It is submitted that as many planning applications contain separate and divisible elements, the test of severability should be applied. But where the application is not severable, then the test of substantial difference would be appropriate.

4.   Planning permission for buildings

Where planning permission is granted for the erection of a building, then, if no purpose is specified, the permission will authorise the building to be used for the purpose for which it is designed (section 33 of the 1971 Act). A planning permission for the *use* of land will not, however, authorise the carrying out of building operations: *Sunbury-on-Thames U.D.C.* v. *Mann* [1958]; therefore planning permission for "warehousing" is not permission for building operations to erect warehouses: *Wivenhoe Port Ltd.* v. *Colchester B.C.*

98 Development and Planning Law

[1985]. Strictly planning permission is for a material *change* of use, not simply a *use*: see the *Cynon Valley* case (above).

5. Planning permission for existing buildings, works or use of land

Planning permission may be sought, and granted, for the retention on land of buildings or works, or the continuance of a use of land, where these matters exist at the time of the application and do so in breach of planning control (section 32 of the 1971 Act).

6. Planning permission and time limits

Every planning permission is to be granted subject to a condition, that development must be begun within 5 years of the grant. In the absence of an express condition, every planning permission is deemed granted subject to such a condition. The local planning authority may grant, in appropriate cases, planning permission subject to a longer or shorter time limit, having regard to the provisions of the development plan and to any other material considerations (section 41 of the 1971 Act).

Where outline planning permission is granted for building or other operations, it shall be granted subject to a condition that application for approval of the "reserved matters" must be made within three years from the outline planning permission. The development must begin within five years of the outline planning permission or two years from the final approval of the reserved matters, whichever in the later date (section 42).

A development is begun on the date when the following "specified operations" have been carried out: any work of construction of a building; digging of foundation trench; laying of mains or pipes; laying or constructing a road or part of one; and certain specified changes of use (section 43 of the 1971 Act). The laying of pipes and a road constitute "specified operations" even if the pipes are not quite in accordance with the plans: *Spackman* v. *Secretary of State for the Environment* [1977]; and in *Malvern Hills D.C.* v. *Secretary of State for the Environment* [1982], the pegging out of an estate road amounted to a specified operation within section 43(2)(b).

If the development authorised by a planning permission is begun before the expiry of the time limit, but the time limit has expired before the development has been completed, the local planning authority may serve a completion notice requiring the development to be completed within a stated period of not less than 12 months.

Failure to comply with the notice means that the planning permission ceases to be valid. There are certain rights of appeal (section 44 of the 1971 Act).

7. Planning permission unnecessarily obtained

Interesting questions arise if planning permission is unnecessarily obtained in the belief that a proposed activity is development; this situation is most likely to involve a change of use. Are the previous existing use rights thereby lost, and is one bound by conditions attached to the planning permission? In *Newbury D.C.* v. *Secretary of State for the Environment* [1980] H.L. where, as it turned out, planning permission was not necessary to use some former hangars as warehouses, it was decided that the owners could rely on their previous existing use rights and ignore any planning conditions (although for the validity of these, see page 102).

8. Outline planning permission

For applications for outline planning permission, and for the approval of reserved matters, see chapter 7; for tine limits, see section 6 above on Duration of planning permission.

9.3 Planning conditions

1. The statutory power to impose conditions

A local planning authority "... may grant planning permission ... subject to such conditions as they think fit" (section 29(1)(a) of the 1971 Act).

Apart from this apparently wide power, a local planning authority may impose conditions:

> "... for regulating the development or use of any land under the control of the applicant (whether or not it is land in respect of which the application was made) or requiring the carrying out of works on any such land, so far as appears to the local planning authority to be expedient for the purposes of or in connection with the development authorised by the permission ..." (section 30(1)(a) of the 1971 Act).

Section 30(1)(a) can only be used if the land made subject to the conditions is under the "control" of the applicant. Such conditions may affect land not the subject of the planning application. "Control" does not necessarily mean ownership, and what amounts to control is a question of fact and degree: *George Wimpey & Co Ltd.* v. *New Forest D.C.* [1979].

There is a further power:

> "... for requiring the removal of any buildings or works authorised by the permission, or the discontinuance of any use of land so authorised, at the end of a specified period, and the carrying out of any works required for the reinstatement of land at the end of that period ..." (section 30(1)(b) of the 1971 Act).

The conditions referred to in section 30(1)(b) above would apply to a temporary or limited period permission.

Where planning conditions are imposed in a planning permission, the conditions only become effective if the permission is implemented: *Kerrier D.C.* v. *Secretary for the Environment* [1980].

To the extent that the conditions are otherwise valid, they will bind successors in title to the affected land. The existence of planning conditions will normally be discovered as those imposed after July 1977 in express planning permissions are registrable as local land charges. A failure to register does not render the conditions unenforceable. In *Atkinson* v. *Secretary of State for the Environment* [1983], where land was sold between the application for, and the grant of planning permission, a condition affecting the land sold was triggered by the implementation of the permission on the vendor's retained land. The purchaser was bound by the condition.

2.   The limit on the statutory power

At an early stage of the history of planning law the courts, in considering the legality of conditions, established a set of useful criteria:

> *Pyx Granite Co.* v. *Ministry of Housing and Local Government* [1958] CA
> Conditions governing the crushing and screening of granite were imposed in a permission to quarry granite. If complied with the conditions would have retricted a previous lawful use of certain plant. Lord Denning M.R. said that despite the wide power to impose conditions "... to be valid [they] must fairly and reasonably relate to the permitted development ... [and] the planning authority are not at liberty to use their powers for an ulterior object, however desirable that object may seem to them to be in the public interest". The conditions were held to satisfy these requirements.

Fawcett Properties Ltd. v. *Buckingham C.C.* [1961] HL
In a planning permission for a cottage in the green belt, a condition was imposed restricting its occupation to persons employed or last employed in agriculture. Lord Denning (again) added two further criteria, to that contained in *Pyx*: the condition must not be so uncertain as to have no sensible or ascertainable meaning (ambiguity is not uncertainty); and an authority entrusted with a discretion must not impose a condition that is so unreasonable no reasonable council could have imposed it. In this case the condition was also upheld as it satisfied the objects of the green belt policy.

Hall & Co v. *Shoreham-by-Sea U.D.C.* [1964] CA
A planning condition required the developer to construct an ancillary access road and provide rights of access over it to other persons. The Court of Appeal decided the condition was void for two reasons: it required the developer to provide extensive rights of access to other persons over his own private land, and there was an alternative procedure under the Highways Acts for the acquisition at public expense and on the payment of compensation. Wilmer L.J. referred to *Colonial Sugar Refining Co Ltd.* v. *Melborne Harbour Trust Commissioners* [1927] where Lord Warrington said: "a statute should not be held to take away private rights of property without compensation unless the intention to do so is expressed in clear and unambiguous terms".

The whole question of legal validity was reconsidered by the House of Lords in *Newbury D.C.* v. *Secretary of State for the Environment* [1980], which approved three broad principles: a condition must not be totally unreasonable that no reasonable authority would impose them; it must relate to the permitted development; it must serve a planning purpose and not some other ulterior motive; and it must not be uncertain as to meaning. Over the years the cases have collected other problems which are considered below. Circular 1/85—the use of conditions in planning permissions, sets out guidance for imposing planning conditions. The guidance is concerned not only with the legality of conditions, but their necessity, precision and relevance in planning terms.

3. Unreasonableness

This criterion is really about the application of the *Wednesbury* principles (see chapter 19), and restrains an authority from abusing a power granted by Parliament. The question is whether there has been a perverse use of the power to impose conditions. It is arguable that the criteria that follow this are but more specific applications of the "unreasonableness" criterion. A condition requiring an applicant to provide land, construct a road upon it and grant rights of passage over it was held to be totally unreasonable in *Hall & Co. Ltd.* v. *Shoreham-by-Sea U.D.C.* [1964] CA, on the basis that the local authority would obtain the benefit of a public road without having to pay for it. They had alternative powers under the highways Acts to achieve a similar object, but at their cost.

In *R.* v. *Hillingdon L.B.C. ex parte Royco Homes Ltd.* [1974] DC, two conditions imposed in a planning permission for residential development required the completed dwellings to be first occupied by persons on the authority's housing waiting list, and that they should have security of tenure. These were held to be invalid as they went beyond anything Parliament could have intended, or a reasonable authority could have imposed, as they required the developer to discharge at his expense the duties of the local housing authority.

A condition that reduces the permitted development below the development applied for is not totally unreasonable provided the permitted development is not substantially different from that in the application so as to deprive those entitled to be consulted of that opportunity: *Bernard Wheatcroft Ltd.* v. *Secretary of State for the Environment* [1980] (where the condition reduced the area for residential development from 35 acres to 25 acres—see also page 97).

4. Relate to the permitted development

A simple example may illustrate this criterion. If an applicant submits a planning application to redevelop his petrol filling station in Queenstown, the authority cannot impose a condition that affects another of his filling stations in Kingstown. The cases involve more difficult questions than this in practice.

In *Penwith D.C.* v. *Secretary of State for the Environment* [1977] planning permission had been granted for a factory extension subject to conditions that restricted the use of, and emission of noise from, the old factory as well as the extension. The extension was the permitted development; but the conditions also affected the old factory. They were held to be lawful as the new extension enabled the old factory to be more intensively used, and without the conditions the extension would not have been permitted.

The House of Lords had the opportunity of considering this problem in *Newbury D.C.* v. *Secretary of State for the Environment*

[1980]. A rubber company had acquired an interest in some existing hangars, and applied for planning permission to use them for warehouses. This was granted subject to their removal at the end of a specified period. It was held that as the permitted development was a permission for a change of use, a condition requiring the removal of the hangars was invalid as removal of the hangars had nothing to do with the use of them as warehouses. (This case involved other issues, see chapter 3.)

One way of deciding whether a condition relates to the permitted development is to consider whether the condition helps to eliminate the detrimental consequences of the proposed development: *Gill* v. *Secretary of State for the Environment* [1985].

5. Serve a planning purpose

The condition in the *Fawcett* case (see above) served a valid planning purpose as it furthered the maintenance of green belt policies. It was accepted that the condition requiring the removal of the hangars in the *Newbury* case (see above) served a valid planning purpose— the improvement of the amenity of the area. But the conditions in the *Royco* case (see page 102), although void for unreasonableness, could be said to have served a housing purpose rather than a planning purpose. This criterion may therefore often overlap with that concerning unreasonableness, as a condition imposed for some ulterior motive may be struck down as unreasonable. An ulterior motive may involve a non-planning object. The courts are more familiar with considering the question of unreasonableness, rather than deciding what is a planning purpose.

Some guidance as to what is a planning purpose may, it is submitted, be found in the matters which should be the subject of policy and proposal statements in development plans (see chapter 6).

6. Certainty as to meaning

Lord Denning M.R., in the *Fawcett* case (see page 101) said that a planning condition is only void for uncertainty if it can be given no meaning or no sensible or ascertainable meaning: ambiguity or a meaning that may lead to absurd results can be construed by the courts. A condition in *Britannia Ltd.* v. *Secretary of State for the Environment* [1978] required the provision of a small village type social/shopping centre, and this condition the Secretary of State decided was void for uncertainty as the words were incapable of definition and therefore impossible to give effect to. Although the judge thought this condition could be given a meaning, he, unfortunately, did not actually decide whether it was valid or not because he quashed the Secretary of State's decision on another matter.

A condition reserving for future approval the density of the proposed development in an outline planning permission, is not within the definition of reserved matters. Such a condition is not regarded as uncertain: *Inverclyde D.C.* v. *Inverkip Building Co. Ltd.* [1983].

7.   Taking away existing rights

The *Hall* case (see above) was decided on the basis that the condition requiring the provision of land and its dedication as a public road did involve taking away property without compensation, and was therefore invalid as being totally unreasonable. This was applied in *City of Bradford* v. *Secretary of State for the Environment* [1986] where road improvement was required on land outside the applicant's control. However, the trend of recent cases is to allow conditions that interfere with or take away existing proprietary rights provided the conditions are otherwise valid; the argument is that the applicant only loses his existing rights if he makes use of the planning permission.

A condition in *City of London Corpn.* v. *Secretary of State for the Environment* [1972] restricted the use of office premises to those of an employment agency. This prevented a change to any other office use within the same class of the Use Classes Order, a change which would not have been development (see section 22(2) of the 1971 Act). The condition was upheld as valid.

In *Kingston-upon-Thames L.B.C.* v. *Secretary of State for the Environment* [1974], the effect of a condition imposed with a planning permission to redevelop a railway station, required certain other land of British Rail to be made available for car parking. This would have interfered with their existing lawful use of that other land without payment of compensation. Relying on the earlier case of *Prossor* v. *Minister of Housing and Local Government* [1968], the court upheld the validity of the condition. In any event, the provisions of section 30(1)(a) of the 1971 Act (see page 99) seemed to confirm this use of a condition.

A planning condition may restrict development that would otherwise be permitted by a development order (see *Gill* v. *Secretary of State for the Environment* [1985]). As the condition is only triggered by the implementation of the express planning permission, it will be in the applicant's interest to initiate the permitted development first.

8. Conditions dependent on matters outside control of applicant

Conditions imposed under section 30(1)(a), for regulating the development or use of land, whether the subject of the planning application or not, but necessary for the permitted development, can only be imposed in respect of land under the control of the applicant (see above page 99). There may be cases where a condition under section 29 is imposed which anticipates the applicant fulfilling an undertaking or acquiring land or other rights not in his control at the time of the application.

In *Augier* v. *Secretary of State for the Environment* [1978], the applicant gave an undertaking that he would secure rights over land not in his ownership to secure visibility splays to an access road. On the strength of that undertaking, planning permission was granted subject to a condition that the undertaking would be fufilled. It was held that the condition was valid and binding as the applicant could not later be heard to suggest that the undertaking could not be complied with, having encouraged the grant of permission on the strength of it. But in *City of Bradford* v. *Secretary of State for the Environment* [1986], a condition requiring road improvements on land not in the applicant's ownership or control was held to be manifestly unreasonable and ultra vires.

The problems associated with undertakings are better secured by a planning agreement considered in the next section of this chapter.

9. Negative conditions

It can be seen so far that a condition requiring the applicant to provide land for a highway at his expense, or to do something on land not in his control, may be struck down as unreasonable and ultra vires. In *Grampian R.C.* v. *City of Aberdeen* [1984] Lord Keith in the House of Lords said that there are many uncertainties in the development process, and a condition worded to prevent the commencement of development until matters (including those not within the applicant's control) necessary for the development were achieved would be valid. In the *City of Bradford* case it was also suggested that the road improvements could also have been validly provided for by a suitably worded negative condition.

10.   The effect of an unlawful condition

If a condition is unlawful, what is the effect on the permission to which it is attached?

In *Kent C.C.* v. *Kingsway Investments* [1970], the House of Lords suggested that if a condition was fundamental to the permission, both should be quashed if the condition was held to be invalid. That was the case in the *Pyx Granite, Shoreham* and the *Royco* cases (see above). There is therefore a danger to the applicant who successfully challenges a condition that he will lose the whole planning permission.

Although there is dicta in the *Kingsway* case suggesting circumstances where a void condition may alone be severed, because it is not fundamental to the development permitted, there is little reliable case authority to support this. In *Allnatt London Properties* v. *Middlesex C.C.* [1964] a condition was found void because it affected existing use rights, and the planning permission remained severed of the condition; but that case has been doubted following the *Kingston* case (see above). *Hartnell* v. *Minister of Housing and Local Government* [1965], which involved the same sorts of issues, turned on the unfortunate consequences of certain transitional legislation. The advice to an applicant must be that a successful challenge of a condition in the courts may leave you without the planning permission.

11.   The circumstances in which conditions may be imposed

So far we have been considering the legal validity of some doubtful conditions. In practice, a great many conditions are imposed, and their legal validity is never in question. They are imposed in cases where the application would otherwise be refused, and the details of the application do not, or cannot, make reference to the matters which are the subject of the conditions. For example, in a planning permission to redevelop a petrol filling station, conditions may be attached which limit the total lumens of light onto the forecourt, or which restrict the range of products sold at the cash point to motor accessories such as tyres, batteries and lightbulbs. Such matters would not otherwise be the subject of planning controls.

A condition may also be imposed to reinforce some matter of particular importance to the planning authority which may anyway be in the application. The fact that it is highlighted in this way may further the possibility that it will be secured: a breach of a condition is clearly a breach of planning control.

A useful memorandum on the use of planning conditions is found in Circular 1/85.

9.4   Challenging planning conditions

There are various ways of challenging planning conditions. They may be invalid in law, for the reasons considered in the preceeding section of this chapter, or they may be unnecessary or irrelevant on planning grounds.

A planning condition may be challenged by appeal to the Secretary of State for the Environment where the applicant is aggrieved by the decision to impose conditions (section 36 of the 1971 Act). The planning merits of the conditions can then be considered by the Inspector appointed by the Secretary of State (this is more fully considered in chapter 16). A further appeal from the decision of the Secretary of State, or his inspector, may be taken to the High Court, but only to question the legal validity of a planning decision. Because the Secretary of State, in determining this type of appeal, may reconsider the whole of the original planning permission, it is often preferable to submit a planning application to the local planning authority seeking the removal or modification of the conditions. If this is refused, and an appeal is taken to the Secretary of State, the original planning permission cannot be affected by his determination.

An alternative procedure is available if the applicant believes the planning condition is legally invalid: he may apply direct to the court for a declaration to that effect (*Pyx Granite Co.* v. *Ministry of Housing and Local Government* [1958]); or for order of certiorari to quash the decision of the authority (*R.* v. *Hillingdon L.B.C. ex parte Royco Homes Ltd.* [1974]). (See further on this in chapter 19.)

A further possibility is to proceed with the development without complying with the condition, and then in any appeal to the Secretary of State against an enforcement notice that may be served in respect of the noncompliance, the legal and planning merits can be raised. This procedure has some obvious difficulties, but there is an advantage in that if the conditions are found unnecessary or unlawful, the development will usually be permitted to remain, whereas a successful challenge of a condition at an earlier stage in the courts may leave you with no planning permission.

9.5 Planning agreements

1. The statutory basis

Agreements between local authorities and developers and land-owners are common. They are used for a number of purposes. There is a general power for local authorities to make or receive payments or enter into agreements "calculated to facilitate, or is conducive or incidental to, the discharge of their functions": section 111, Local Government Act 1972. There is a specific power in section 38 of the Highways Act 1980 for a developer to make an agreement for the provision and adoption of a road as a public highway; and power in section 278 of the same Act for a highway authority to agree with a developer to carry out road works in return for a contribution by the developer towards the costs. There is also power in section 18 of the Public Health Act 1936 for agreement to the adoption of new sewers as public sewers.

In relation to planning agreements, especially those containing continuing obligations on the part of the landowner, it is necessary that such agreements are enforceable against successors in title to the affected land.

Section 52(1) of the Town and Country Planning Act 1971 provides that:

> "A local planning authority may enter into an agreement with any person interested in land in their area for the purpose of restricting or regulating the development or use of the land, either permanently or during such period as may be prescribed by the agreement; and any such agreement may contain such incidental and consequential provisions (including provisions of a financial character) as appear to the local planning authority to be necessary or expedient for the purposes of the agreement."

This provision contains the necessary enabling powers for local planning authorities to enter into agreements with landowners for the purpose of restricting or regulating the development or use of land. To ensure that such agreements are enforceable against subsequent owners of the subject land, further provision is made to ensure that they are enforceable as if they were restrictive covenants (section 52(2)).

As positive covenants, that is undertakings that are more onerous than those required for the purpose of "restricting or regulating the development or use of land" are not enforceable against successors in title, an additional power was enacted. Section 33 of the

Local Government (Miscellaneous Provisions) Act 1982 provides that positive covenants in planning agreements can be enforced against successors in title, not only where they relate to the carrying out of works, or are to facilitate the development of land, but also if they are concerned with regulating the *use* of land.

2.   Agreements cannot fetter statutory powers

There is a general principle that a body with statutory powers cannot by contract agree not to use its statutory powers (*Ayr Harbour Trustees* v. *Oswald* [1883]). It is also wrong for a local planning authority to decide a planning application in order to fulfill an agreement. In *Stringer* v. *Minister of Housing and Local Government* [1971], the planning authority had an agreement with the owners of Jodrell Bank radio telescope to restrict development that might interfere with its operations; the court decided that proper consideration must be given to every planning application, and a decision could not be given merely to fulfil such an agreement.

A planning agreement may contain terms that the local planning authority will not exercise one or more of its powers under the 1971 Act (i.e. not take enforcement action, or not refuse permission for a certain application). These terms would ordinarily be ultra vires as an authority cannot contract not to exercise a statutory power: *Ransom and Luck Ltd.* v. *Surbiton B.C.* [1949]. Section 52(3) provides that an agreement cannot restrict the use of powers exercised in accordance with the provisions of the development plan. This, and the principle that an agreement cannot fetter the exercise of statutory powers was considered in *Windsor and Maidenhead Royal Borough* v. *Brandrose Investments Ltd.* [1983]. The planning authority made an agreement allowing the redevelopment of certain buildings. They later extended a conservation area and sought to exercise their statutory powers to prevent the demolition of the buildings, the exercise of those powers being contrary to the agreement. It was decided that the authority was free to use its powers to extend the conservation area, and the exercise of that power could not be fettered by the agreement.

Apart from the enabling power in the 1971 Act, there are numerous local Acts, usually of county councils, that contain analagous powers. Many planning agreements are made under these.

3.   The scope of planning agreements

Local planning authorities may insist on planning agreements in many circumstances; and developers, rather than be put to unnecessary delays that may otherwise result, will sign agreements if this advances the grant of an acceptable planning permission. However, they should be advised to resist signing an agreement in the following cases: there would otherwise be no objection to the grant of a planning permission; planning permission is granted subject to a condition that a planning agreement is signed; the agreement requires the payment of money as a contribution to infrastructure costs, and the planning authority have no other objection to the development; or, planning permission will only be granted if a planning agreement is signed, and this contains terms which if they were conditions, would be void. There is a suggestion in *City of Bradford M.B.C.* v. *Secretary of State for the Environment C.A.* [1986] that, a provision in a planning agreement made under section 52, requiring a developer to bear the whole risk and expense of widening a public highway, could be an unreasonable use of powers, and beyond the powers of the authority. That opinion was *obiter dictum*.

The planning agreements commonly used in practice have been reviewed and categorised by Dr. Hawke (1981 J.P.L. 5); they are as follows: restrictions on occupancy of land; restrictions on land uses that may be difficult to control by enforcement controls; prevention of development already authorised by planning permission (thus avoiding payment of compensation); regulation of complex development; agreements in regard to the provision of sewerage or other services; control of the pollution effects of new and existing development; an alternative to regulate existing breaches of development control in place of enforcement notices; and the acquisition to the benefit of the local planning authority of land, facilities or financial contributions for controls over planning gain; see section 7 below.

4.   Enforcement of Planning Agreements

The advantage to the local planning authority of a planning agreement over the normal means of development control is that the remedies for breach are contractual and lie in the field of private law, rather than the statutory procedures of the planning Acts which are subject to appeals and the requirements of administrative fairness.

Where the original party, to the agreement has sold the land, enforcement against successors in title is achieved under the statutory powers as if the covenants were restrictive covenants.

In *Avon C.C.* v. *Millard* [1985] the Court of Appeal decided that where a breach of a planning agreement also involved a breach of planning control, the local planning authority was entitled to restrain the breach of the agreement by the remedy of injunction; the authority was not obliged to first exhaust the planning remedy of an enforcement notice.

5. The discharge or modification of covenants in a planning agreement

Reference has already been made to the fact that an agreement is enforceable against successors in title to the land as if it was a restrictive covenant. Restrictive covenants may be discharged or modified by the Lands Tribunal under section 84(1) of the Law of Property Act 1925 if it is satisfied the covenants are obsolete; they restrict the reasonable use of the land, or impede such use as to deny either practical benefits of substantial value or advantage, or are contrary to the public interest, and money will compensate any loss by reason of the discharge or modification; the beneficiary of the restriction agrees; or, no beneficiary will be injured.

The Lands Tribunal allowed a modification of a covenant in a planning agreement in *Beecham Group Ltd.'s Application* [1980]. Although planning permission had been granted following an appeal to the Secretary of State, Beecham's could not develop in breach of the planning agreement. The Lands Tribunal considered the decision of the Secretary of State highly relevant in deciding that the covenant could be modified. The fact that the local planning authority would suffer no injury by the modification because they owned no land capable of being benefited by the restriction, and that no objection to the development had been put forward by the authority on aesthetic grounds, seemed important to the Tribunal. It is curious that a private law approach is applied to an important matter of public law, in this case planning. But the Tribunal has allowed the modification of an agreement in *Re Cox's Application* [1985], to permit the sale of an old farm house.

In *Abbey Homesteads (Developments) Ltd. v. Northampton C.C.* [1986] the Court of Appeal decided tht the Tribunal was wrong in considering that a restriction reserving land for school purposes could be modified once the land was acquired by the educational authority. Because of surrounding development, that land had to be reserved for a school on a permanent basis, and it would be wrong to regard the restriction as no longer necessary.

4. Planning agreements and public planning

Although planning agreements are not necessarily private documents, they are often negotiated behind closed doors, and the usual influences on the making of planning decisions are not present. This is because there is no opportunity for the scope of an intended agreement to be considered by the public, and they cannot make representations or objections as is the case with many other types of planning decisions made under the Planning Acts. Because of this aspect of agreements, the High Court may be prepared to consider the validity of any planning decision that arises as a result of an agreement, and not as a result of an open, impartial consideration by the local planning authority. An authority that agreed to use its best endeavours to secure a particular planning permission, and to pay damages to a developer if it failed to obtain the permission by a stated date, has a biased interest in granting the planning permission. A local society successfully obtained a declaration that a planning decision of this nature was void, in *Steeples* v. *Derbyshire C.C.* [1981], on the grounds of a breach of the rules of natural justice (see Chapter 19). However the mere presence of a financial interest will not itself constitute bias. The test today is whether the authority has taken into account the proper considerations, and ignored the improper: *R.* v. *Sevenoaks D.C. ex parte Terry* [1984].

5.   Planning gain

Planning agreements are not synonomous with what is usually called planning gain, but they are frequently used to achieve planning gain. This is defined as some expenditure, surrender, concession or benefit which the developer agrees or is obliged to provide and which cannot be embodied in a valid planning condition: see Property Advisory Group—"Planning Gain" (1981).

Circular 22/83—Planning Gain defines planning gain where a developer is obliged to carry out works not included in the development for which he seeks planning permission, or where he confers some extraneous right or benefit in return for being permitted to develop. The Circular advises that an obligation should not be imposed where it is otherwise reasonable to grant the requested planning permission. An applicant's need for planning permission is not an opportunity to obtain some extraneous benefit or advantage. The tests of reasonableness are posed in the circular, and relate to the need for facilities to enable the development to proceed; and are required to relate directly to the proposed development.

In *Richmond-upon-Thames L.B.C.* v. *Secretary of State for the Environment* [1983] it was decided that an inspector would be wrong to give preference to the PAG Report, which was critical of planning gain, over a clear policy requiring the provision of planning gain in the development plan. Although it was equally wrong in *Westminster Renslade Ltd.* v. *Secretary of State for the Environment* [1983] for a planning authority to refuse planning permission for development that was otherwise acceptable merely because planning gain was not being offered by the developer.

PART III

SPECIAL CONTROLS

Chapter 10

Listed Buildings, Conservation Areas and other Special Areas

Introduction   117
Control over Listed Buildings   117
Conservation areas   123
Ancient Monuments and Archaeological areas   125
Protection of the countryside   126

10.1 Introduction

There is a special control, additional to the development controls dealt with in the earlier part of this book, that applies to buildings of special architectural or historic interest. This special control has a more detailed relevance to the problem of the preservation of such buildings. This chapter also deals with the related policy concerning conservation areas: the object here is the preservation and enhancement of areas of special architectural or historic interest. A number of special areas that give further protection to the countryside, and the protection to ancient monuments and archaeological areas, are more briefly described.

Useful additional guidance on Historic Buildings and Conservation Areas is contained in Circular 8/87.

The Historic Buildings and Monuments Commission was established by the National Heritage Act 1983. Known simply as "English Heritage", it has an advisory role, but is also concerned more generally with the preservation of, and the promotion of interest in, ancient monuments and historic buildings. The commission has more specific powers of control in relation to buildings in London.

10.2 Control over Listed Buildings

1. Listing

Apart from buildings temporarily protected by a building preservation notice, and discussed below, a building must be listed by the Secretary of State for the Environment to enjoy the controls considered in this chapter. In deciding to list a building, consideration

117

is given not only to the building itself, but the contribution its exterior makes to a group of buildings; and the desirability of preserving any feature of the building consisting of a man-made object or structure fixed to the building or on the land within the curtilage of the building. The important criterion being that the building is of special architectural or historic interest (section 54 of the 1971 Act).

If a building is listed, notice is served on every owner and occupier, and a copy of the list is registered as a local land charge. The local planning authorities are informed, and copies of the list are available for public inspection (section 54(4)–(8)). There is no appeal against listing at this stage.

The consequences of lising can be seen in *Amalgamated Investment and Property Co. Ltd.* v. *John Walker and Sons Ltd.* [1976]. The purchaser of a warehouse had contracted to pay its value of £1,700,000. The building was listed after the exchange of contracts, and before completion. The effect of listing was to reduce its value to £200,000; the purchaser was obliged to complete the purchase at the original contract price.

2.   Meaning of a building

A listed building includes "any object or structure fixed to a building, or forming part of the land and comprised within the curtilage of a building, shall be treated as part of the building" (section 54(9)). In *Att.-Gen.* v. *Calderdale B.C.* [1983], a terrace of cottages connected by a bridge to a mill, were regarded as listed as the mill was a listed building. The House of Lords in *Debenhams plc.* v. *Westminster City Council* [1987] decided that the reference in the Act to a "structure" meant something ancillary to the principal building, and would not include an independent building even if connected by a bridge or tunnel.

3.   Certificate of immunity from listing

If planning permission has been granted for any development consisting of the alteration, extension or demolition of a building, any person may apply to the Secretary of State for a certificate that the building will not be listed for five years (section 54A(1)). The effect of this is to prevent the Secretary of State from listing the building, or the local planning authority from serving a building preservation notice, for the five years. There must be some doubt about the usefulness of this provision, as the Secretary of State is unlikely to issue his certificate if he believes the building may have the special interest, and in cases where it clearly has no such interest, no-one will bother to apply in the first place. There is an intention to charge for a certificate of immunity.

4. Building Preservation Notice

It may appear to a district planning authority that an unlisted building is of special architectural or historic interest, and is in danger of demolition or of alteration in such a way as to affect that interest. The district planning authority may then sever a building preservation notice on the owner and occupier. The effect of such a notice is to give to the building the legal protection it would enjoy were it listed and to inform the parties concerned that the Secretary of State will be asked to list (section 58 of the 1971 Act). If the Secretary of State does so list the building, it will then, of course, enjoy permanent legal protection. If he chooses not to list, the building preservation notice will cease to have effect. It only lasts for six months in any event. An owner, whose building has been the subject of a building preservation notice, but which is not ultimately listed, is entitled to compensation for any loss or damage directly attributable to the effect of the notice. This would include sums paid to contractors for any breach of contract caused by the cancelling of work (section 173 of the 1971 Act).

5. Need for Listed Building Consent

It is a criminal offence to demolish a listed building or to carry out any works of alteration or extension which would affect its character as a building of special interest without listed building consent (section 55). The erection of a fence under the general development order is not "demolition, alteration or extension" requiring listed building consent: *Cotswold D.C.* v. *Secretary of State for the Environment* [1985]. Whether any work will affect the character of a building of special interest is a question of fact and degree for the local planning authority: in one case the painting of a door in yellow was regarded by the Secretary of State as such work (although by the time the appeal was heard the painted door was acceptable because the yellow paint had meanwhile faded!).

Application for listed building consent is made to the local planning authority. Additionally, in the case of the demolition of a listed building, one month's notice has to be served on the Historic Buildings and Monuments Commission, and an opportunity given to them to record the building; they may state that either they have recorded the building or they do not wish to do so. Where work has been carried out without listed building consent, then, although that remains a criminal offence, provision is made for written consent to be granted to retain the works of demolition, alteration or extension, as the case may be: the works will then be authorised from the date of the grant of that consent (section 55(2)).

If listed building consent is granted subject to conditions, it is similarly a criminal offence not to comply with these conditions (section 55(4)).

In determining the fine, the court shall have regard to any financial benefit which arises from the unauthorised work (section 55(5)). It is a defence to a prosecution that the work was urgently necessary in the interests of safety or health, or for the preservation of the building, and that a notice was given to the local planning authority (section 55(6)). But this defence is limited to where it can be shown that temporary support or shelter was not reasonably practicable; the minimum measures necessary were taken; and, the notice contains reasons justifying the works undertaken.

The criminal offence is one of strict liability. This means that a magistrates court would be wrong in dismissing a charge against a building contractor for doing work on a building without listed building consent merely because the builder was ignorant of the listed building status: *R. v. Wells Street Metropolitan Stipendiary Magistrate, ex parte Westminster City Council* [1986].

6. Application for Listed Building Consent and Planning Permission

If the proposed works affect the special interest of a listed building, and also constitute development, both listed building consent and planning permission are required after 13 November 1980 (Local Government, Planning and Land Act 1980, schedule 15, para. 7). Clearly certain work to the interior of a building, or which does not materially affect its external appearance, or a demolition, whilst requiring listed building consent, may not need planning permission.

If planning permission is required, it may be applied for either before or at the same time as the application for listed building consent. A fee is payable for a planning application, none is payable for a listed building consent application.

Application may now be made for outline listed building consent, subject to the approval of reserved specific details (section 56). Application for a listed building consent is made in the first place to the district planning authority. (Town and Country Planning (Listed Buildings and Buildings in Conservation Areas) Regulations 1987; regulation 3.) The application must be accompanied by a certificate of ownership or a certificate that the applicant has notified the owner along the lines of the certificate that must accompany a planning application (regulation 6).

The district planning authority must then advertise the application in a local newspaper and by way of a site notice stating where the proposals may be inspected, and inviting representations. Any representations received must be taken into account. Advertisement is not necessary if the application relates only to interior work to Grade II—listed buildings (regulation 5). All applications for grade I and grade II starred buildings must be notified to the Historic Buildings and Monuments Commission.

The Secretary of State may give a direction to call-in an application (or such applications as he specifies) for his decision (Schedule 11 to the 1971 Act). The Secretary of State must be notified of any application which the local planning authority propose to grant— thus enabling him to call-in if he chooses (Schedule 11, para. 5). Additionally any application to demolish a listed building must be notified to a number of specified and interested bodies and societies (Circular 8/87). It was decided in *R. v. North Hertfordshire D.C. ex parte Sullivan* [1981], that, in this connection, if works of extension to a listed building involved some demolition of part of the building, the application had to be notified to the appropriate bodies and societies: the 1971 Act defining a building as including a part of a building. The decision of the local planning authority to grant listed building consent was quashed (of interest, is that the application for judicial review was brought by a disatisfied neighbour).

There is an appeal to the Secretary of State against a decision of the local planning authority to refuse consent, or to grant consent subject to conditions. The applicant may, as one of his grounds of appeal, claim that the building should not be listed (para. 8 Schedule 11 to the 1971 Act).

Further provisions regarding applications and appeals are found in Schedule 11 to the 1971 Act, and in the Town and Country Planning (Listed Buildings and Buildings in Conservation Areas) Regulations 1987.

In deciding whether to grant listed building consent, the local planning authority, or the Secretary of State, are required to have special regard to the desirability of preserving a listed building (section 56(3)).

7.   Conditions and time limits

Listed building consent may be granted subject to conditions, and in particular, conditions with respect to the preservation of particu-

lar features of the building; the making good of damage caused
to the building by the works so authorised; and the reconstruction
of the building, or any part, with the use of original materials where
practicable (section 56(4)).

Listed building consent for the demolition of a listed building
may be granted subject to a condition that the building shall not
be demolished before a contract for the carrying out of works of
redevelopment of the site has been made, and planning permission
for the redevelopment granted (section 56(5)). It is not clear with
whom a contract is to be made nor, indeed, precisely what would
suffice as such a contract: would a contract with one's secretary
satisfy the condition? The purpose of such a condition is to prevent
premature demolition.

Listed building consents are now subject to a condition that the
authorised works must be commenced within five years (section
56A).

Provision is now made for an application to vary or modify any
condition attached to a listed building consent (section 56B).

8.   Exempted buildings

Listed building consent is not required, and a building preservation
notice cannot be served, in respect of certain buildings. These
exempted buildings are ecclesiastical buildings used for ecclesiastical
purposes, and ancient monuments (section 56(1) and 58(2)). In *A–G*
v. *Howard United Reformed Church* [1975], the House of Lords
decided that if a church was to be demolished, it would not then
be used for ecclesiastical purposes, and that therefore, if listed, listed
building consent would be needed for the demolition. This would
not apply to a church to be demolished under the Redundant
Churches and other Religious Buildings Act 1969.

The Housing and Planning Act 1986 contains new powers for
the Secretary of State to make regulations to limit the exemptions
enjoyed by ecclesiastical buildings.

9.   Enforcement

There are certain enforcement provisions available to local planning
authorities that apply to listed buildings. These are fully described
in chapter 14. They include powers to require repairs to be carried
out. If an owner of a listed building is refused listed building consent,
he may be entitled to some compensation, or to serve a purchase
notice compelling the authority to acquire his interest. (See further
chapters 17 and 18.)

10.3 Conservation areas

1. Duty to designate conservation areas

Every local planning authority shall determine which parts of their area are of special architectural or historic interest. These are areas, the character or appearance of which it is desirable to preserve or enhance. The areas identified are then designated as conservation areas (section 277(1) of the 1971 Act).

Conservation areas are selected for their comprehensive interest, and may include a whole town or part of one, a village, or perhaps only a street or square. The area may contain listed buildings: very often many of the buildings will not, individually, be worthy of attention, but as a group, they provide the necessary interest.

Designation has certain consequences (see below), and therefore the fact of designation has to be notified to the Secretary of State, advertised, and registered as a local land charge (section 277(6)–(9)).

The local planning authorities publish their proposals for preservation and enhancement; these are considered at a public meeting (section 277B). A local planning authority may therefore have a particular policy with regard, not only to development in a conservation area, but also to positive steps to enhance the attractiveness of the area such as traffic management and restrictions, parking restrictions, and removal of unsightly advertisements and street furniture. See Circular 8/87—Historic Buildings and Conservation Areas—for further guidance.

2. Legal consequences of conservation area designation

There are a number of legal consequences that may or will affect development in or near a conservation area.

(a) Any planning application for development that in the opinion of the local planning authority may affect the character or appearance of a conservation area, must be advertised by the authority in a local newspaper and by way of site notice. The authority must then take into account any representation received, and may not determine the application within 21 days of the advertisements (section 28 of the 1971 Act). See *R. v. Lambeth L.B.C. ex parte Sharpe* [1986], where an application made by an officer of a local authority was not given the proper consideration as required.

(b) The demolition of buildings, with some exceptions, in conservation areas needs conservation area consent of the local

planning authority (section 277A). Conservation area consent follows listed building consent in some respects (see
Town and Country Planning (Listed Buildings and Buildings in Conservation Areas) Regulations 1987). Conse-
quently a number of the provisions in the 1971 Act that
apply to listed buildings also apply to an application to
demolish a building in a conservation area (see the Town
and Country Planning (Listed Buildings and Buildings in
Conservation Areas) Regulations 1987, regulation 12). A
proposal may therefore require consent to demolish and
a planning permission.

The buildings that are exempted the need for conservation area consent for demolition are: listed buildings
(already the subject of demolition control); ecclesiastical
buildings used for ecclesiastical purposes that are to be par-
tially demolished, but not if they are to be totally demolished (applying *A–G. v. Howard Reformed Church*
[1975]) unless within the Redundant Churches and other
Religious Buildings Act 1969; ancient monuments (already
controlled); and a number of small buildings, temporary
buildings and agricultural and industrial buildings erected
under the general development order as permitted development (see chapter 4).

(c) Trees in conservation areas may be afforded the degree
of protection that would be available under a tree preservation order (section 61A); there are a number of exemptions
and these are more fully considered in chapter 12.

(d) Development permitted by the General Development Order
1977 (as amended) is limited in a conservation area by
special development orders such as the Town and Country
Planning (National Parks, Areas of Outstanding Natural
Beauty and Conservation Areas) Special Development
Order 1985. This means that whereas the cubic content
of a dwelling-house may be enlarged up to 70 cubic metres
or 15% (whichever is the greater), and an industrial building may be enlarged up to a further 20% of cubic content
and within a floor space limit of a further 750 square metres
in other areas, in a conservation area (and a National Park
and an Area of Outstanding Natural Beauty), the limits
are 50 cubic metres and 10% for dwelling-houses, and 10%
extra cubic content and 500 square metres of floor space
for industrial buildings. Other limitations are more fully
considered in chapter 4 where the development orders are
discussed.

(e) The local planning authority may make use of its power to issue an Article 4 Direction, and thereby withdraw the automatic planning permission available under the General Development Order 1977 for certain development that would otherwise be permitted in a conservation area. The article would specify the development no longer automatically permitted (see further in chapter 4).

(f) For the purposes of advertisement control (see next chapter), a conservation area may involve the use of discontinuance notices to discontinue advertisements which have deemed consent but which are contrary to the amenity interests; a conservation area may also be an area of special control of advertisements which places greater restrictions on the display of advertisements.

10.4 Ancient Monuments and Archaeological areas

1. Monuments

Under the Ancient Monuments and Archaeological Areas Act 1979, the Secretary of State may compile a schedule of monuments; it then becomes an offence to carry out certain works to a "scheduled monument" without consent. A scheduled monument may include a building, structure or work, or a site comprising the remains of such things. The proscribed work includes work of demolition, damage, destruction, removal, repair, alteration or addition, or flooding or tipping operations (section 1). There are a number of defences (section 2). In *Essex County Council* v. *A.H. Philpott & Sons Ltd.* [1987] a farming company was fined £1,500 for laying a drain through the site of a roman villa.

Scheduled monument consent is obtainable from the Secretary of State (section 2). Consent may be granted with or without conditions. Conditions may specify how the work is to be carried and by whom, i.e. an archaeologist. The Secretary of State may grant scheduled monument consent by an order: this may relate to certain categories of work, and in respect of specified classes of scheduled monuments (section 3). This power is similar to the general development order in general development control.

The Act also makes provision for the general protection of ancient monuments. These include both scheduled monuments and others of great interest and defined by the Secretary of State. Either the Secretary of State or a local authority may become the guardian of ancient monument, with the consent, of the owner (section 12).

Responsibility for upkeep passes from the owner. Unless scheduled monument consent exists, it is an offence to destroy or damage any scheduled monument or any ancient monument which is the subject of guardianship (section 28).

2.   Archaeological areas

The 1979 Act contains powers enabling the Secretary of State or a local authority to designate an area of archaeological importance (section 33). It then becomes an offence to carry out operations that disturb the ground, or flooding or tipping that affect the area without first giving notice to the district council (section 35). There are then certain powers of entry for the Secretary of State and others to make investigations before the operations are carried out (sections 38–40).

10.5   Protection of the countryside

There are several special areas that are accorded particular titles in planning legislation and practice. These are very briefly described; some do and some do not have legal consequences for the development of land; they are all significant in their own way on the planning decision process and all are directed to the protection of the countryside.

1.   National Parks

These have been created under the National Parks and Access to the Countryside Act 1949. Under this Act, and the Countryside Act 1968, local planning authorities have particular obligations with regard to: access to the countryside, by access agreements or orders; management and maintenance of foot paths and bridleways; and the conservation of natural beauty. The Countryside Commission is a national body concerned with the provision and improvement of facilities for the enjoyment of the countryside; the conservation and enhancement of natural beauty and amenity; and the need to secure public access. It has interests and duties in all the countryside, and not just in National Parks.

The local planning authority in a National Park (either the county council or a joint planning board if the Park covers more than one authority) will exercise its planning functions to safeguard the interests of the National Park: not only will development inconsistent with National Park policies not be allowed, but the authority may make particular use of its positive planning powers to enforce planning control and discontinue non-conforming uses (see chapters 16–17).

Several of the classes of permitted development are more restricted in National Parks and the other special areas: see chapter 4 and the Town and Country Planning (National Parks, Areas of Outstanding Natural Beauty, Conservation Areas, etc.) Special Development Order 1985. In the case of the erection of agricultural or forestry buildings, or the construction of private roads, notice must be given to the local planning authority, and work cannot commence for 28 days. Town and Country Planning (Agricultural and Forestry Development in National Parks etc.) Special Development Order 1986. The authority may serve a notice during the 28 day period that its prior approval is required. If approvals refunded, compensation may be payable.

2. Areas of Outstanding Natural Beauty

These are usually smaller areas than National Parks, and may be designated following the proposals of the Countryside Commission or the local planning authority: National Parks and Access to the Countryside Act 1949, sections 87–88.

In an AONB, the local planning authority may decide that such an area should be particularly protected from uncontrolled permitted development by the use of an article 4 direction withdrawing one or more classes of permitted development (see chapter 4). The Town and Country Planning Agricultural and Forestry Development in National Parks etc.) Special Development Order 1986 applies to certain areas of natural beauty. This order is unexplained above under National Parks, and in chapter 4.

3. Sites of Special Scientific Interest

The Nature Conservancy Council has a duty to notify the local planning authority, and every owner and occupier concerned, of a site of special scientific interest. The notification will specify the flora, fauna, or geological or physiographical interest, and the operations which are likely to damage the features giving rise to that interest (section 28, Wildlife and Countryside Act 1981). Anyone proposing to carry out any of the potentially damaging operations must first give notice to the NCC.

Where it appears to a local planning authority that development proposed in a planning application is likely to affect a site of special scientific interest, they must consult with, and take into account the views of, the Nature Conservancy Council (General Development Order 1977, article 15).

The Secretary of State may make an order designating a site of special scientific interest for the purpose of securing the survival of any kind of animal or plant or of complying with an international obligation, or in the case of a site of national importance, for the purpose of conserving any of its flora, fauna, or geological or physiological features (section 29, Wildlife and Countryside Act 1981). It is then an offence to carry out operations proscribed by the designation order unless notice has been given to the Nature Conservancy Council, and they have given written consent; the operations are permitted under an agreement between the Council and the landowners; or three months have elapsed from the written notice. During the three month period the Council may come to an agreement with the landowner, or decide to compulsorily acquire the site. However, it is not an offence to carry out the prohibited operations if planning permission is first obtained [section 29(9)].

4. Management Agreements in the Countryside

A management agreement may be made between an owner or occupier and the local planning authority (in a National Park, the county planning authority) for the purpose of conserving or enhancing the natural beauty of any land (section 39(1) of the Wildlife and Countryside Act 1981).

Such an agreement may impose restrictions on the owner "as respect of the method of cultivating the land, its use for agricultural purposes or the exercise of rights over the land and may impose obligations on that person to carry out works or agricultural or forestry operations or do other things on the land". An agreement may also permit the authority to carry out works on the land; and provide for the payment of money by either party to the other (section 39(2)).

A management agreement will bind successors in title to the land, unless it provides otherwise. It is not clear if this means that it is enforceable in the same way as planning agreements under section 52 of the 1971 Act; that is, as if they were restrictive covenants. If so, they could be the subject of modification upon application to the Lands Tribunal (see chapter 9).

5. Green Belts

The purpose of a green belt is to check the unrestricted sprawl of built-up areas; to prevent neighbouring towns from merging into one another or to preserve the special character of a town (see Circular 42/1955). A green belt is a matter of planning policy rather than planning law; although it will have an inevitable effect on the decision making process. A local planning authority should have regard to a green belt policy, but they are not bound to slavishly follow it (see *Enfield L.B.C.* v. *Secretary of State* (1975)).

6.   Environmentally Sensitive Areas

A new form of land designation was introduced by the Agriculture Act 1986. ESA designation provides voluntary protection for important landscape areas by the use of management agreements. The agreements encourage conservative farming practices, and may provide for payments. The first ESA covered the marshes of the Norfolk Broads.

Chapter 11

Advertisements, Enterprise Zones and other Controls

Introduction	131
Advertisement Controls	131
Advertisements excluded from control	132
Advertisements that may be displayed without consent	133
Advertisements requiring express consent	136
Advertisements: Areas of Special Control	136
Enterprise Zones	137
Pollution and Hazardous Materials	141

11.1 Introduction

In this chapter the reader will find the special controls over the display of advertisements. Enterprise zones are also described. These represent a very different policy from many of the special controls. Their purpose is in fact to free selected areas of unnecessary planning control, and to provide other incentives to encourage the development of the zones.

There is a brief description at the end of this chapter of the controls over dangerous and hazardous materials.

11.2 Advertisement Controls

The display of advertisements is controlled by the Town and Country Planning (Control of Advertisements) Regulations 1984. The reason for control is for amenity and public safety interests (section 63(1) of the 1971 Act).

A district planning authority (in a National Park, a county planning authority), may propose that the Secretary of State approve an order for an Area of Special Control. In such an area there is a greater restriction on the display of advertisements than elsewhere (section 63(4)).

The Regulations exclude certain advertisement displays from control; and give deemed consent to a number of other displays of advertisements. It is an offence to display any other advertisement without the consent of the district planning authority. The offence can be committed either by the owner or occupier of the land, or by the person whose goods or business is advertised (section 109).

131

There is a defence if the person charged can show that the advertisement was displayed without his knowledge or consent. This defence succeeded in *John* v. *Reveille Newspapers Ltd.* [1955] where the newspaper company were able to prove that an advertisement of theirs was displayed on a public urinal without their consent. But the defence failed in *Preston* v. *British Union for the Abolition of Vivisection* [1985] because the offence was regarded as a continuing one, and the advertiser had been informed of the display.

Advertisements are defined in the Regulations as:

> "any word, letter, model, sign, placard, board, notice, device or representation, whether illuminated or not, in the nature of, and employed wholly or partly for the purposes of, advertisement, announcement or direction (excluding any such thing employed wholly as a memorial or as a railway signal), and includes any hoarding or similar structure or any balloon used, or adapted for use, for the display of advertisements ..."

Any consent under the Regulations for the display of an advertisement also operates as a planning permission to the extent that the display involves development (i.e. building or engineering operation, or a material change of use) (section 64).

11.3   Advertisements excluded from control

The following displays of advertisements are specifically excluded from control by the Regulations (Regulation 3 and 12):

(a) Advertisements displayed on enclosed land, and not readily visible from the outside, or from a public right of way through the land.

(b) Advertisements displayed within a building. This exclusion will not include advertisements that are visible from outside the building, and are illuminated, or displayed in a building used principally for advertisement display, or displayed within 1 metre of any external door, window or opening: these advertisements are within control, although, in fact, deemed consent may be available (see below).

(c) Advertisements displayed on or in a vehicle that is normally used for its mobility.

(d) Advertisements displayed on, or which consists of, a balloon flown at a height more than 60 metres above ground level.

(e) Advertisements incorporated in, and forming part of, the fabric of a building which is not principally used for advertisement displays.

(f) Advertisements on an article for sale or on the package or other container in which an article is sold, or displayed on the pump, dispenser or other container from which an article is sold; the advertisement must only refer to the article for sale, must not be illuminated, and must not exceed 0.1 square metre in area.

(g) Advertisements on or consisting of a lettered balloon flown at any height on a site for not more than 10 days in any calendar year, and not in an area of special control, a National Park, area of outstanding natural beauty or a conservation area.

11.4   Advertisements that may be displayed without express consent

Although all the advertisements in this group are within control, consent is deemed granted by the Regulations. This is subject to the right of the district planning authority to challenge an advertisement in some of the cases. The deemed consent is more retricted in areas of special control. (Part III of the Regulations.)

1.   Election notices, statutory advertisements and traffic signs

Consent is granted for the display of these advertisements (regulation 9). The district planning authority has no power to serve a discontinuance notice (see below) in respect of such advertisements (regulation 16).

2.   Advertisements displayed on 1st August 1948

These may continue to be displayed without express consent (regulation 11). But the district planning authority may serve a discontinuance notice in respect of any such advertisement—see below (regulation 16).

3.   Advertisements displayed within buildings

Where an advertisement within a building is illuminated, or displayed in a building used principally for displaying advertisements, or is displayed within 1 metre of a door, window or other opening through which it is visible from outside, the advertisement may be displayed without consent. However, the local planning authority may require its discontinuance under Regulation 16.

4. Display of advertisements after expiration of express consent

Every express consent to the display of an advertisement is for a limited period, usually five years (regulation 20). However, there is deemed consent to continue the display after the expiration of this period unless the district planning authority serve a discontinuance notice (regulation 13).

5. Specified Classes

Consent is granted for the display of these advertisements under regulation 14, although the district planning authority may serve a discontinuance notice under regulation 16:

> Class I—Functional advertisements of local and statutory authorities, and public transport undertakers;
> Class II—nameplates, professional or business names (not exceeding 0.3 square metre in area), advertisements of religous, educational, cultural, recreational, or medical institutions, or of hotels, inns, or public houses, flats, clubs, boarding houses or hostels (not exceeding 1.2 square metres in area);
> Class III—temporary advertisements such as "to let" or "for sale" boards (one advertisement not exceeding 2 square metres);
> Class IV—advertisements on business premises relating to the business or other activity, the goods sold or services provided; the advertisement must be displayed below the level of any first floor window, and if on a shop, only on the wall containing the shop window; (in areas of special control, there is a limit on the proportion of the face of the building taken up by advertisement);
> Class V—advertisements on the forecourts of business premises for the same purposes as in Class IV but subject to an area limit of 4.5 square metres;
> Class VI—flags on a single flagstaff in an upright position on the roof of a building containing the name or device of the occupier.
> Class VII—displays on hoarding around building sites not being in an area of special control, conservation area, National Park, or area of outstanding natural beauty.

The following conditions apply to these advertisements:

(a) apart from Class I, the height of any letters, figures, symbols, emblems or devices shall not exceed 0.75 metre, or 0.3 metre in an area of special control;

(b) apart from Class I and VI, no advertisement can be displayed above 4.6 metres from ground level, or 3.6 metres in an area of special control. (There is some relaxation for "for sale" and "to let" boards);

(c) no advertisements can be illuminated except those in Class I, and those in Classes II and IV that relate to medical or similar matters.

Advertisements on the modern petrol filling station need to attract customers from outside the premises. In *Heron Service Station Ltd. v. Coupe* [1973], the House of Lords had to decide if advertisements on the edges of the canopy, and on the kerbs of the concrete islands, were within class IV as being advertisements displayed on business premises. Because business premises are defined as a building in the regulations, it was held that the advertisement on the canopy (being a building) was permitted, but that on the kerbs was not. The case also decided that business premises and forecourts of business premises are mutually exclusive for the purposes of Class IV and V.

The Secretary of State has power, by a direction, to withdraw the deemed consent for the advertisements in the specified classes. He may do so in respect of a class or a description, in any particular area, or case (regulation 15). He must allow an opportunity for objections to be made to such a direction.

6.   Discontinuance Notices

These have already been mentioned. In the case of advertisements that may be displayed by a deemed consent under the regulations, the district planning authority may serve a discontinuance notice "in the interests of amenity or public safety" requiring the display of the advertisement to cease (regulation 16). It has already been noted that this power is not available in respect of the statutory notices (see 1 above).

In the case of the specified classes (see 5 above), a discontinuance notice cannot be served unless the notice "is required to remedy a substantial injury to the amenity of the locality or a danger to members of the public" (regulation 16). It is then an offence if the advertisement is not removed by the specified time. There is right of appeal.

11.5 Advertisements requiring express consent

All other advertisements that are not either excluded from control (see 11.3 above), or for which consent is deemed granted (see 11.4 above), need the express consent of the district planning authority (regulation 17).

The authority is required to consult with certain bodies (regulation 18) and it may then grant consent, grant consent subject to conditions, or refuse it (regulation 19). Every consent is normally for a limited period of 5 years (regulation 20), but may, if appropriate, be for a longer or shorter period.

In exercising their powers, the authority should consider the general characteristics of the locality and the presence of any feature of historic or architectural interest; and have regard to the safety of persons who may use roads etc., and the effect of an advertisement on any traffic sign, railway signal etc. (regulation 5). There can be no control over the content of an advertisement other than in the interests of amenity and public safety.

The applicant may appeal to the Secretary of State against an adverse decision (regulation 22).

11.6 Advertisements: Areas of Special Control

These have already been referred to (see 11.2 above). The district planning authority (in National Parks, the county planning authority) may propose that the Secretary of State approve an order for such an area (section 63(4) of the 1971 Act). The area must then be kept under review (regulation 26). The section states that such areas can be either rural areas, or other areas that appear to require special protection on grounds of amenity.

In an area of special control there is some restriction on the advertisements that have deemed consent under the regulations (9, 12, 14, and 23). These restrictions were described in relation to those regulations at 11.4 above.

In respect of other advertisements, the power of the local planning authority is limited in an area of special control; it may only grant express consent for the advertisements specified in the regulations (regulation 27). These advertisements include temporary advertisements for local events; a necessary announcement or direction for buildings or other land; advertisements necessary for public safety; and advertisements in the specified classes, which exceed the limitations contained therein (see regulation 14), but can be reasonably allowed.

Section 63(4) additionally contains powers for the Secretary of State to make special regulations for advertisement control in conservation areas. None have so far been made.

11.7 Enterprise Zones

Part XVIII of the Local Government, Planning and Land Act 1980 made provision for the designation of enterprise zones. Substantial relaxation of planning control, and exemption from rates for non-domestic hereditaments, is seen as the tonic for the areas selected, together with other fiscal incentives.

The Government sees the purpose of these zones as an experiment to test how far industrial and commercial activity can be encouraged on a few selected sites. Areas with problems of economic and physical decay are likely to be chosen; and zones will generally not exceeed 500 acres.

There is some optimism that significant impact can be achieved through increased economic activity and development and improvement of the physical environment. Enterprise zone designation orders, to be laid before Parliament, are likely to last about 10 years.

1. Initiation of enterprise zone schemes

The Secretary of State may invite any district council, London borough council, new town corporation or urban development corporation to prepare a scheme relating to the development of an area with a view to its designation as an enterprise zone. His invitation may specify an area and contain directions as to the form and content of a scheme and of any consultations to be made (para 1 of schedule 32).

Any authority or corporation receiving such an "invitation" may prepare a draft scheme (para 2(1)). There appears to be no obligation on a reluctant body to prepare a scheme; indeed, it is clear that the Secretary of State is unlikely to invite such a body.

2. Publicity

A body that prepares a draft scheme with a view to the designation of an enterprise zone must give the scheme provisions adequate publicity (para 2(2)). A scheme for an area in Greater London must be given publicity in Greater London—elsewhere in England and Wales, publicity must be given in the county in which the area lies; in new town areas or urban development areas, publicity must

be given in those areas. The detailed requirements of the publicity
are not specified in the schedule: presumably they will be contained
in the invitation.

The body preparing the scheme must ensure that any persons
"who may want to make representations ... are made aware that
they are entitled to do" and are given an opportunity of making
such representations. The body is particularly directed to consider
a representation made on the ground that some development in
the scheme should not be granted planning permission (para 2(2)–
(3)). The question of planning permission is considered below.

3.   Adoption of an enterprise zone scheme

When the period for making representations has expired, the body
who made the draft scheme may, by resolution, adopt it. Modification may be made to a draft scheme to take into account any representations (para 3(1)–(3)).

A copy of the adopted scheme is sent to the Secretary of State
and a further copy is made available for public inspection. These
matters must then be advertised, together with the fact that if the
Secretary of State designates the scheme area as an enterprise zone,
his order will grant planning permission in accordance with the
scheme (para 3(7)).

4.   Challenging a scheme

The Secretary of State may designate the area to which a scheme
relates as an enterprise zone. He will do so without those familiar
steps of public local inquiry (or written representations) and his
inspector's report.

Apart from making representations, the only means provided by
the schedule for a person to challenge a scheme is by application
to the High Court for judicial review (para 4). This expensive and
unsatisfactory procedure is restricted to a challenge that the scheme
is not within the powers conferred by the schedule (*ultra vires*);
and any person making such an application must show he is "a
person aggrieved". (See chapter 19.)

If the High Court is satisfied that the scheme is wholly or to
any extent outside the powers in the schedule, or that the interests
of the applicant would be substantially prejudiced by a failure to
comply with any requirement, it may order that no designation
order shall be made until further steps are taken to comply with
the requirements of the schedule (para 4(2)).

5. Designation of an enterprise zone

Once a body has adopted its prepared scheme, the Secretary of State may, by order, designate the area it covers as an enterprise zone (para 5(1)). Although he cannot make such an order until at least six weeks after the advertisement of the adoption has appeared or any court proceedings have been disposed of, whichever is later.

The order is subject to annulment by a resolution of either House of Parliament. This means the order will have validity without the express approval of Parliament; to prevent an order, either House has to pass a resolution against it. The order also needs Treasury consent (para 5(3)).

The order itself will specify the date designation is to take effect; the period of time the area is to remain an enterprise zone; the boundaries of the zone; and the authority, usually the local (district) planning authority, that is to be the enterprise zone authority (para 5(4)). Yet further advertisement is to occur, this time of the making of the order (para 6).

6. Planning

When the order designating an area as an enterprise zone is duly made, this has the effect of granting "planning permission for development specified in the scheme or for development of any class so specified" (para 17(1)). Thus, it is not the case that the need for planning permission for all development is dispensed with: planning permission is available only for development in the scheme.

It is predictable that local planning authorities will therefore draw up schemes in some detail, and they will take their time in doing so, to ensure that only development they would have permitted in the ordinary way is specified in the scheme. It is also predictable that local planning authorities will fail to consult the landowners in the area *before* making a draft scheme to establish *their* proposals and resources. Where development initiative lies with landowners and private developers, it would seem important for the landowners to be partners in the scheme-making process.

The planning permission granted by the designation order may be subject to conditions or limitation specified in that order (para 17(3)). Certain matters may also be specified in the order as reserved for approval by the enterprise zone authority (para 17(6)). Planning delays are still foreseeable!

Even though the designation order has granted planning permission for development in the scheme, the enterprise zone authority may direct, with the approval of the Secretary of State, that planning permission shall not apply in certain cases. These may involve a specified development, a specified class of development or a specified class of development in a specified area (para 17(4)–(5)).

It can be seen that the freedom from planning controls may be illusory. If the zones are not to continue as areas of physical and economic dereliction, guarantees of substantial freedom from controls should be forthcoming.

The planning permission granted by the designation order does not have the limited duration of five years ordinarily provided for in the 1971 Act. Unless the scheme contains a condition as to time-limit, it will last for the duration of the enterprise zone. However, the scheme will not authorise the carrying out of operations after the termination, even if they commenced before termination (paras 18 and 22).

7. Relief from rates

A further benefit of an enterprise zone is that there is no liability to pay rates in respect of exempt hereditaments during the period of designation (para 27(1)). Exempt hereditaments are non-domestic hereditaments; rates will remain payable for a dwelling house, private garage or private storage premises. Rates will also remain payable for the hereditaments of certain public utilities, or occupied by public utility undertakers and valued, for rating purposes, on the profits basis (para 27(3)).

No rates will be payable in respect of the non-domestic part of a mixed hereditament. In this case the valuation officer will determine the portion of the rateable value attributable to part of the hereditament used for domestic purposes: rates will then be paid only on that portion of the rateable value (para 28).

This relief from liability to pay rates will naturally cause loss to the rating authorities. The lost revenue will be made good by grants from the Secretary of State (para 29).

8. Other fiscal incentives

Further provisions concerning fiscal incentives in enterprise zones are found in the Finance Act 1980. For a period of 10 years, 100 per cent capital allowance in respect of commercial and industrial buildings are to be available for income and corporation tax purposes.

11.8 Pollution and Hazardous Materials

It is beyond the scope of this work to detail the legislative controls over pollution and hazardous materials. There are a number of provisions giving powers to deal with noise, pollution of water supplies and the atmosphere, and the storage and use of hazardous materials. These controls are largely additional to, and do not replace any requirement to obtain planning permission for the erection of buildings or the material change of use of buildings or other land.

1. Pollution to Water

Part II of the Control of Pollution Act 1974 contains provisions for controlling pollution to inland and coastal waters. A number of criminal offences are defined in relation to unauthorised discharges of pollutants. Apart from this Act, a local planning authority is bound to consult the water authority in respect of proposed development that may affect a water course.

2. Noise

Part III of the Control of Pollution Act 1974 contains provisions to control noise. It amends the procedures for dealing with specific noise problems and includes powers for local authorities to designate noise abatement zones. These are zones where noise levels can be monitored, and steps taken to reduce noise levels for the improvement of the local environment.

3. Pollution to the Atmosphere

Pollution to the atmosphere in the form of factory, power station or other discharges is not the subject of satisfactory controls in all cases. Specific provisions deal with specific forms of discharge. Examples include the Alkali Works Regulation Act 1906, which covers certain industrial processes, and the Clean Air Acts 1956–68 which introduced smokeless zones. Acid rain discharges from powers stations are outside existing legislative controls.

4. Hazardous Materials

In the past the proper control and siting of the storage, use and processing of hazardous materials has not been satisfactory. The Health and Safety Executive possesses certain powers under the

Health and Safety and Work Act 1974; and the nuclear inspectorate had powers under the Nuclear Installations Act 1965.

New powers are given to local planning authorities in the Housing and Planning Act 1986. District councils and London boroughs are to become "hazardous substances authorities", and the Act states that a "hazardous substances consent" will be required for the presence on any land (with certain exceptions) of hazardous substances. The substances are to be defined in regulations to be made by the Secretary of State. A number of criminal offences are defined in relation to failure to comply with the control requirements. Provision is also made for dealing with contraventions, the revocation and modification of consents, and for the payment of compensation. Transitional provisions allow a deemed consent for hazardous substances present on land when the regulations take effect.

Chapter 12

Trees, Minerals and Caravans

Trees: General   143
Tree Preservation Orders   143
Trees and Felling Licences   147
Trees in Conservation Areas   147
Control over Mineral Workings   148
Caravans   153

12.1 Trees: General

There are two principal controls that protect trees: one is found in planning legislation, and concerned with the protection of trees because of the interests of amenity; and another is found in the Forestry Act 1967 and controls felling, through the issue of felling licences, with a view to the proper conservation and management of timber resources.

There is a general duty, in section 59 of the 1971 Act, on a local planning authority to impose conditions, where appropriate, in a grant of planning permission for the preservation or planting of trees, or to make tree preservation orders to give effect to such conditions or otherwise.

12.2 Tree Preservation Orders

A local planning authority may make a tree preservation order (TPO) in the interests of amenity for the preservation of such trees, groups of trees or woodlands as may be specified in the order (section 60(1)). Most TPOs are made by district planning authorities; county planning authorities can only make TPOs in relation to a grant by them of a planning permission, in relation to land covering more than one district planning authority area, where the county hold an interest in the land, or in relation to land in a National Park (section 60(1A)).

The TPO may contain provisions (section 60(1)):

    (a) for prohibiting the cutting down, topping, lopping, uprooting, wilful damage or wilful destruction of trees without consent;

(b) for securing the replanting of any part of a woodland area felled in the course of felling operations permitted by the order;

(c) for the application of certain provisions of the 1971 Act as may be specified. (The provisions that may, and are usually specified, are those that apply to an application for planning permission—in other words, where a TPO is in force, and consent is needed for some prohibited work, application for consent is by way of an application for planning permission, and is subject to most of the rules that apply to such an application, or planning permission.)

A map detailing the trees protected by a TPO must be deposited for public inspection for as long as the TPO is in force: *Vale of Glamorgan B.C.* v. *Palmer* [1984]. A failure to deposit the map, or register a local land charge may mean that criminal prosecutions will fail.

1.   Criminal Offences

It is a criminal offence to contravene a TPO by the cutting down, uprooting, wilful destruction, or wilful damage, topping or lopping of a tree without consent (section 102(1)). Other contraventions of a TPO attract lighter penalties (section 102(2)). The offence is one of strict liability; the tree feller who fells a tree in ignorance of the TPO is commiting an offence, and is liable to the stiffer penalty: *Maidstone B.C.* v. *Mortimer* [1980]. The landowner who orders the tree felling is only liable to the lighter penalty as his offence of causing or permitting the felling appears to fall under section 102(2)) (*R.* v. *Bournemouth Justices, ex parte Bournemouth Corpn.* [1970]).

Where a TPO covers an area of woodland, it may be important to determine what is a "tree", as it is only in relation to trees that an offence may be committed. In *Kent C.C.* v. *Batchelor* [1976], Lord Denning M.R. opined that a tree should be something of 7″ or 8″ in diameter. This case was not followed in *Bullock* v. *Secretary of State* [1980], where the landowner had argued that a coppice does not contain trees, as what grew in a coppice were too small and anyway were cut in rotation which was inconsistent with a TPO. This argument did not prevail, the word tree should be given its ordinary meaning, and trees in a coppice can be the subject of a TPO; provision can also be made for the proper management of a coppice.

The penalty does not include imprisonment, but in case of deliberate and threatened contravention, the court may grant an injunction, which, if disobeyed amounts to contempt; the court may then imprison see *A.G.* v. *Melville Construction Co. Ltd.* [1968].

It is not an offence to do work to a tree if it is dying, dead, or has become dangerous, the work is required by some other statute, or is necessary to abate a nuisance (section 60(6)). But a replacement tree must be planted (section 62). There is provision for enforcement, and a right of appeal (section 103).

2. Procedure for making a TPO

Section 60(5) provides for the making of regulations: these are currently the Town and Country Planning (Tree Preservation Order) Regulations 1969 as amended by the Town and Country Planning (Tree Preservation Order) (Amendment) Regulations 1981. Further guidance is found in Circular 36 of 1978—Trees and Forestry.

The regulations specify the form of the TPO. It is the TPO itself, it will be recalled, that not only carefully identifies the trees, groups of trees, or woodland to be protected, but also sets out the prohibited acts in relation to the trees, and the provisions of the 1971 Act that are to apply to any application for consent required by the TPO (regulation 4).

The local planning authority, after making the TPO, must deposit details for public inspection, and serve a copy of the TPO on the owners and occupiers of the affected land (and the Conservator of Forests and District Valuer). The owners and occupiers are also entitled to a notice of the grounds for making the TPO and to be informed that objections and representations may be made to the authority (regulation 5).

If no objections or representations are received within 28 days, the TPO may be confirmed by the local planning authority (regulation 6). If objections or representations are made, and they must include the grounds upon which they are based, the local planning authority must take these into consideration. They may then decide to confirm the TPO with or without modifications, or not to conform it. Presumably a public local inquiry would be held, and if so, the Inspector's report must be fully considered by the local planning authority (regulation 8).

When the TPO is confirmed, the local planning authority must notify the owners and occupiers of the affected land, the Conservator of Forests and the District Valuer (regulation 9). The TPO is also registered as a local land charge: this is good notice to any purchaser.

3. Provisional Tree Preservation Order

A TPO does not take effect until the local planning authority has confirmed it (section 60(4)). Because this may involve several months delay, and the trees concerned may meanwhile be felled or otherwise damaged, the local planning authority may, in making a TPO, include a direction that section 61 of the 1971 Act shall apply. The effect of this is that the TPO takes effect on a specified date, and before it is confirmed. It is then a provisional TPO, lasting for six months, or until confirmed, and protects the trees for the time being as if the TPO were confirmed (section 61(2)).

4. Consents under a Tree Preservation Order

A TPO must be made substantially in the form of the model TPO contained in the 1969 Regulations. The model TPO form sets out the procedure for obtaining consents, making appeals, and making claims for compensation.

If a person wishes to do any of the prohibited acts to trees protected by a TPO, he must do so by applying for consent from the district planning authority. The application is treated as an application for planning permission. If permission is granted, it may be subject to such conditions as the authority think fit (such as to require replacement trees). The TPO may contain a power for the authority to issue a direction as to replanting.

The model form of TPO provides that no consent is required for the cutting down of trees which are the subject of a forestry dedication covenant, and the cutting down is in accordance with an approved plan of operations; or which are the subject of an approved plan of operations under a Forestry Commission grant scheme.

Where the TPO covers woodland, the model TPO form provides that consent to fell in accordance with the principles of forestry must be granted unless refusal is necessary in the interest of amenity to maintain the special character of the woodland, or the woodland character of the area. Such a consent cannot be the subject of conditions requiring replacement or replanting.

The model form contains a right of appeal to the Secretary of State against an adverse decision of the local planning authority. There is also a right to claim compensation if consent is refused for certain matters prohibited by the TPO (section 174 of the 1971 Act). (See page 231.)

5. Replacement of Trees

The Town and Country Planning (Amendment) Act 1985 extends
section 62 of the 1971 Act. This section now imposes a duty on
the landowner to replace any trees removed, uprooted or which
are destroyed or die unless the local planning authority dispense
with the requirement. The duty is fulfilled by planting another tree
of an appropriate size and species at the same place as soon as
reasonable. In the case of trees in a woodland, the same number
of trees should be planted on or near the land where the original
trees stood, or as may be agreed with the local planning authority.

12.3   Trees and Felling Licences

Unless the developer is felling a large number of trees, he is unlikely
to need a felling licence under the Forestry Act 1967. In any event
no licence is required if the felling is necessary for the purpose of
carrying out development for which planning permission has been
granted (section 9(4) of the Forestry Act 1967).

   If an application is made to the Forestry Commission for a felling
licence in respect of trees which are the subject of a TPO, the Commission may, and must if they propose granting the licence, refer
the application to the local planning authority (section 15(1) of
the Forestry Act 1967). If the authority object to the granting of
a licence, the matter is referred to the Secretary of State.

   Where a person has been convicted of felling trees without a
felling licence, the Forestry Act 1986 contains powers for the
Forestry Commission to require the restocking of the felled land
with trees.

12.4   Trees in Conservation Areas

Section 61A of the 1971 Act provides protection for trees in conservation areas. The protection is equivalent to the protection afforded
to trees which are subject to a TPO. The prohibited acts are those
found in section 60 (see above). It is a defence to any criminal
proceedings that the person charged either obtained consent for
the prohibited acts, or he gave notice to the local planning authority
and six weeks have elapsed since that notice and the act is done
not more than two years from the date of the notice (this is to
give time, if appropriate, for the making of a draft TPO) (section
61A(3)).

   This protection does not apply to dead or dying trees, trees within
a forestry dedication or approved forestry plan made with the
Forestry Commission, trees for which a felling licence is granted,

trees on land owned by the local planning authority where the prohibited acts are done with their consent, and to trees less than 75
millimetres in diameter (or 100 millimetres if the work is done to
improve the growth of the trees): see the Town and Country Planning (Tree Preservation Order) (Amendment) and (Trees in Conservation Areas) (Exempted Cases) Regulations 1975.

12.5   Control over Mineral Workings

Although somewhat outside the scope of this book, there follows
a very brief outline of the control over mineral workings; certain
aspects of which may interest the general developer. The control
of mineral workings is now largely found in the Town and Country
Planning (Minerals) Act 1981, which enacts many of the recommendations of the Stevens Committee "Planning Control over Mineral
Workings" (1976). Most of the provisions of the Act came into
force in May 1986, and consist of amendments to the 1971 Act.

Policy guidance is found in Circular 11/86 which describes the
provisions of the 1981 Act. (Further guidance on specific matters
is found in Circulars 21/82—Aggregates, 25/85—Restoration, and
24/85—Silica Sand.)

1.   Wider definition of mining operations

It will be recalled that planning control arises in respect of development, and development is defined to include mining operations (section 22(1) of the 1971 Act). Mining operations are now defined
to include the removal of material of any description from a mineral
working deposit, a deposit of pulverised fuel ash, furnace ash or
clinker, or a deposit of iron, steel or other metallic slags; and the
extraction of minerals from a disused railway embankment (section
3A). A mineral working deposit is that left after the extraction of
minerals from land (section 264(1A)). Minerals include all minerals
and substances in or under land of a kind ordinarily worked for
removal by underground or surface working (section 290(1)).

The purpose of this wider definition is to bring the working of
slag and other waste heaps clearly within control.

2.   Mineral planning authority

The 1981 Act defines a new mineral planning authority: the county
planning authority (in Greater London, the London borough councils). The Local Government, Planning and Land Act 1980 had
already identified the county planning authority as being responsible

for the development control over mineral related activities (see definition of county matter in chapter 5).

There is a duty on every mineral planning authority to undertake at appropriate intervals reviews of every site in their area where the winning and working of minerals is, or has, been carried out, or is authorised by planning permission and has not yet started. The authority must then consider whether to revoke or modify any planning permission (not possible when acted upon); to serve a discontinuance order to prevent further use of a site; or to prohibit the resumption of mining operations or order a suspension (these last two orders are new to planning control and are outlined below) (section 264A).

3. Permitted Development

Two new classes of permitted development were added to the general development order in 1985. Class XXVI permits certain mineral exploration work for up to 28 days, and exploitation testing for up to 4 months, subject to stringent conditions. Class XXVII permits the removal of materials from stockpiles and from smaller temporary mineral-working deposits.

4. Notification and publicity for planning applications

In connection with an application in respect of underground mining operations, notice of the application must be given to all owners of land (including those with an interest in a mineral in the land except oil, gas, coal, gold or silver) (section 27(1)(cc)).

5. Aftercare conditions

Conditions may be imposed upon the grant of planning permission to ensure the restoration and aftercare of land after the completion of mining operations. A restoration condition requires the site to be restored by the use of soils; and an afercare condition requires steps to be taken to bring the land to a required standard for agriculture, forestry or amenity uses (section 30A(1)–(2)).

Aftercare may include planting, cultivating fertilising, watering, draining or otherwise treating the land: a period of time may be specified for any of these steps; the aftercare period itself being 5 years after compliance with the restoration condition (section 30A(6)–(7)).

The required standard for agriculture is that which prevailed before the mining operations, where the original use was agriculture, provided the Minister of Agriculture has stated what the original physical characteristics of the land were, and it is practicable to achieve these characteristics again (section 30A(9)).

There are also provisions defining the required standard for agriculture (in other circumstances), forestry or amenity uses (section 30A(10)–(12)).

In *R. v. Derbyshire C.C. ex parte N.E. Derbyshire D.C.* [1980] a question arose as to whether a condition imposed in a planning permission to extract minerals, that the excavated land should be filled with the remaining overburden and other fill that may be necessary, to restore the area, authorised the use of the land for tipping waste. The divisional court decided that the condition did authorise the tipping of waste because if the condition required infilling of the site, it must authorise the necessary activities, and these could include infilling with waste.

Where planning permission for mineral extraction has been granted subject to conditions requiring the restoration of the quarry, and an application for tipping waste materials finished with a topsoil covering is approved, that approval may be treated as approval of the restoration conditions which had originally been reserved: see *R. v. Surrey County Council and another ex parte Monk* [1986].

6. Duration of planning permission

Unless some other period is specified, planning permission for the winning and working of minerals lasts for 60 years. That period also applies to planning permissions granted before section 7 of the 1981 Act comes into force. The permitted operations must cease within the period of time (section 44A).

7. Positive planning powers

These have already been mentioned. One of the objects of the 1981 Act is to give increased powers to mineral planning authorities to deal with sites where the winning and working of minerals becomes inconsistent with the proper planning of their areas. It may be a site that has not yet been worked, is in the process of being worked, or work has been abandoned. The use of a site may become inconsistent with adjoining uses or development, become an eyesore; or, in some cases, prevent the land from being used for some other purpose.

The ordinary powers of making revocation or modification orders to an existing planning permission; or a discontinuance order requiring a use to cease and buildings or works removed, are available under the 1971 Act subject to some amendments (sections 45 and 51). For the purpose of a discontinuance order, use includes the winning and working of minerals; and plant or machinery can be ordered to be removed as well as buildings or works (section 51(1A)–(1C)). In respect of any of the foregoing orders, aftercare conditions may be added. The basis of compensation is considered below.

The 1981 Act provides for two new planning powers: an order prohibiting the resumption of the winning and working of minerals where that work appears to have permanently ceased; and a suspension order in cases of the temporary suspension of the winning and working of minerals.

A prohibition order may be made where work has not been carried out to any substantial extent for two years, and it appears that it is unlikely to be resumed. The order may specify the steps to be taken to remove plant or machinery and to safeguard the amenities; it may include a restoration condition and an aftercare condition. The order must be confirmed by the Secretary of State, to whom there is a right of appeal (section 51A).

A suspension order may be made where any work has been suspended temporarily for 12 months, but may be resumed. The purpose of the order is to require that steps be taken for the protection of the environment. The steps mean those necessary for the preservation of the amenities of the area during suspension, the protection of the area from damage, and the prevention of any deterioration in the condition of land (section 51B). A suspension order must be confirmed by the Secretary of State, to whom there is a right of appeal (section 51C). The winning and working of minerals, suspended by an order, may be recommenced: a notice must first be served on the mineral planning authority. If they fail to revoke the order within two months, application may be made to the Secretary of State, for revocation (section 51F). Section 108 of the 1971 Act is amended to include these new orders: it is an offence to contravene a prohibition or suspension order without planning permission.

8. Compensation in connection with positive planning powers

Compensation is ordinarily available to a person with an interest in land following an order revoking or modifying planning permission, or a discontinuance order (see chapter 18). In either case, a person entitled only to an interest in the mineral may now be entitled to compensation (section 164(1) and 170(2)). Other amendments are made to provide a right to claim compensation in connection with prohibition and suspension orders.

Because the use of these new powers to control mining operations and the aftercare and restoration would have imposed a large compensation burden on planning authorities, there is a different basis of compensation where "mineral compensation requirements" are satisfied. The object here is to reduce the amount of compensation that a claimant may otherwise be entitled to: see chapter 18, and in particular the case of *Hobbs (Quarries) Ltd.* v. *Somerset C.C.* [1975]. This different basis, known as "mineral compensation modifications", puts part of the cost of compliance on the mining industry and is set out in the Town and Country Planning (Compensation for Restrictions on Mineral Working) Regulations 1985 (section 178A). It is important to realise, that these regulations only apply in the circumstances now detailed in the Act as "mineral compensation requirements".

In relation to an order revoking or modifying a planning permission, the mineral compensation requirements are:

(a)   the order modifies a planning permission for the winning and working of minerals;

(b)   the order does not restrict the winning and working of minerals; or modify any existing such restriction;

(c)   the owners and district council were previously consulted; and

(d)   the permission was granted more than 5 years before the order; or if granted before the commencement of section 30A (power to impose after care conditions), there is an aftercare condition but no other; or, any previous modification order was at least 5 years before the order (section 164A).

If these requirements are satisfied the "mineral compensation modifications" apply and there is a reduction of compensation liability payable by the planning authority. Any orders outside the scope of the "mineral compensation requirements", for example containing limits on the duration, size of area, depth, rate, commencement or other restriction on the quantity of minerals permitted to be excavated (section 178C) will mean full compensation, not the reduced compensation basis introduced by the 1981 Act.

The mineral compensation requirements also apply, with adaptation, to compensation for a discontinuance order: the order must impose conditions on the continuance of the use of land for the winning and working of minerals, or require buildings, works, plant or machinery for the same to be altered or removed; and—

(a) the winning and working of minerals began more than 5 years before the order;
(b) the order does not impose restrictions, or modify existing restrictions on the winning and working of minerals (see above for the meaning of this); and
(c) the owners and district council were previously consulted (section 170B).

In relation to compensation for a prohibition order, the mineral compensation requirements are satisfied if (a) and (c) above are fulfilled (section 170B(3)). And in relation to compensation for a suspension order, if (c) above is satisfied (section 170B(4)).

12.6 Caravans

The ordinary developer is unlikely to be concerned with the problems of caravans; what follows is therefore a very brief outline of the appropriate controls.

Caravans are the subject of general planning control as well as the special controls found in the Caravan Sites and Control of Development Act 1960. The 1960 Act was passed because of the enforcement difficulties experienced by planning authorities in applying the development controls of the planning Acts.

1. Control under the 1971 Act

Under the 1971 Act, the use of land for caravans may involve a material change of use requiring planning permission: see *Guildford R.D.C.* v. *Fortescue* [1959]. But in a Ministerial decision (Bulletin of Selected Appeal Decision No. IX No. 18), it was decided that the stationing of a caravan in the drive or garden of a private dwelling-house during such times as it was not used for holiday purposes was not development; no planning permission was required; provided that it was not used for any residential purpose.

If a caravan becomes a permanent fixture to land, perhaps because its wheels are removed or it is connected to services, it may be regarded as a building or structure within Lord Parker C.J.'s tests in *Cheshire C.C.* v. *Woodward* [1962]: see chapter 2.

But where a caravan is stationed on agricultural land and used for the storage of feed for agricultural purposes, this involves no material change of use: *Wealden D.C. v. Secretary of State for the Environment* [1986].

2.   Control under the 1960 Act

Any person who wishes to use land as a caravan site must first obtain planning permission in the ordinary way under the 1971 Act (see above). Appropriate conditions may be attached to any such permission.

Having obtained planning permission, the occupier of the land still cannot use it as a caravan site unless he obtains a site licence under the 1960 Act. Failure to do so is a criminal offence (section 1). A caravan site "... means land on which a caravan is stationed for the purposes of human habitation and land which is used in conjunction with land on which a caravan is stationed" (section 1(4)).

The first Schedule to the Act contains a list of exemptions to this requirement of a site licence (section 2). The exemptions include: land within the curtilage of a dwelling house if the use is incidental to the enjoyment of that dwelling house; land used for a person travelling with a caravan, staying not more than two nights, and which is otherwise not so used more than 28 days in the preceding 12 months, and only by one caravan at a time; land that exceeds 5 acres and which is not used by a caravan on more than 28 days in the preceding 12 months, and with no more than 3 caravans at a time (caravans on farms during holiday seasons); land used by an organisation holding a certificate of exemption; land approved by exempted organisations (maximum 5 caravans); land used by meetings of exempted organisations (maximum 5 days); seasonal accommodation of agricultural or forestry workers on agricultural or forestry land; use of land, adjoining a site where building or engineering operations are taking place, for accommodation of building or engineering workers employed on the site; use of land by a certified travelling showman; and, the use of land by the local authority.

It must be emphasised that these are exemptions from the need for a site licence, planning permission may still be required in some of these cases.

Application for a site licence is made to the district or borough council. Planning permission must first be obtained; if granted, otherwise than by a development order (see chapter 4), the site licence must be issued within 2 months (section 3). A site licence cannot be issued for a limited period only, unless the planning permission is limited in duration, in which case the site licence expires when the period limited in the planning permission ends (section 4).

Conditions may be attached to the site licence: they may restrict the numbers of caravans, their type and state of repair and distribution on the site; they may concern the preservation and enhancement of the amenities; the provisions for fire prevention; and the proper arrangements for sanitary facilities (section 5). Apart from these particular matters, conditions are otherwise imposed in the interests of the caravan dwellers, other persons, or of the public at large (section 5(1)).

There is a right of appeal, against any condition that is unduly burdensome, to the magistrates court within 28 days of the issue of the site licence. The court may vary or cancel any condition having regard to the "Model Standards" issued by the Department of the Environment (section 7).

Conditions may be varied, deleted, or added to a site licence at any time by the local authority. The licence holder may first make representations. He then has a right of appeal to the magistrates court within 28 days of the written notification of the altered site licence (section 8).

It is an offence if the occupier fails to comply with a condition of a site licence. Persistent offenders risk the revocation of the licence (section 9).

PART IV

POSITIVE PLANNING AND ENFORCEMENT

Chapter 13

Revocation, Modification and Discontinuance Orders

Revocation or Modification of a Planning Permission   159
Discontinuance Orders   161

13.1 Revocation or Modification of a Planning Permission

A local planning authority may, by order, revoke or modify any planning permission that has been granted upon an application. They may do so having had regard to the provisions of the development plan and to any other material considerations (section 45 of the 1971 Act). This power is used sparingly; first, because compensation may be payable; and secondly, because the validity of a planning permission, that is not made use of, expires after five years; outdated planning permissions will hopefully just lapse.

1. General

The power to revoke or modify a planning permission may only be exercised before the carrying out of the building or other operations have been completed, or before a change of use has taken place. A revocation or modification order cannot affect any building or other operations already carried out (section 45 (4)). Once the building or other operations have been completed, or the change of use taken place, the local planning authority is limited to the use of a discontinuance order (see below) if it wishes to take positive action against development that is unacceptable in planning terms, but is otherwise perfectly lawful. A revocation or modification order is registrable as a local land change.

There are two procedures for the making of these orders by the local planning authority; the second of these will be appropriate where the landowner is not going to oppose the order; this may be the case if the local planning authority are prepared to grant an alternative planning permission.

2. Procedure where order is likely to be opposed

Notice of the making of an order, and its submission to the Secretary of State for his approval, must be served on the owner and occupier of the land affected, and upon any other person who in the opinion of the local planning authority will be affected by the order. Any person upon whom the notice has been served may require that he be heard before a local inquiry or hearing. The Secretary of State, having considered, if the order is opposed, any report made by his inspector, may confirm the order, with or without modifications; the order only then takes effect (section 45(2)–(3)). The costs of a successful objector at an inquiry may be awarded against the local planning authority (Circular 2/87).

3. Unopposed procedure

Orders made under this procedure do not need the confirmation of the Secretary of State. The procedure may be used where the owner and occupier of the affected land, and any other person affected by the order, have notified the local planning authority in writing that they do not object to the order. The local planning authority must advertise the fact that they have made an order under section 45, and also notify the parties who have previously said in writing that they will not object.

Any person who may be affected by the order may give notice to the Secretary of State that they wish to be heard before a local inquiry or hearing (section 46(2)–(3)).

If no notice of objection is made, and the Secretary of State, who must have been sent a copy of the advertisement, does not call in the order for his consideration, the order then takes effect without the Secretary of State's confirmation at the end of a period of time specified in the advertisement (section 46(4)–(5)).

4. Compensation and Purchase

An order may cause a depreciation in land values or give rise to other costs; the land may be rendered incapable of reasonably beneficial use. The remedies of compensation (see chapter 18) or a purchase notice (see chapter 17) may be available to the landowner.

5. Mining operations

The Town and Country Planning (Minerals) Act 1981 allows mineral planning authorities to modify planning permissions by the imposition of restoration and aftercare conditions. There is a modified compensation basis.

13.2 Discontinuance Orders

If it is considered by a local planning authority that it would be in the interests of the proper planning of their area, or in the interests of amenity, that:

(a) any use of land should be discontinued, or that any condition should be imposed on the continuance of a use of land; or

(b) any buildings or works should be altered or removed,

They may then achieve such objectives by the making of a discontinuance order, due regard being paid to the provisions of the development plan and to any other material consideration (section 51(1) of the 1971 Act). The importance of a discontinuance order is that it may be directed against any existing lawful use of land, or require the removal of alteration of any building or works that are lawful. Its limitation is that compensation becomes payable.

The storage and sorting of scrap, an activity that might well be the subject of a discontinuance order, was held in *Parkes* v. *Secretary of State for the Environment C.A.* [1979] to be a use of land within (a) above, and therefore properly within the scope of these orders.

The demolition of a disused coastguard lookout station was held in *Re Lamplugh* [1967] to be within the scope of (b) above: (b) was a separate case for the use of a discontinuance order, it was not necessarily ancillary to (a) which refers to a discontinuance of a use.

A discontinuance order will specify the steps to discontinue the use, or to alter or remove the buildings or works, or it will specify the conditions being imposed. It may grant planning permission for any development of land to which the order relates; or grant planning permission for the retention of buildings or works or the continuance of a use of the land which existed or commenced, as the case may be, before the order was submitted for confirmation (section 51(1)–(3)).

A discontinuance order does not take effect until confirmed by the Secretary of State (section 51(4)). He may vary the order to include a grant of planning permission (section 51(5)). The reason for including a power, either for the local planning authority, or the Secretary of State, to grant a planning permission for the affected land, is to ensure that the owner is able, following the discontinuance order, to use his land for some lawful purpose.

Notice that the discontinuance order has been submitted to the Secretary of State for confirmation must be served on the owner and occupier of the affected land, and on any other person who the local planning authority believe will be affected by the order. Such persons may then require that their objections be heard before a local inquiry or hearing (section 51(6)).

Once the Secretary of State has confirmed the order, the local planning authority must serve a notice to that effect on the owner and occupier of the affected land (section 51(7)). These orders are registrable as land charges.

Unless planning permission has been obtained, it is a criminal offence to use the land for the purpose that is required to be discontinued by an order; or to use land contrary to any conditions imposed by an order. It is also an offence if a person causes or permits the affected land to be so used in contravention of an order (section 108(1)).

If the discontinuance order required the alteration or removal of any buildings or works, and this has not been achieved within the specified time, the local planning authority may do the work. (section 108(2).)

For the payment of compensation in respect of compensation in respect of discontinuance orders, see chapter 18. And for purchase notices see chapter 17.

Chapter 14

Enforcement

Introduction   163
Breach of Planning Control   163
The Enforcement Notice   169
Appeals against the Enforcement Notice   173
Prosecution and Enforcement   176
Enforcement and Listed Buildings   179

14.1 Introduction

It may seem curious, but it is not an offence to carry out development of land without planning permission. Although it is, paradoxically, unlawful (section 23(1)). The principal sanction against unlawful development is the issue, by the local planning authority, of an enforcement notice: if this is not complied with, the owner and occupier of the land are then committing a criminal offence. With some of the special controls, such as those affecting trees, advertisements or listed buildings, a breach of the special control does immediately involve a criminal offence. The reason for this distinction is presumably because the special controls would be ineffective unless backed by immediate and strict criminal liability; and, in the case of general planning control, the local planning authority must first consider whether the unlawful development is in fact unacceptable.

The principal enforcement provisions have now been amended by the Local Government and Planning (Amendment) Act 1981: reference in this chapter is to the 1971 Act as amended.

14.2 Breach of Planning Control

A local planning authority may commence enforcement action "where it appears" to them that there has been a breach of planning control since 1963 [section 87(1)]. The words "where it appears" mean that the authority do not have to establish that there has been a breach, only that there is sufficient evidence to show that a breach may have occurred (*Miller-Mead* v. *Minister of Housing and Local Government* [1963]). An enforcement notice may even be issued before the erection of a building is completed where there is real doubt from the physical appearance as to whether the building is authorised: *Green* v. *Secretary of State for the Environment* [1985].

It is clear that the authority has a discretion as to the use of the enforcement powers, even where there is a clear breach of planning control (*Perry* v. *Stanborough (Developments) Ltd.* [1978]). However, the discretion must not be abused. A failure to consider the use of the enforcement powers can form the subject of a complaint to the Local Ombudsman.

Section 87(1) provides that an enforcement notice, requiring the breach to be remedied, may be issued if the authority "consider it expedient to do so having regard to the provisions of the development plan and to any other material considerations". The point is that there is no point in taking enforcement action against unauthorised development if planning permission could have been granted for it.

This point is emphasised in Circular 22/1980 where paragraph 15 states that the permissive power to issue an enforcement notice should only be used "where planning reasons clearly warrant such action, and there is no alternative to enforcement proceedings". The Circular continues by stating that where the activity involved is one which would not give rise to insuperable planning objections if it were carried out somewhere else, then the planning authority should do all it can to help in finding alternative premises before initiating enforcement action.

1.   Breach of Planning Control

A breach of planning control consists of the following (section 87(3)):

   (a) development carried out without planning permission; or
   (b) non-compliance with any conditions or limitations imposed on a planning permission.

The meaning of development was dealt with in Chapters 2 and 3; many of the cases considered there having arisen out of enforcement action. A planning permission may be subject to conditions (see chapter 9), but the word "limitations" in (b) above is not wholly clear: it may refer to a particular type of planning condition that requires the removal of buildings or works, or the discontinuance of any use, at the end of a specified period. A planning permission subject to this type of condition is known as "planning permission granted for a limited period" (section 30). In *Cynon Valley B.C.*

v. *Secretary of State for Wales* [1986], it was said that where planning permission was granted by a general development for shop use except certain excluded uses, the permission was subject to a limitation.

2. Time Limits

Any breach of planning control that occurred before 1 January 1964 is now immune from enforcement action. In the case of a material change of use, it is advisable for the owner or occupier of land or buildings to apply for a certificate of established use where a use has commenced without planning permission before 1964 (see chapter 3); this certificate is then conclusive against enforcement action.

The four-year rule
In respect of certain breaches of planning control, the enforcement action must commence within four years of the breach (section 87(4)).

The reason for this rule is twofold; a particular breach of planning control cannot be very objectional, in planning terms, if no-one is bothered to take action within a reasonable time from the commission of the breach; and, secondly, great uncertainty and injustice may arise if innocent persons acquire buildings or land which may at any time be the subject of enforcement proceedings.

The breaches of planning control that are subject to the four-year rule, and therefore immune from enforcement action after this period of time are:

(a) the carrying out without planning permission of building, engineering, mining or other operations;
(b) non-compliance with any condition or limitation, which relates to the carrying out of the operations at (a) above, and imposed in a planning permission;
(c) change of use of any building to a single dwelling-house without planning permission; and
(d) failure to comply with a condition that prohibits a change of use of any building to use as a single dwelling-house, or has that effect.

Any other breach of planning control occurring after 1963 does not therefore enjoy the same immunity from enforcement action.

Apart from the exception at (c) and (d) above, a material change of use, and a breach of condition not within (b) are outside the immunity for the four-year rule.

Difficult questions have arisen in relation to (a) above. If the building of a house commences more than four years before enforcement action, and is not finished until within that period of time, does the breach occur at the commencement of work, or does it continue for the duration of the building operations? The date of completion is usually the relevant date for the application of the four year rule: *Howes* v. *Secretary of State for the Environment* [1984]. Is the construction of the house one operation or a series of operations, and can enforcement action only be taken against the building work carried out within the four years?

In *Copeland B.C.* v. *Secretary of State for the Environment* [1976], it was said that the erection of a building was one operation, not a series of operations, so that if any part of the construction was not in accordance with a planning permission, the whole building was in breach of planning control (following *Garland* v. *Minister of Housing and Local Government* [1968]). It would seem to follow that if any part of such a building operation continues to a date less than four years before enforcement action, not only is there a breach within the time limit, but the whole operation can be the subject of enforcement action, and not just that carried out within the time limit.

This argument was accepted in *Ewen Developments Ltd.* v. *Secretary of State for the Environment* [1980] in relation to engineering operations. Lord Widgery C.J. said that the construction of earth embankments amounted to one operation, so that even if some of the work was carried out more than four years before the enforcement action, the whole operation was a breach if carried out without planning permission, and the whole of the embankments, not just that part made within the four years, could be required to be removed.

Different considerations seem to apply to mining operations. In *Thomas David (Porthcawl) Ltd.* v. *Penybont R.D.C.* [1972], Lord Denning M.R. decided that every shovelful of excavation is a mining operation, and if any such mining operation occurred within the four years before enforcement action, that was a breach even if the series of mining operations commenced before the four-year period. The Court of Appeal therefore held that although the enforcement action could stop and prevent further mining operations, and could require restoration of the work carried out within the four years, it could not deal with mining operations that took place before the time limit.

3. Problems with conditions

Because of the significance of the immunity provided by the four-year rule, the distinction between a breach of planning control within (a)–(d) above, which is subject to the rule, and a breach of planning control not affected by the rule becomes important:

> *Bilboe* v. *Secretary of State for the Environment* [1980] C.A. Planning permission had been granted in 1950 to use an old quarry as a tip subject to a condition which restricted the type of material to be deposited. Between 1950–1963 materials were deposited in breach of this condition; further materials were deposited in 1975, also in breach of this condition. The Court held that the breach of planning control in this case was a material change of use; tipping was a use of land, not an operation; therefore although the use continued to within four years of the enforcement notice, the breach occurred when the material change of use took place. As that was before 1964, it was now immune.

Although the tipping was said to be a material change of use, it was also in non-compliance of the original condition. The Court of Appeal did not consider whether non-compliance with a condition involves a once and for all breach, or is a continuing breach. If non-compliance with a condition is a continuing breach, enforcement is possible if the breach continues after 1963; the four-year rule only providing immunity to non-compliance with a condition relating to the carrying out of the operations, not one relating to a material change of use. Perhaps the Court of Appeal did not give due consideration to the breach of condition point because they were aware that had the appellant's proceeded to tip without any planning permission from before 1964, they would have been in a better position than tipping in contravention of a conditional planning permission, as the change of use would have been immune from action.

The distinction between continuing breaches of a planning condition and a once-and-for-all breach was considered in *Peacock Homes Ltd.* v. *Secretary of State for the Environment* [1984]. Planning permission for a warehouse was granted for a limited period, and a condition required its removal by 1974: it had not been removed by the time of the enforcement notice in 1980. It was decided that the condition was one that related to a building operation, and the four year time limit had therefore expired.

The fact that a breach of planning control may be non-compliance with a condition relating to use and at the same time be unauthorised development enjoying the protection of the four-year rule also arose in *Backer and another* v. *Secretary of State* [1981]. It was held that the appellants were entitled to the protection afforded by the four-year rule if their circumstances fell within it, which they did. (The protection of the four-year rule was extended in 1981 by paragraph (d) above following this case.)

4. Triggering the conditions

There can be no breach of a planning condition if the planning permission it is attached to is not implemented: *Newbury D.C.* v. *Secretary of State for the Environment* [1980].

The fact that an appellant who carries out development without any planning permission may be in better position then a person who has planning permission, but does not comply with a condition attaching to it, was recognised in the *Bilboe* case; the Court of Appeal deciding that there should be no disadvantage to the latter person. So if a person builds a house without permission, and no enforcement action is taken within four years, he cannot be made to take it down, and he is entitled to occupy it without any restriction. No advantage of this nature was conceded in the following case:

> *Kerrier D.C.* v. *Secretary of State for the Environment and Brewer* [1981] D.C.
> Planning permission was granted in 1973 for the erection of a bungalow subject to a condition that it be occupied by a person employed in agriculture. The bungalow that was built did not comply with the planning permission, it was materially different. Further, the occupancy condition was not complied with and an enforcement notice was served in 1979 requiring compliance with this condition. The argument was that if the bungalow did not comply with the planning permission, it was unauthorised; and if unauthorised, it meant the permission had not been implemented; and if that was right, the condition was not binding as conditions are only binding if the permission to which they are attached is implemented.

The Divisional Court dealt with this intriguing argument by first finding that the planning permission was implemented in the sense that without it no bungalow would have been built; it would be strange if an occupier could avoid a condition by simply not building in accordance with the approved plans. The condition was therefore binding, and non-compliance with it resulted in a breach of planning control. The Court did not think the *Garland* and *Copeland* cases were applicable.

14.3 The Enforcement Notice

1. Persons to be served

Until 1981, an enforcement notice was required to be served on all owners and occupiers of the land. This presented a number of difficulties if a number of people were involved, and the notices could not be served on the same date. Since 1981, an enforcement notice is first "issued" by the local planning authority (section 87(1)). Copies of the enforcement notice must then be served, within 28 days of its issue, on the owner and occupiers of the land, and on any other person with an interest in the land which the authority consider is materially affected by the notice. The copies of the notice must be served on these persons at least 28 days before the date, specified in the notice, on which the notice is to take effect (section 87(5)). Failure to specify this date will render the notice invalid: *Burgess* v. *Jarvis* [1952].

An enforcement notice may be a nullity and of no effect if the requirements of section 87(5) are not satisfied. But a person challenging a notice on such a ground must show that he has been prejudiced by a failure to serve a copy of the notice on him, and that there has been some malfeasance on the part of the authority: *R*. v. *Greenwich L.B.C. ex parte Patel* [1985].

2. The contents of an Enforcement Notice

The Town and Country Planning (Enforcement Notices and Appeals) Regulations 1981 directs an authority to specify in an enforcement notice the reasons why they consider it expedient to issue the notice, and the precise boundaries of the land to which the notice relates.

The principal contents of an enforcement notice are otherwise specified by the 1971 Act. The notice must state the matters which are alleged to constitute a breach of planning control (section 87(6)). This was held, in *Eldon Garages Ltd*. v. *Kingston-upon-Hull C.B.C.* [1974], to mean that the notice must specify whether the breach is development without planning permission, or non-compliance with any condition or limitation—a reference to the two matters that may constitute a breach of planning control (see section 87(3)). In *Scott* v. *Secretary of State for the Environment* [1983], where the land was used for scrap metal, storing caravans and a building had been erected all without planning permission, the enforcement notice did not state whether the breach of planning control was an operation or a material change of use. It was held that there was nothing in the Act to require that sort of detail.

The breach must be sufficiently specified so that the recipient of the notice knows "what he has done wrong" (*Miller-Mead* v. *Minister of Housing and Local Government* [1963]).

The enforcement notice must specify any steps which are required by the authority to be taken to remedy the breach (section 87(7)(a)). Although the authority are entitled to under-enforce (*Copeland B.C.* v. *Secretary of State for the Environment* [1976]; the notice cannot require over-enforcement, that is, more than is necessary to comply with planning control. The problem of overenforcement is considered below under the *Mansi* principle.

Practical problems have arisen out of these two requirements, where planning permission has been granted and the breach consists of a material variation from the permission, as in the *Copeland* case (wrong colour tiles), the whole development is a breach, and must be so specified in the notice. The same point arose in *Garland* v. *Minister of Housing and Local Government* [1968] where development exceeded the limits of the General Development Order; the whole development constituted a breach and had to be removed. The 1981 Act has amended section 87 to enable the enforcement notice to specify that only part of a building be removed to make the remaining development comply with the terms of any planning permission (section 87(10)(a)).

It is now also possible for the enforcement notice to specify steps for removing or alleviating any injury to amenity which has been caused by the unauthorised development (section 87(10)(b)). If those steps are carried out, and the breach consisted of the erection of a building or the carrying out of works without planning permission, planning permission is then deemed to have been granted for the retention of the building or works as they are as a result of complying with the enforcement notice (section 87(16)).

The enforcement notice must specify a date when it takes effect. That date must be at least 28 days after the service of the copy of the notice on all the affected parties (section 87(5)).

The enforcement notice must also state the period or periods within which the steps that are specified to be taken by the notice are to be completed (section 87(8)). The period of time must be adequate and reasonable in all the circumstances. If the period is too short, not only is this a ground of appeal (see below), but it may make the enforcement notice invalid: *Smith* v. *King* [1969].

An enforcement notice that is so unclear, imprecise or ambiguous, that the recipient does not know what is alleged, or what he is required to do, is a nullity: see the *Miller-Mead* case (above) and *Metallic Protectives Ltd.* v. *Secretary of State for the Environment* [1976].

3. The Mansi Principle and unauthorised change of use

There is a special problem where the breach of planning control involves a change of use without planning permission. It will be recalled that "development" only takes place if there is a material change in the use of any buildings or other land; and that the commencement of incidental or ancillary uses within the planning unit, or a change in the degree of use, may not be development requiring planning permission (see chapter 3). Therefore an enforcement notice should not prohibit so much of a use that is not development, as to this extent there can be no breach of planning control. The point is that an enforcement notice remains valid, once issued, to prevent any change of use within its scope, at any time in the future, and it would be wrong to prevent what is not even development.

The problem is illustrated in the case which gives its name to the principle:

Mansi v. *Elstree R.D.C.* [1965] D.C.
A greenhouse had been used for horticulture since 1922, and there had been some incidental retail sales. The sales use became more significant, and eventually constituted the main use of the building. An enforcement notice required the shop use to cease. The Divisional Court held that, as some incidental or ancillary retail sales in association with the horticultural activity would not have been a breach of planning control, the enforcement notice went too far in prohibiting all sales.

The principle was applied in *Trevor Warehouses Ltd.* v. *S.S.E.* [1972] to an enforcement notice that prohibited a use that had commenced before 1st January 1964, such a use became an established use right, and was immune from enforcement action (see section 87(1)). In the case, a wholesale warehouse had an incidental retail sale use established before 1964, the breach of planning control was an unauthorised change of use to retail supermarket, the enforcement notice could require the discontinuance of retail sales as a main use of the property, but not the incidental retail sales established before 1964.

However, if the incidental or ancillary use had ceased before the breach of planning control, that use can be regarded as abandoned, and any enforcement notice subsequently issued may then lawfully prohibit some previous, but now abandoned incidental use. The *Mansi* principle had therefore no application in *Jones* v. *Secretary of State for the Environment* [1974] where an incidental trailer manufacturing use ceased in 1966: an enforcement notice could prevent any manufacturing of trailers.

In cases of creeping intensification, it is clear that some degree of intensification of an existing use can be enjoyed by the landowner before he passes the line over which there is a material change of use (see chapter 3). Lord Widgery C.J. dealt with this, and the application of the *Mansi* principle in:

> *De Mulder* v. *Secretary of State for the Environment* [1974] "In these so-called intensification cases the material change of use occurs at a point when the landowner has already exercised every right which the planning Acts give him, in other words it is not until the material change of use occurs that enforcement action can be taken, and when the enforcement action is taken any latitude of the kind to which I referred in *Mansi* has already been absorbed and enjoyed."

Lord Widgery C.J. then added that provided the enforcement notice prohibited only that degree of use that occurred from immediately before the point at which a material change of use took place, the planning authorities would then have made the necessary adjustment required in *Mansi*.

The *Mansi* principle protects existing rights from an excessive enforcement notice. But in cases where a new building is erected under a planning permission, any previous rights are extinguished (*Petticoat Lane Rentals Ltd.* v. *Secretary of State for the Environment* [1971]) and the only rights flow from the permission itself. In *Hilliard* v. *Secretary of State for the Environment* [1978] (reversed by the Court of Appeal on a different point), the *Mansi* principle was therefore held to have no application to safeguard rights destroyed by the implementation of a planning permission.

One final matter involves a point which is similar to the *Mansi* principle. An enforcement notice cannot prohibit something which is expressly permitted by the planning Acts. In *Day and another* v. *Secretary of State for the Environment* [1979], an enforcement notice wrongly prohibited activities for which the landowner had permission under section 23(9) of the 1971 Act (see page 36).

14.4 Appeals against the Enforcement Notice

The 1971 Act provides an appeal to the Secretary of State on a number of specified grounds (section 88). Legal, fact and planning questions may be raised in this appeal. The appeal is also a deemed application for planning permission for the alleged unauthorised development.

The decision of the Secretary of State may be further appealed to the High Court on a point of law only. If an enforcement notice is not complied with so that a prosecution takes place, there is a further possibility of appeal from the magistrates court, but not on any of the grounds upon which an appeal can be made to the Secretary of State. Appeals to the High Court against enforcement notices, or to challenge the validity of such notices, are dealt with in chapter 19. This chapter concentrates on the appeal to the Secretary of State.

1. Statutory appeal to Secretary of State

Any person who has an interest in the land affected by an enforcement notice may appeal to the Secretary of State at any time before the date on which the notice states it will take effect (section 88(1)). An appeal must be received by the Secretary of State before the date when the enforcement notice takes effect: *Lenlyn Ltd.* v. *Secretary of State for the Environment* [1985]. A person with a licence to occupy the land has a right to appeal (Town and Country Planning Act 1984, section 4(2)). An appeal must be in writing, specifying the grounds of appeal and the facts on which the appellant proposes to rely. The Enforcement Notices and Appeals Regulations 1981 also require that the local planning authority provide a statement containing the submissions they will rely on, and whether they would have granted a planning permission for the development, conditional or otherwise. The Regulations contain time limits for these requirements to be met.

Each appellant against an enforcement notice will have to pay the appropriate fee (see page 70) as such an appeal is also a deemed application for planning permission (Reg. 8 of the Town and Country Planning (Fees for Applications and Deemed Applications) Regulations 1983).

The grounds of appeal are as follows (section 88(2)):

(a) that planning permission ought to be granted for the unauthorised development, or the condition or limitation not being complied with should be removed;

(b) that the matters alleged in the notice are not a breach of planning control;

(c) that the breach of planning control alleged in the notice has not taken place (this new ground of appeal meets the criticism in *Hammersmith L.B.C.* v. *Secretary of State for the Environment* [1975] that there was no power to accept an appeal if the facts alleged in the notice differ from those on the ground).

(d) in cases where the four-year rule applies (see above), that period has elapsed at the date of the issue of the enforcement notice;

(e) in cases not covered by the four-year rule (material change of use—with minor exceptions), the alleged breach of planning control occurred before 1st January 1964;

(f) copies of the enforcement notice were not served as required;

(g) that the steps required to be taken to remedy the breach are excessive, or go further than making the development comply with any existing planning permission, or exceed the purpose of removing or alleviating any injury to amenity caused by the development;

(h) that the period or periods specified in the notice for the steps required to be taken are less than should be reasonably allowed.

Appellants are advised to appeal on more than one ground, selecting whichever seem most appropriate. Once an appeal has been made, the enforcement notice ceases to have any effect until the appeal is decided by the Secretary of State or is withdrawn (section 88(10)). The suspension does not continue through the legal process of appealing the Secretary of State's decision to the High Court: *Dover D.C.* v. *McKeen* [1985]. Although where such an appeal is actually made, the Court has jurisdiction to stay legal proceedings for the prosecution of any offence for failing to comply with the enforcement notice until after the High Court has decided the appeal: *London Parachuting Ltd.* v. *Secretary of State for the Environment* [1986].

The Secretary of State may dismiss the appeal if the appellant does not state his grounds of appeal and provide any further information required by the regulation within the time limit; and he may quash the enforcement notice if the local planning authority fail to comply with any requirements of the regulations (section 88(6)). The burden of proof in an appeal falls on the appellant: *Nelsovil* v. *Minister of Housing and Local Government* [1962].

It is on the balance of probabilities: *Thrasyvoulou* v. *Secretary of State for the Environment* [1984].

If either the appellant or the local planning authority so require, an inspector will be appointed to hear both parties (section 88(7)). The appeal may be heard by the inspector at a public local inquiry or by way of written representations. The new regulations may require the authority or the appellant to give notice of the appeal; this may give rise to third party representations (section 88(5)(d)). The Secretary of State may dispense with the public local inquiry if he is dismissing the appeal because of a failure by the appellant to provide the required grounds and other information within the specified time; he may similarly dispense with the inquiry if the authority has failed to comply with the regulations, and he is going to quash the notice (section 88(8)).

2. The Decision of the Secretary of State

The Secretary of State may allow the appeal on one or more of the grounds, and quash the enforcement notice; or he may dismiss the appeal, and uphold the enforcement notice. However, his decision is not usually as simple as this and he is required to give directions for giving effect to it (section 88A(1)). Accordingly, where the Secretary of State concluded that an enforcement notice was wider in its allegations and requirements than could be legally justified (or indeed justified on planning merits), he may direct the precise scope of the notice: *Miller-Mead* v. *Minister of Housing and Local Government* [1963]. In any event, his decision may be legally challenged if he fails to give a proper reason, or makes a decision which no reasonable person considering the relevant facts would have made: *Camden L.B.C.* v. *Secretary of State for the Environment* [1980].

The Secretary of State is entitled to correct any informality, defect or error in the enforcement notice, or vary its terms, if he is satisfied that this can be done without causing injustice to the appellant or to the local planning authority (section 88A(2)). In *Wealden D.C.* v. *Secretary of State for the Environment* [1982], it was said that the power to vary could include changing the allegation of a breach of planning control due to operational development to one of a material change of use.

The power to correct the notice was said in *Miller-Mead* "to be wider than 'the slip-rule'", but not so wide that it could be used to correct a notice regarded as a nullity, i.e. so defective it was not an enforcement notice. In *Kensington and Chelsea R.B.C.* v. *Secretary of State for the Environment and Mia Carla Ltd.* [1981], the Divisional Court, in holding that the power of correction was limited, decided that it could not be used to correct a notice alleging change of use of a garden to a restaurant to an allegation of a change of use by intensification of the restaurant use, in a case where the authority had made a mistake in deciding the planning unit. Errors of description have been corrected under this power (lodging-house more accurate than guest-house: *Hammersmith L.B.C.* v. *Secretary of State for the Environment* [1975]). But in *H. T. Hughes & Sons Ltd.* v. *Secretary of State for the Environment* [1985], where the inspector corrected an enforcement notice which alleged a breach of planning control after 1963, to an allegation of a breach within the last four years, the court decided this went to the substance of the notice which could not be so corrected without an injustice.

The power to vary the terms of the notice were added in 1981, and may widen the previously limited power of correction. But does the word "terms" apply only to the steps required to be taken, or the time limits, or, more doubtfully, the description of the breach?

Failure to serve a copy of an enforcement notice on a person so entitled need not be a ground for quashing the notice if neither the appellant nor that person has been substantially prejudiced (section 88A(3)).

The Secretary of State, in deciding an appeal, may (section 88B):

> (a) grant planning permission for the unauthorised development, or part of it, or for development of part of the land affected by the notice.

In considering this possibility, he must have regard to the provisions of the development plan and any other material considerations. Any permission he grants may be to retain or complete any buildings or works, or to do so without complying with any previous conditions.

> (b) discharge any condition or limitation, or substitute another condition or limitation, whether more or less onerous; or
> (c) determine any purpose for which the land may be lawfully used in relation to any past use or any planning permission.

This is a useful possibility in cases involving a material change of use; his decision may resolve doubts about lawful uses.

14.5   Prosecution and Enforcement

1.   Prosecution

The enforcement notice comes into effect on the date it specifies. This date may be suspended if an appeal is made to the Secretary of State (section 88(10)), and it will remain suspended until that appeal is decided. For the effect of the suspension, see page 174 above. But once the notice is effective, and the periods specified for compliance have expired, a criminal offence is committed if the steps required to comply with the notice have not been taken (section 89).

It is the owner of the land at the time of the offence who is generally liable for this offence. Where a planning application is submitted in respect of certain land, and part of that land is sold before planning permission is granted, the purchaser may be bound by conditions attached to the permission of which he had no knowledge: *Atkinson* v. *Secretary of State for the Environment* [1983].

It is not possible to raise questions in the Magistrates Court on any matter that could be a ground of appeal to the Secretary of State (section 243(1) of the 1971 Act, as amended in 1981) *Smith* v. *King* [1970] is therefore no longer good law.

2. Execution of work in default

If an enforcement notice requires steps to be taken, other than the discontinuance of a use, and any of the steps are not taken within the required period, or extended period, the local planning authority may enter the land to carry out the necessary work, and recover their reasonable expenses from the owner (section 91).

3. Stop Notice

It may be desirable that the activities believed by the local planning authority to be a breach of planning control should cease at the earliest opportunity rather than await the date specified in the enforcement notice, a date which may be put off by an appeal. Accordingly, where an enforcement notice has been served, an authority may serve a stop notice to prevent the carrying out of any activity included within the matters believed to be a breach of planning control (section 90(1)). The activities prohibited by the stop notice must be all or part of the activities alleged to be a breach of planning control by the enforcement notice: *Welsh Aggregates Ltd.* v. *Secretary of State for Wales* [1983].

A stop notice cannot prevent the use of a building as a dwelling-house, the use of land for a caravan occupied as a sole or main residence, or any of the steps required by the enforcement notice to remedy the breach. Further, if the activity commenced at least 12 months earlier, the stop notice cannot prevent that activity unless it is, or is incidental to, building or other operations or the deposit of refuse or other materials (section 90(2)).

The stop notice takes effect on a date specified at least three but not more than twenty-eight days from its service (section 90(3)). And it ceases to have effect if the enforcement notice is quashed or withdrawn, the stop notice itself is withdrawn, or the compliance period in the enforcement notice expires (section 90(4)). A site notice must be displayed on the land giving notice of the stop notice, and that a breach is a criminal offence.

It is an offence to fail to comply with a stop notice (section 90(7)). Where a person is prosecuted for breach of a stop notice, the defendant may challenge the validity of the stop notice in the criminal proceedings against him: *R.* v. *Jenner* [1983].

A person with an interest in the land may be entitled to compensation for any loss or damage arising out of the effect of the stop notice if the enforcement notice or the stop notice is withdrawn, or the enforcement notice is quashed on appeal because there was no breach of planning control, or the breach is immune from enforcement, or copies of the enforcement notice were not served on those entitled (section 177). See further *Scott Markets Ltd.* v. *Waltham Forest L.B.C.* [1979], *Bristol Stadium Ltd.* v. *Brown* [1980] and Circulars 4/87.

4.   Injunction

A local authority may prosecute or initiate proceedings if it considers it expedient for the promotion or protection of the interests of its inhabitants (section 222, Local Government Act 1972). An injunction may be obtained to prevent a person acting in breach of planning control, and it will be granted to prevent a deliberate and flagrant flouting of the law and a plain breach of the law. In *Westminster C.C.* v. *Jones* [1981], planning control powers proved ineffective to restrain the use of a shop as an amusement arcade pending the outcome of an appeal; the defendant's only ground of appeal was that planning permission ought to be granted. An injunction was granted in this case. Failure to obey an injunction is contempt of court and the offender may be committed to prison: *Kent C.C.* v. *Batchelor* [1979].

It was said in the House of Lords case of *Stoke-on-Trent City Council* v. *B. & Q. Retail Ltd.* [1984] that a deliberate and flagrant flouting of the law was necessary before a court should grant an injunction. But in *Runnymede B.C.* v. *Ball* [1986], the Court of Appeal said that all the facts must be considered, including the past conduct of the wrong-doer, and whether the activity is irreversible.

5. Continuing Effect of an Enforcement Notice

If planning permission is granted after the enforcement notice for the activities which are the subject of the notice, the notice ceases to have effect (section 92(1)). This does not excuse any offence committed before the planning permission.

Unless planning permission is obtained, the enforcement notice remains effective and is not discharged by compliance (section 93(1)). Where one caravan is removed in compliance with an enforcement notice, the notice remains in force to prevent the stationing of a second caravan: *Prosser* v. *Sharp* [1985]. Where land enjoys an established use, one in respect of which there would be a good ground of appeal against an enforcement notice, a failure to appeal will mean that the notice will take effect, and the established use rights will be lost: *Nash* v. *Secretary of State for the Environment* [1985]. To assist those concerned with discovering whether any land is affected by an enforcement or stop notice, there is now a provision for a register of these notices (section 92A).

14.6 Enforcement and Listed Buildings

1. Listed Building Enforcement Notice

There are parallel provisions for the issue of a listed building enforcement notice where it appears to the local planning authority that there has been a contravention of the requirement to obtain listed building consent for certain work (section 96(1)). Since 1981, the steps required by a notice need not include the full restoration of the building to its former state where this is not reasonably practicable, or would be undesirable, but may be limited to works "necessary to alleviate the effect of the works carried out without listed building consent" (section 96(1)(b)(ii)).

The grounds of appeal are as follows (section 97(1)):

(a) the building is not of special architectural or historic interest;

(b) the matters alleged are not a contravention of the requirement to obtain listed building consent;

(c) the alleged contravention has not taken place;

(d) the works were urgently necessary in the interest of safety or health or for the preservation of the building and that it was not practicable to secure safety, health or preservation by temporary works of repair or support, and the work done was the minimum;

(e) listed building consent ought to be granted, or any condition discharged or substituted;

(f) copies of the notice were not properly served;

(g) except where authorised by section 96(1)(b)(ii) or (iii) (see above) the steps required for the restoration of the building go too far;

(h) the period specified for the steps required to be taken are less than should be reasonably allowed;

(i) the steps specified for restoring the character of the building to its former state would not serve that purpose;

(j) the steps required by virtue of section 96(1)(b)(ii) exceed what is necessary to alleviate the effect of the unauthorised works;

(k) the steps required by virtue of section 96(1)(b)(iii) exceed what is necessary to make the building conform to the terms of a listed building consent.

The enforcement provisions are otherwise, with technical differences, similar to those described for general development control (sections 97–99).

2. Urgent works for preservation of listed buildings

The provision described here applies to a listed building, or any building in a conservation area on the direction of the Secretary of State (section 101). The local planning authority or the Secretary of State, after giving seven days notice to the building owner, may enter and execute works which are urgently necessary for the preservation of the building (section 101(4). If the building is occupied, works may only be carried out to those parts which are not in use (section 101(3)). The owner may be required to pay the expenses of any work so executed. In this last matter he has a right of appeal to the Secretary of State (section 101A). The powers in section 101 can be used by the Historic Buildings and Monuments Commission (section 101(5)).

In *R.* v. *Secretary of State for the Environment, ex p. Hampshire* C.C. [1981], a notice under this section was considered inadequate in not specifying with some degree of particularity the works to be carried out. In *R.* v. *Camden L.B.C. ex parte Comyn Ching & Co. Ltd.* [1983] a requirement to take all such steps as may be necessary to preserve the building was also too imprecise and held to be invalid. Works and supports of a temporary nature may now be required.

3. Compulsory Purchase

The final measure available to a local planning authority where a listed building is allowed to fall into disrepair, is compulsory purchase of the building (section 114). Minimum compensation, which excludes any development value, may be directed by the Secretary of State if he is satisfied that the building has been deliberately allowed to fall into disrepair for the purpose of justifying its demolition and the development or redevelopment of the site, or adjoining site (section 117).

However, compulsory purchase may not commence unless at least two months previously a repairs notice was served on the owner of the building (section 115). The repairs notice must specify works necessary for the proper preservation of the building, and explain the effect of the compulsory purchase powers if the notice is not complied with.

Chapter 15

Development by Public Authorities

Introduction   183
Land Acquisition and Development Powers   185
Public Authorities and Planning Permission   187
New Towns   189
Urban Development Areas   189
The Land Authority for Wales   191
Register of land held by Public Bodies   192

15.1 Introduction

There is plenty of precedent for a development role for public authorities. The consequences of the Great Fire of London were such that wide powers of street improvement were conferred upon the Corporation. In the nineteenth century, the new local authorities exercised a wide range of powers to provide and improve highways, sewers and water supplies; and to deal with unsatisfactory houses. In this century, the erection of houses, and the building of the new towns have been significant elements in the development process. But it has always been a matter of great debate as to whether public authorities should have wider development powers.

This chapter deals with some of the present development powers conferred upon certain public authorities. But by way of introduction, some history of past attempts to secure a wider development role for public authorities needs to be considered.

Present development control has its genesis in the Town and Country Planning Act 1947; from 1st July 1948, all development required planning permission. A necessary corollary of development control was the existence of development plans to provide the basis for the implementation of development control decisions. In effect the Act nationalised development rights, they were thereafter no longer part of a landowner's property rights. Landowners who lost development value as a consequence of this Act in 1948 made a claim for compensation. On the other hand, landowners securing a planning permission for development could not, logically, keep any development value that arose: they were required to pay a charge to the state. The 1947 Act did not contain wide powers for public authorities to purchase and develop land; the powers were limited to deal with the post-war problems for existing urban areas.

A change of government in 1951 left the main provisions of the 1947 Act on the statute book, but eventually removed the land-owners' obligation to pay the development charge upon obtaining planning permission, and limited his rights to claim compensation. Rather illogically, development rights remained nationalised, but development value could be retained whenever it arose. During the course of the Conservative government's years in office, others, including the Labour Party, were arguing for more public control over the ownership of land in order to secure its development in accordance with perceived social policies.

Undoubtedly the existence of public control over the planning and development of land is not easily reconciled with the con-tinuance of private ownership of suitable development land. There are two basic problems. First, the decision to develop or not remains with the private landowner, and his development ideas may be influenced by economic considerations rather than social policies as expressed in development plans. For example, Blackacre is con-sidered as appropriate for residential development in a development plan, but because of its location, it would enjoy a higher "rent" if available for industrial development.

The second problem lies in the complex tapestry of landowner-ship: a development plan may consider a certain form of develop-ment as appropriate for a particular area, but the complexity of landownership in the area may mitigate against the realisation of that development; however willing some landowners may be, de-velopment may not be possible without the co-operation of all; and, there may be tenants with unexpired leases and security of tenure effectively preventing the release of such an area.

Some argue that these two problems can easily be met by a better co-operation between planners and landowners (see *Prospects of Co-operative Planning*—D. R. Denman 1974). Others that the pub-lic ownership of development land is the only solution; thus bringing together the planner and the landowner in one entity. The Labour Party have made two attempts when in office to partly realise this solution; the Land Commission Act 1967, and more recently, the Community Land Act 1975. Both were repealed by the succeeding Conservative governments. However, the powers described in this chapter are now certainly more extensive than those of the 1947 Act. In part recognition of these problems, the Land Authority for Wales, enjoying wide powers of land acquisition, and originally established by the Community Land Act 1975, remains to deal with some of the problems in the Principality. (For further reading, see the Uthwatt Report, Cmnd 6386 of 1942, and the White Paper "Land", Cmnd 5730 of 1974.)

15.2 Land Acquisition and Development Powers

1. Compulsory Purchase

The principal powers of compulsory purchase of land for planning purposes are now found in sections 112 and 113 of the 1971 Act.

A local authority may be authorised by the Secretary of State to acquire compulsorily the following land in their area (section 112(1)):

(a) Land which is suitable for and required to secure development, redevelopment and improvement; and

(b) Land required for a purpose which it is necessary to achieve in the interests of the proper planning of an area in which the land is situated.

In deciding whether land is suitable for development, redevelopment or improvement, the following are considered: the provisions of the development plan; whether a planning permission is in force; and any other matters that would be material considerations if a planning application were submitted for the land (see page 88) (section 112(13)). Since 1968, designation of land for compulsory purchase is no longer required in a development plan as a prerequisite for the use of these compulsory purchase powers. Indeed, in *Company Developments Ltd.* v. *Secretary of State for the Environment* [1978], it was held that this power is now available even if the development plan for the area has not been finally approved.

Where land is being compulsorily purchased under the above powers, any adjoining land required for executing works for facilitating the development or land use of the principal land, and any exchange land needed to replace any common land, open space or fuel or field garden allotment being acquired, may also be compulsorily purchased (section 112(1B)).

Land may still be compulsorily purchased for the purposes set out above even if the local authority acquiring the land do not propose to carry out the development or improvement themselves (section 112(1C)).

This enables the land to be developed by private developers, or another authority with the necessary powers, following a sale, lease arrangement, or a partnership agreement.

The Secretary of State enjoys wide powers of compulsory purchase of land necessary for the public service under section 113.

2. Purchase by Agreement

Land may also be acquired with the agreement of the owner for any of the purposes for which it may be compulsorily acquired under section 112. In addition, a local authority may acquire any building appearing to it to be of special architectural or historic interest, and other surrounding land required for the preservation, amenity, access or management of such a building (section 119).

3. Disposal and Development

Land that has been acquired, or appropriated to, planning purposes, may be sold or leased by the local authority in whatever manner and subject to whatever conditions that will secure the best use of that or other land, or that will secure the development of that land needed for the proper planning of the area (section 123). This section may enable a partnership scheme between a local planning authority and a developer to be agreed (see *Jones* v. *Secretary of State for Wales* [1974]).

Many local authorities use powers in local Acts to secure partnership scheme agreements, although adequate power would seem to be available under section 123. The power in section 52 to make a planning agreement is limited to circumstances where the land is not owned by the local authority and the need is to restrict or regulate the development or use of that land.

Local authorities are authorised to carry out any development themselves by the erection or construction of buildings or works (section 124). This power is hedged about with a number of restrictions, not least being those of a financial nature exercised by the Secretary of State.

Where persons are displaced from land following local authority acquisition, and the subsequent development, the authority should offer accommodation or business or other premises to such persons on completion of the scheme, "so far as may be practicable" (section 123(7)). Whether it is so practicable is a question for the local authority to decide, not for a court: *Crabtree & Co Ltd.* v. *Minister of Housing and Local Government* [1965].

The genesis for the use of these powers of acquisition and development may be (the definition in an old development plan of an area of comprehensive development, or) the indication of an action area in a structure or local plan (section 7 of the 1971 Act). An action area is one selected for comprehensive treatment during a period by development, redevelopment or improvement of the whole or part of the area, or partly by one and partly by another method.

Town centre redevelopment schemes: the provision and improvement of land for industry; and facilities for recreation and leisure may constitute aspects of a development plan or a policy accepted by a local planning authority. These matters can then be achieved with the statutory powers so far discussed.

The procedure for the acquisition of land by a public authority, and for assessment of compensation, is dealt with in the author's companion volume "Law of Compulsory Purchase and Compensation" (Estates Gazette, 1985).

15.3 Public Authorities and Planning Permission

1. The Crown

The planning Acts, with minor exceptions, do not affect the Crown. The Crown does not therefore need planning permission for development (see *Ministry of Agriculture, Fisheries and Food* v. *Jenkins* [1963]). The minor exceptions are found in section 266 of the 1971 Act and include the indication of proposals for the use of Crown land on a development plan and the listing of a building on Crown land. Tenants and lessees of Crown land will require planning permission for development; they may be served with an enforcement notice; and may themselves serve a purchase notice.

"The Crown" for these purposes includes Her Majesty in right of the Crown, and "Crown Land" includes land so owned and the land of any Government department (section 266(7)).

However, as a matter of policy, Government departments are required to consult with local planning authorities before proceeding with any development. The Secretary of State may, where appropriate, hold a public local inquiry to consider objections and representations (see Circular 18/84).

Because planning permission could not be granted for Crown land, difficulties began to arise over the disposal of surplus Crown land. To enable such land to be sold with the benefit of planning permission, listed building or conservation area consents, the Town and Country Planning Act 1984 was passed to authorise applications for these purposes. The Act also permits suspended tree preservation orders for Crown land, the use of enforcement notices against non-Crown interests in Crown land (such as tenants) and permits planning agreements to restrict existing Crown uses after the disposal of the land.

2.   Local Planning Authorities

A local planning authority is subject to development control, and requires planning permission for any development of its own land or of any land of which it is the local planning authority as well as an applicant for consent. Permission may be granted in the General Development Order for certain minor forms of development (see chapter 4). For all other development, the procedure for dealing with an application for planning permission by the local planning authority is governed by the Town and Country Planning General Regulations 1976 (section 270 of the 1971 Act). The details of the procedure are beyond the scope of this work, but because the procedure may result in the local planning authority giving planning permission to itself, the courts are often strict about the proper and full compliance with it. In *Steeples* v. *Derbyshire C.C.* [1981], planning permission granted to the county council was declared null and void because of a failure to comply with all steps of the procedures involved; the council was also bound by the rules of natural justice and had failed to show lack of bias in relation to an agreement with a developer to take all reasonable steps to obtain planning permission for a partnership scheme.

More recent cases involving a possible conflict of interest between an authority's role as planner, and as developer, have not followed the test of bias, based on the "reasonable man" in the *Steeples* case: see further section 8.8 in chapter 8 above.

Where a local government officer makes an application for permission for development that will affect a conservation area, there must be strict compliance with the regulations: *R.* v. *Lambeth L.B.C.* [1986].

3.   Statutory Undertakers

These bodies include railway, road and water transport undertakers, and any undertaking for the supply of electricity, gas, or water. Special provisions are found in Part XI of the 1971 Act where development is to be carried out by these bodies in respect of their operational land. Apart from development authorised by the General Development Order (see chapter 4), planning permission is required for the development of operational land. But where the matter comes before the Secretary of State following a call-in or an appeal, the Secretary of State makes his decision in conjunction with the Minister appropriate to the undertaking concerned.

Where development proposed by a local authority or a statutory undertaker requires the express consent of a Government department, that consent may state that planning permission is deemed granted (section 40 of the 1971 Act).

British Telecom, and any licensed communications operator, is subject to planning control in the ordinary way, but the installation and replacement of apparatus is largely permitted by the General Development Order (see chapter 4).

15.4 New Towns

The urban development corporations described below are modelled on the legislative provisions pertaining for new towns. Because of the topicality of the former, their powers are more fully described than are those of the new towns in this section.

The legislative powers in respect of new towns originated in the New Towns Act 1946, but with amendments along the way, the present statute is the New Towns Act 1981. The essential features of these powers is that the Secretary of State designates an area of land as a new town; a development corporation is then established to secure the laying out and development of the new town; and the development corporation is granted the necessary powers to achieve these objects. Certain local authority functions such as planning control, public health and highways are modified; there are compulsory purchase powers to take land; and there is now provision for the eventual sale of the development corporation's assets, and then for the dissolution of the development corporations.

15.5 Urban Development Areas

The Secretary of State has power to designate any area of land as an urban development area (UDA) (section 134 of the Local Government, Planning and Land Act 1980). He will do so in the national interest to regenerate urban areas. The first two designations were the Docklands in London, and the South Docks on Merseyside.

To regenerate a UDA, an urban development corporation (UDC) is established for the area (section 135(1)). The principal object of a UDC is "to secure the regeneration of its area" and this is to be achieved "by bringing land and buildings into effective use, encouraging the development of existing and new industry and commerce, creating an attractive environment and ensuring that housing and social facilities are available to encourage people to live and work in the area" (section 136).

A UDC will have the following powers:

(a) to acquire, hold, manage, reclaim and dispose of land and other property;
(b) to carry out building and other operations;
(c) to seek to ensure the provision of water, electricity, gas, sewerage and other services;
(d) to carry on any business or undertaking for the purposes of the object; and
(e) generally do anything necessary or expedient for the purposes incidental to those purposes (section 136(3)).

These powers are its powers as a statutory corporation. Further specific powers are necessary to authorise such matters as compulsory purchase of land.

1. Planning Control in a UDA

The Secretary of State may approve, with or without modification, proposals for the development of land submitted by a UDC after consulting the local planning authority (section 148(1)).

The Secretary of State may then grant planning permission for any development of land, subject to conditions, if any, by a special development order under section 24 of the 1971 Act. The conditions may require details of proposed development to be submitted to the local planning authority (section 148(2)). In view of the likely attitude of local authorities towards a UDC, this provision is a recipe for conflict and delay.

Perhaps to avoid conflict with the local planning authority, and certainly to speed decision-making, the Secretary of State may provide, by order, that a UDC shall be the local planning authority only for the purposes of the development control provisions of Part III of the 1971 Act (section 149(1)).

However, the Secretary of State may, again by order, confer further planning functions on a UDC (section 149(3)). The order will specify the functions from a list contained in Part I of Schedule 29. The list includes the additional control in respect of listed buildings, tree preservation orders and advertisements; the enforcement notice powers in relation to general and special planning controls; and the powers and duties of local planning authorities in relation to conservation areas. Although a corporation is a local planning authority for its area, it will not have the powers of a "local authority" to bring proceedings by way of an injunction to prevent a breach of planning control under section 222 of the Local Government Act 1972: *London Docklands Development Corpn.* v. *Rank Hovis McDougall Ltd.* [1985].

Part II of Schedule 29 contains modifications to the 1971 Act which may apply if specified in an order made under section 149(3).

Section 150 enables the Secretary of State to limit the powers of a local highway authority to impose restrictions on a grant of planning permission to those specified in a development order. This will apply where a UDC is the planning authority under section 149.

2. Building Control in a UDA

The Secretary of State may provide, by order, that a UDC shall exercise building control functions for the whole or any part of the UDA. The order may specify the extent of the building control functions and any necessary modifications (section 151).

Building control functions means the functions of local authorities under the building regulations, or, in inner London, the functions exercisable under the London building legislation.

15.6   The Land Authority for Wales

Despite the repeal of the Community Land Act 1975, the Land Authority for Wales is continued (section 102(1) of the Local Government, Planning and Land Act 1980). Schedule 18 of the 1980 Act sets out its constitution and makes provision for its membership.

1.   Functions

The Land Authority has "the function of acquiring land in Wales which in its opinion needs to be made available for development and of disposing of it to other persons (for development by them) at a time which is in the Authority's opinion appropriate to meet the need" (section 103(1)). Before acquiring, the Authority is to consider certain matters (section 103(2)). After acquisition, it may execute works (with the Secretary of State's consent) and "manage and turn to account the land pending its disposal to other persons for development by them" (section 103(3)).

The Authority may advise and assist certain local and other authorities in Wales about land disposal, and give development advice to county and district authorities (section 103(5) and (6)). It may charge a reasonable fee for such advice or assistance (section 103(7)).

2.   Power of Acquisition

The Authority has power to acquire, by agreement or compulsorily, land suitable for development; any adjoining land required for works to facilitate development; exchange-land for any common land, open space or allotments taken; and new rights over land, required for the Authority's functions (section 104(1) and (2)).

Schedule 20 contains certain provisions concerning the preparation and confirmation of compulsory purchase orders (paras 1–4); a provision extinguishing private rights over acquired land (para 6); a power to provide rights, easements and advantages to other land by building or other work done on the acquired land in accordance with planning permission (para 7); and a power to use common land, open space or allotments in any manner in accordance with planning permission (para 9).

Where rights over land are extinguished, or easements or other rights overridden, compensation is payable (paras 6(5) and 7(4)).

3.   Requisitioning of Sewers

The Land Authority is given the power to requisition sewers from the water authority. It is intended that these would be sewers for domestic drainage of buildings to be erected on development sites (section 105).

15.7   Register of Land held by Public Bodies

Part X of the Local Government, Planning and Land Act 1980 provides for a register of land held by public bodies and contains powers for the Secretary of State to direct a sale of any land entered on the register. It is said that much derelict or unused land in urban areas is owned by public bodies. The Secretary of State wants information and powers to deal with the situation.

1.   The Public Bodies

The bodies affected are set out in Schedule 16. They include not only local authorities but many of the nationalised industries and all statutory undertakers. Private companies authorised to run docks or harbours are therefore presently included in the list. Further bodies can be added to or deleted from the list by statutory instrument (section 93).

2. Areas

The Secretary of State may make orders specifying the registration areas for the operation of this Part of the Act (section 94).

3. The Register

The Secretary of State may compile the register "in such form as he thinks fit". Land may be entered on the register if it satisfies certain conditions: either a freehold or a leasehold interest is held by one of the affected public bodies or a subsidiary; it is in a registration area or adjoins land which is in such an area; and "in the opinion of the Secretary of State the land is not being used or not being sufficiently used for the purposes of the performance of the body's functions or of carrying on their undertaking" (section 95).

Although government departments are not in the list of affected public bodies (see above), the Secretary of State may enter any Crown land on to the register (section 95(4)).

4. Public Access

A copy of the register for any area (including any amendments) shall be sent to the district council concerned. This shall be made available for public inspection. Copies of any information in the copy of the register shall be supplied to any member of the public upon payment of a reasonable charge (section 96).

5. Powers of the Secretary of State

The Secretary of State will have power to require information from a public body (section 99). He may also direct that a public body takes steps to dispose of land entered on the register (section 98(1)). Before giving a direction, the Secretary of State will serve a notice of his intention on the public body; it may then make representations within a period of 42 days. He may not issue his direction to a public body which has made representations unless he is satisfied that the land can be disposed of without causing serious detriment to the performance of that body or the carrying on of its undertaking (section 99).

Any direction issued to a local authority to sell surplus land operates as consent to sell under section 123 of the Local Government 1972: the sale can therefore be by auction and without a reserve (*R. v. Secretary of State for the Environment ex parte Manchester City Council* [1987]).

PART V

RIGHTS AND REMEDIES

Chapter 16

Appeals and Inquiries

Introduction   197
Appeal to the Secretary of State   198
Public Local Inquiry   199
Written Representations   204
The Decision of the Secretary of State or Inspector   205
Costs   206

16.1 Introduction

The local planning authority possesses wide discretionary powers to implement planning policies and make development plans; that discretion is also present in its development control powers and duties. Probably because planning and development control were regarded in 1948 as interferences to private interests in property rights, the planning Acts still contain many opportunities for the merits of the decisions of local planning authorities to be appealed to the Secretary of State. The right of appeal is granted to the applicant for planning permission or the landowner. The merits of development control decisions cannot be appealed by disappointed neighbours or pressure groups. There is an exception to this in relation to the making of development plans, any person may make representations or objections, and these may be considered at a subsequent examination in public of a structure plan, or a public local inquiry for a local plan. There is also an exception where a decision of a local planning authority is being challenged because it is wrong in law, or the proper procedure has not been followed; a person with sufficient interest (a group of local residents: *Covent Garden Community Association Ltd.* v. *Greater London Council* [1981]) may seek the High Court prerogative order of certiorari to quash a planning decision (see *R.* v. *North Herts D.C. ex p. Sullivan* [1981] where wrong procedure used).

This chapter deals with the more usual appeal to the Secretary of State against a refusal of planning permission by the local planning authority, and the manner in which such an appeal is heard. Some 85% of such appeals are determined by written representations, with the occasional private hearing, and the balance by

197

public local inquiry. Appeal also arises in connection with revocation or modification orders, discontinuance orders, refusal of listed building consent, and many other matters. The appeal against an enforcement notice was considered in chapter 14, but the form of the public inquiry is similar to that dealt with here.

16.2 Appeal to the Secretary of State

Section 36 of the 1971 Act makes provision for an appeal where the following applications have been made to a local planning authority:

(a) planning permission to develop land;
(b) for any consent, agreement or approval of that authority required by a condition imposed on a grant of a planning permission; or
(c) for any approval of that authority required under a development order,

and that permission, consent, agreement or approval is refused or granted subject to conditions. Appeal is also allowed where a determination under section 53 is made as to whether an activity is development and needs planning permission, or where the local planning authority fail to reach a decision within 8 weeks, or the application is referred to the Secretary of State under section 37.

Notice of appeal must be made within six months of the decision or, where no decision is made within the time limit, within six months of the expiration of the time limit (General Development Order 1977). There is a special form, obtainable from the Department of the Environment, that must be completed and returned with copies of all relevant documents. The appellant is now required to send a duplicate copy of the appeal form to the local planning authority.

In a case where a decision appears bad in law, and is not simply disputed on its planning merits, application may be made direct to the High Court for certiorari to quash that decision (*R. v. Hillingdon L.B.C. ex p. Royco Homes Ltd.* [1974]). The legal validity of planning conditions may also be tested by seeking a declaration in the High Court (*Pyx Granite Co. v. Ministry of Housing and Local Government* [1960]). These remedies should only be considered in place of the statutory appeal where the issues are solely legal and do not involve planning merits.

If either the applicant or the local planning authority request it, the Secretary of State must afford to each an opportunity of being heard by an inspector, before the appeal is determined (section

36(4)). This is either by a public local inquiry or by written representations. Appeals in respect of applications for planning permission,
and appeals against enforcement notices are now determined by
an inspector appointed by the Secretary of State. The only appeals
now decided by the Secretary of State himself are those by statutory
undertakers and which concern their operational land (Town and
Country Planning (Determination of Appeals by Appointed Persons)
(Prescribed Classes) Regulations 1981 (S.I.804)), although he may
direct that he will hear any appeal if he so decides (Schedule 9
to the 1971 Act). Inspectors were given the power to determine
appeals relating to listed building consents (except application to
demolish listed buildings, or to alter grant aided grade I and grade
II* buildings), conservation area consents and enforcement notices
under the Determination by Appointed Persons Regulations 1986.

16.3   Public Local Inquiry

The public local inquiry is a familiar process in many fields of public
administration, apart from planning and development control. It
is a quasi-judicial process in that the inspector who conducts it
is impartial and also an expert with knowledge and experience of
the area of administration being considered. The public local inquiry
tends to mirror court procedure in being adversarial rather than
inquisitorial. In other words it depends on the parties present to
put their "case" and not upon the inspector to take the major initiative in examining the disputed decision; although he may well ask
questions to clarify matters necessary for him to reach his own
conclusions. In any adversarial process parties are likely to be represented by persons skilled and qualified in advocacy whose task is
to present their respective clients' evidence, and to test, by cross-
examination, the evidence of opposing parties. It is not unusual
for a non-lawyer to present a "case" at a public local inquiry, indeed
he deserves every encouragement, but the advantages of a legal presence should be that the matters of dispute can be identified from
the common ground, and the procedure conducted fairly to ensure
that the irrelevant and hearsay are excluded.

The conduct of an inquiry, where the Secretary of State is to
determine the appeal, is subject to the Town and Country Planning
(Inquiries Procedure) Rules 1974 (S.I.419); where the inspector is
to determine the appeal, the Town and Country Planning Appeals
(Determination by Appointed Persons) (Inquiries Procedure) Rules
1974 (S.I.420) and in respect of appeals against enforcement notices,
the Town and Country Planning (Enforcement) (Inquiries Procedure) Rules 1981 (S.I.1743). Although there are number of differ-

ences in detail between these inquiries procedure rules, they share the common objective of the Franks Committee (1957) recommendation that such inquiries must be conducted openly and fairly. The rules are made under section 11 of the Tribunals and Inquiries Act 1971 after consultation with the Council on Tribunals.

It can be argued that the inquiry process has now become too judicial; that the trend of the decisions of the Courts when reviewing post-inquiry decisions places such a constraint on what the inspector may or may not refer to in his written decision that his main task is to use the right "incantation" in that decision; and, that as a consequence, planning decision-making suffers because alternatives and solely planning issues seem subordinated to the requirements of a fair procedure. Perhaps all this is inevitable so long as many planning decisions are issues between the landowner/applicant and the local planning authority.

The various inquiries procedure rules share a number of features. What is described here are the more important rules in relation to a planning appeal.

1. Preliminary information and Notification of Inquiry:

The local planning authority may be required to provide details of persons entitled to be informed of an application and who have made representation under section 29 of the 1971 Act (i.e. owners and certain tenants); and of any directions or advice received from a government department.

The Secretary of State will fix the date, time and place of the inquiry giving at least 42 days notice. He may request that the inquiry be advertised in a local newspaper and by way of a site notice.

2. Exchange of Statements before Inquiry

Not later than 28 days before the inquiry the local planning authority shall serve on the applicant (and section 29 parties, i.e. owners and certain tenants) a written statement of any submission which the authority propose to put forward at the inquiry (Rule 6). A copy is sent to the Secretary of State. Any documents, plans or maps that may be referred to or put in evidence shall be listed, and the parties given an opportunity to inspect these, and make copies. Any Ministerial directions, considerations or advice must similarly be made available. It is wise practice to obtain the local planning authority's written confirmation that no other submissions than those the subject of this preliminary exchange will be made at the inquiry. If required by the Secretary of State, the applicant is also to provide a written statement of the submission and documents he will be relying on. These must then be served on the other parties.

The inspector has discretion during the inquiry to allow any party to add to or vary these statements. But he must ensure that if this is permitted, the other parties have an adequate opportunity to consider any fresh submission or document. This may mean an adjournment, and the party responsible may have to bear the costs.

Even if there is compliance with this rule of procedure, where there is a breach of the rules of natural justice, prejudice to the party involved is irrelevant for, "justice must be seen to be done", see *Performance Cars Ltd.* v. *Secretary of State for the Environment* [1977].

3. Appearances at Inquiry

The persons entitled to appear at the inquiry include the applicant; the local planning authority; the county or district council if not the local planning authority; the section 29 parties (owners and certain tenants of the land); the parish or community council where it has made representations; and other persons specified by the Secretary of State. Any other person has no right to appear, but may do so at the inspector's discretion.

A party may appear on his own behalf or may be represented by counsel, solicitor or any other person (such as a town planning consultant, surveyor or agent).

4. Representatives of Government Departments:

Where a government department is involved because of a direction or has given advice, the applicant may make a request at least 14 days before the inquiry that a representative of that department be available at the inquiry. Such a person may give evidence and be cross-examined, although he cannot be required to answer any question which in the opinion of the inspector is directed to the merits of government policy.

5. Representatives of Local Authorities:

This rule parallels the rule above where a local authority has issued a direction, or otherwise expressed views, and is not itself the local planning authority in the appeal. Only here, the representative may state the reasons for the direction, or explain the views expressed by his authority.

6. Procedure at the Inquiry

The procedure is at the discretion of the inspector to the extent that the rules do not otherwise apply. The applicant will ordinarily begin, and has the right of final reply. The practice is for the applicant to make an opening speech outlining his case and the evidence he is going to rely on; he calls his expert witness or witnesses who read their proofs of evidence. They may then be cross-examined by the other parties entitled to the present at the inquiry. The purpose of this cross-examination is to enable the evidence to be tested by direct questions. The local planning authority will present its case in a similar manner, and its expert witnesses may also be cross-examined.

Ordinary objectors who are present at the discretion of the inspector are generally limited to making a statement. They are not usually allowed to call evidence or to cross-examine other witnesses. This is very much at the discretion of the inspector.

The local planning authority close their case with a speech urging the relevance and significance of their evidence; and the applicant then makes his own final reply in a similar vein.

The inspector will record all the evidence called before him, and make a note of the main points argued by the parties. He will be in breach of the rules of natural justice if he relies on any other evidence not before the inquiry, or not in issue at the inquiry, even if that evidence comes to him because he is an observant expert in his own right and sees something he thinks relevant at his site inspection: *Fairmount Investments Ltd.* v. *Secretary of State for the Environment* [1976].

7. Site Inspection

The inspector may make an unaccompanied site visit before the inquiry. He may, and must if requested, make a site visit after the inquiry. On the second occasion, the parties entitled to be present at the inquiry may accompany him. The purpose of this is to identify any features referred to during the course of the inquiry. Because no further arguments can be put to the inspector, the lawyers are not present at these site visits.

8. Procedure after Inquiry

Where the decision is that of the Secretary of State, the inspector will make a report in writing with his findings of fact and recommendations. In other cases the inspector will proceed to formulate his decision and his reasons.

If the Secretary of State is deciding the appeal and differs from his inspector on a finding of fact, or wishes to take into consideration new evidence or any new issue of fact (not government policy) not considered at the inquiry, and as a consequence disagrees with a recommendation of his inspector, he must inform the parties. They may make further representations, or, where new evidence or a new issue of fact is raised, may ask that the inquiry be re-opened. A difference of opinion on the merits of siting a house in a walled garden is not a difference on a finding of fact: *Lord Luke of Pavenham* v. *Ministry of Housing and Local Government* [1968]. The test is between a finding on an existing state of affairs as opposed to a subjective opinion as to the future (*Pyrford Properties* v. *Secretary of State for the Environment* [1977]). Only if the Secretary of State disagrees with the former, need he re-open the inquiry. The Secretary of State cannot decide an appeal on a ground not considered at all at the inquiry (*Webb* v. *Secretary of State for the Environment* [1972]).

The inspector is bound by the rules of natural justice to give the Secretary of State a fair account of the inquiry but he need not record every irrelevant submission: *N. Surrey Water Co.* v. *Secretary of State* [1977].

Where the inspector decides an appeal he is required to inform the parties if he decides to take into consideration any new evidence, or any new issue of fact not raised at the inquiry. The parties may make representations, and request that the inquiry be re-opened. Where evidence has been presented at the inquiry, or where a site visit has been undertaken, the inspector is entitled to make inferences, such as of architectural values; such inferences will not be new evidence: *Winchester City Council* v. *Secretary of State for the Environment* [1978].

9. Notification of the Decision

The decision, and the reasons for it, are made in writing and notified to the applicant, the local planning authority and the section 29 parties, and to any other person, who has requested to receive it. The decision is final (section 36(6)), although an application may be made to the High Court on a point of law (section 245). This is dealt with partly later in this chapter and partly in chapter 19.

16.4   Written Representations

Some 85% of appeals are now decided on the basis of written representations in place of the public local inquiry. The Town and Country Planning (Appeals) (Written Representations Procedure) Regulations 1987 prescribe time limits for the various stages of the procedure. General guidance is to be found in Circular 18/86—Planning Appeals decided by Written Representations, and Circular 11/87 on the regulations themselves.

When the appellant gives Notice of Appeal to the Secretary of State, he may request that the appeal be disposed of by written representations, and should enclose his written statements of case. Copies of the Notice of Appeal, and all supporting documents must be sent to the local planning authority. Where the Secretary of State accepts that written representations are appropriate, the "starting date" for the procedure laid down in the 1987 Regulations is the date of the receipt by the Secretary of State of the Notice of Appeal.

Within five working days of receipt of the copy of the Notice of Appeal from the appellant, the local planning authority, if they accept the procedure, must notify the authorities and other parties entitled to be consulted over a planning application. These third parties have 28 days from the starting date to submit representations.

The local planning authority must complete a questionnaire and submit this to the appellant and the Secretary of State within 14 days of the starting date. The local planning authority may submit their written representations at this stage, but in any event within 28 days of the starting date. The written representations put in by either party should deal concisely with the facts, the policies applied and the reasons why the appeal should, or as the case may be, should not be allowed.

On receipt of the questionnaire from the local planning authority, the appellant has 17 days within which to make a reasoned reply. If the local planning authority's written statement is not enclosed with the questionnaire, the appellant should wait until that is received, and must then reply with his observations within 17 days of receipt of the written statement. Normally the local planning authority will not need to reply further, but if the appellant's observations raise new material, their final reply must be made within seven days.

The appointed inspector will usually make a site visit within a 2 week target period immediately following the closing date for representations. A decision letter will then be issued within 2 weeks of the site visit, or where the decision is to be that of the Secretary of State, a report will be submitted to the Department within 2 weeks.

The inspector can only decide an appeal on the matters raised in the written representations, he cannot take into account matters which a party has not had an opportunity of considering (*Wontner-Smith* v. *Secretary of State for the Environment* [1977]).

16.5   The Decision of the Secretary of State or Inspector

The Secretary of State may allow or dismiss an appeal, or may reverse or vary any part of the decision of the local planning authority, and may deal with the application as if it had been made to him in the first instance (section 36(3)). An inspector determining an appeal enjoys the same powers.

Because of this wide discretion on the part of the Secretary of State, careful tactics are required in appealing against planning conditions. The Secretary of State may take the opportunity of redeciding the whole or part of the original planning permission. It may be preferable to submit a further application to the local planning authority to have the condition varied or removed; and if refused, then appeal to the Secretary of State. In this way the original planning permission remains.

The decision may be quashed by the High Court if the reasons given are obscure and leave in doubt the matters which the Secretary of State took into account, or did not take into account (*Givaudon & Co. Ltd.* v. *Minister of Housing and Local Government* [1967]). Where the Secretary of State makes a decision following an inquiry and his inspector's report, he is not bound by the recommendations of his inspector; but if he relies on a policy document to which the inspector attached little evidential value, and reaches a contrary conclusion and decision to his inspector, his decision will be quashed if he fails to re-open the inquiry (*French Kier Developments Ltd.* v. *Secretary of State for the Environment* [1977]).

In *Arlington Securities Ltd.* v. *Secretary of State for the Environment* [1985], it was said that inspector must consider three matters in arriving at his decision. First, there is a presumption in favour of planning permission unless there is a clear cut reason for refusing permission. Secondly, any objections to the grant of planning permission should be clearly identified in the decision letter. Thirdly, where there was some new development plan in the offing, that alone should not be a reason for refusing permission unless there was some issue which could not be properly decided.

Policies set out in Ministerial Circulars are material considerations, and where relevant, must therefore be taken into account: *Pye (Oxford) Estates* v. *West Oxfordshire C.C.* [1982]. But it would be wrong for the Secretary of State to apply a policy which is inconsistent with the clear provisions of the development plan unless there are reasons for departing from the plan: *Reading B.C.* v. *Secretary of State for the Environment* [1986].

The Secretary of State is entitled to have a policy, but in determining an appeal, he must give genuine consideration to the issues and merits raised (*Lavender* v. *Minister of Housing and Local Government* [1970]). He is, however, entitled to make reference to a policy statement of another Government department in his decision without having to re-open the inquiry on the basis that he is relying on new evidence (*Kent C.C.* v. *Secretary of State for the Environment* [1977]).

Further grounds for challenging the decision are considered in chapter 19. Undoubtedly the Secretary of State has a difficult task. On the one hand he is deciding an appeal between two parties and is required to show impartiality by reason of the procedure rules and the rules of natural justice. And yet on the other hand he is entitled to regard an appeal as if an application were being made to him for planning permission; the appeal process gives him an opportunity to put into effect ministerial or government policy.

16.6 Costs

There is power to award costs under section 250 of the Local Government Act 1972. In practice costs have usually only been awarded to a party in a case of unreasonable behaviour of another party (*R.* v. *Secretary of State for the Environment, ex p. Reinisch* [1971]).

Circular 2/87—Guidance on the award of costs incurred in planning and compulsory purchase order proceedings—explains the government's policy on the award of costs. Costs are not awarded on the basis of success or failure; they are to be awarded where the unreasonable behaviour of one party has caused another party unnecessary expense. Unreasonable behaviour includes a failure of a local planning authority to make a decision within the statutory time limits; or, the action of an appellant in pursuing an appeal over a refusal of planning permission to build in the green belt where it is clear that no permission would be granted.

In the various inquiries procedure rules, there is also a rule that deals with costs. If a person makes an application for an award of costs, the inspector must make a report on this and on any considerations which may be relevant for the Secretary of State to decide the question. In the case of transferred appeals, where the inspector makes the decision, the inspector now has power to award costs in accordance with the policy in Circular 2/87.

This discretionary power to award costs is no longer limited, in appeal cases against a planning refusal, to those where an inquiry has been held. There is now power to award costs where the appeal is heard by written representations (amendments introduced by the Housing and Planning Act 1986 to section 250 of the Local Government Act 1972). In enforcement notice appeals, the discretion to award costs arises once proceedings have commenced, and therefore costs can be awarded if the enforcement notice is withdrawn or the matter determined by written representations (see Ministerial decision APP/5254/c/79/1736/1742 dated 20 June 1980).

Section 42 of the Housing and Planning Act 1986 provides that where a Minister is authorised to recover costs incurred by him in relation to an inquiry, the costs shall be the entire administrative costs of the inquiry including his departmental overheads. The Minister may make regulation to provide for the recovery of these costs in relation to planning.

Chapter 17

Purchase Notices

Introduction   209
The Planning Decisions   209
Land incapable of reasonably Beneficial Use   211
The Procedure   214

17.1 Introduction

In some situations a decision of a local planning authority may render land "incapable of reasonably beneficial use". This chapter deals with certain rights of a landowner to compel the local planning authority to purchase from him such land. It may also happen that land may be "blighted" by the proposals of a local authority or some other body, or by some indication on a development plan; the affected land may then be difficult to sell. In this case, certain owners have the right to compel the appropriate authority to purchase such land by serving a blight notice. As land is almost invariably blighted by a proposal that ultimately envisages the compulsory purchase of the land, such as a proposed road improvement, blight notices are not considered in this chapter, but in the author's companion volume "Compulsory Purchase and Compensation".

A purchase notice may be served where an owner has an interest in land affected by a planning decision, and must be considered as a remedy against an adverse planning authority decision. An owner for this purpose is a person entitled to receive the rack rent. An owner of a reversionary interest, subject to a lease at a rent less than the rack rent, is not entitled to serve a purchase notice (*London Corpn.* v. *Cusack-Smith* [1955]). A number of matters must be satisfied before a purchase notice compelling a local planning authority to purchase the land can be effectively served. The law and procedure is described in Circular 13/1983—Purchase Notices.

17.2 The Planning Decisions

A purchase notice may only be served in respect of land affected by a planning decision; the decisions giving rise to the right to serve a purchase are found in the 1971 Act:

(a) *Decision in connection with a planning application*
    Where an application has been made for planning permission to develop any land, a decision which is a refusal of permission or a grant subject to conditions (section 180(1)).

(b) *Revocation or Modification Orders*
    An order under section 45, revoking any planning permission or modifying any planning permission by the imposition of any conditions, may enable the owner to serve a purchase notice (section 188). There is an alternative right to claim compensation in those circumstances (see chapter 18).

(c) *Discontinuance Orders*
    Where an order under section 51 requires the discontinuance of any use of land, or imposes a condition on the continuance of a use, or requires the alteration or removal of any buildings or works, the owner may be able to serve a purchase notice (section 189). There is also an alternative right to claim compensation.

(d) *Decisions in connection with a listed building consent application*
    Where an application has been made for listed building consent, a decision which is a refusal of consent or a grant subject to conditions, or a revocation or modification of a listed building consent (section 190). Again, there may be an alternative right to claim compensation in some cases.

(e) *Trees and Advertisements*
    Decisions in connection with tree preservation orders and under the advertisement control regulations may enable the owner of the affected land to serve a purchase notice (section 191).

In each case the decision is usually that of the local planning authority and there is no need to appeal to the Secretary of State before serving a purchase notice.

If planning permission has been granted to develop land and part of that land is restricted by a planning condition or otherwise so as to prevent development of that part, perhaps because it is to be amenity or open space land, a purchase notice may be served in respect of the part so restricted (*Adams and Wade Ltd.* v. *Minister of Housing and Local Government* [1965]). But, in such a case, the Secretary of State need not confirm the purchase notice even if he is satisfied that the land is incapable of reasonably beneficial use (section 184). However, the Secretary of State must confirm the purchase notice if the conditions restricting the development of the land are invalid (*Shepherd* v. *Secretary of State for the Environment* [1975]). The decision in *Plymouth Corpn.* v. *Secretary of State for the Environment* [1972] has been reversed by amendments introduced under the Housing and Planning Act 1986: a purchase notice need not be confirmed where it covers some land restricted by an earlier planning permission decision, and some land not so restricted.

17.3 Land incapable of reasonably Beneficial Use

After establishing one of the appropriate planning decisions, the owner must then claim "that the land has become incapable of reasonably beneficial use in its existing state"; or where he has received a decision subject to conditions, "the land cannot be rendered capable of reasonably beneficial use by the carrying out of the permitted development (or of the works, in the case of listed buildings) in accordance with those conditions".

It was decided in *Wain* v. *Secretary of State for the Environment* [1982] C.A., that the owner can only serve a purchase notice in respect of that part of his land that is incapable of reasonably beneficial use in its existing state. He cannot include other land that is capable of reasonably beneficial use. "Land" is defined as including a building (section 290).

"Incapable" means that the land cannot be put to a reasonably beneficial use because of some practical or legal reason. The words "reasonably beneficial use" must be considered together. The plain meaning suggests that no use can be found for the land that is reasonably beneficial to the owner; thus a reasonably beneficial use must be distinguished from a use that is not reasonably beneficial. The size, location and character of the land will be relevant; for example, a small piece of derelict land adjoining private gardens may have a reasonably beneficial use as an addition to one or more of those gardens, whereas a large area of derelict land in a similar position may have no reasonably beneficial use.

In *Purbeck D.C.* v. *Secretary of State for the Environment* [1982], Woolf J. decided that it would be wrong to confirm a purchase notice where the land had become "incapable of reasonably beneficial use" due to some activity, such as tipping, which was a breach of planning control. The Court of Appeal in *Balco Transport Services Ltd.* v. *Secretary of State for the Environment* [1985] narrowed the effect of the *Purbeck* case by deciding that a purchase notice could be confirmed where, although the land was incapable of reasonably beneficial use due to a breach of planning control, the breach had become immune from enforcement proceedings.

From the cases two tests have emerged which can be applied to determine whether land has become incapable of beneficial use.

1. Is the existing use reasonably beneficial?

In *General Estates Co. Ltd.* v. *M.H.L.G.* [1965] part of the land involved was let to a sports club at a rent of £52 per annum. Although the rent was low in comparison with the potential value of the land with planning permission, had it been granted, this was not considered sufficient to render the land incapable of beneficial use. Similarly it was decided in *R.* v. *M.H.L.G. ex parte Chichester R.D.C.* [1960] that the fact that the land is of less value to the owner than it would have been had the planning decision been more favourable is again irrelevant. In that case, the existing use of the land was as a number of plots let as caravan sites during the summer under a temporary planning permission; this was held to be reasonably beneficial use.

Examples of existing uses that are not reasonably beneficial would include waste or derelict land, the site of a building that has been seriously damaged by fire or has fallen into dereliction, and amenity land or land designated as public open space.

If it is considered that the existing use is reasonably beneficial, no purchase notice can be served; but if the existing use is not reasonably beneficial it will be necessary to consider the second test.

2. Where the existing use is not reasonably beneficial, is some prospective use reasonably beneficial?

The Secretary of State takes the view that any prospective use of the land must be considered even where it is not development and therefore does not need planning permission. In one decision (ref PLUP2/5319/176/1), a small site, in a back-land position in a residential area, was considered to be of reasonably beneficial use as garden ground despite its existing neglected condition. Again, in the *General Estate Co.* case (see above), part of the land could have been let for grazing purpose and this was held to be a reasonably beneficial use. Prospective use for agriculture or forestry would not involve development and could, therefore, be considered in suitable cases.

Section 180(2) of the Act states that in considering any prospective use, any such use that would involve the carrying out of new development must be disregarded. It has been inferred from this (*Brookdene Investments Ltd.* v. *M.H.L.G.* [1970]) that development which is not new development may therefore be considered; this covers any development in the 8th Schedule to the 1971 Act which is often referred to as "existing use development". However, because one is considering whether land is or is not reasonably capable of beneficial use in its existing state, one may only consider 8th Schedule development involving a change of use—e.g., a change of use within the Town and Country Planning (Use Classes for Third Schedule Purposes) Order 1948 (No 955).

If planning permission has been granted for development or the local planning authority or the Secretary of State has undertaken to grant planning permission, the owner serving a purchase notice must show that the land could still not be rendered capable of reasonable beneficial use. However, the limitation in section 180(2) (see above) would seem also to apply here. In other words if you had planning permission for new development, no account should be taken of this in determining whether the land is or is not capable of reasonably beneficial use in its existing state. It is the practice of the Secretary of State not to consider 8th Schedule development that needs express planning permission.

The final point, which applies generally to the problem of reasonably beneficial use, is that, in deciding what is beneficial, it is relevant to make a comparison between the existing use value and the value of the land with the benefit of any relevant 8th Schedule development (see the *Brookdene* case). Such a comparison may be one of the matters which the Minister considers. See also Circular 13/1983—Purchase Notices.

Existing state

One is required to consider whether land is capable of reasonably beneficial use in its existing state. This must mean that land without buildings must be considered as land without buildings: amenity land as amenity land, and so on. It is doubtful whether existing state refers to the state of repair of buildings, although there seems no reason why it should not refer to the age and suitability of a particular building as a description of its general characteristics. A building of the nineteenth century may be in good or bad repair, but its existing state is the present building without improvement. If the building is in a very bad state of repair, a state of dereliction, repair may then be relevant and existing state could in those circumstances refer to the building in a state of dereliction.

Examples
The following examples may clarify some of these points:

1. A strip of land adjoining a highway is used by a nurseryman to grow roses. An application for planning permission to build a petrol filling station is refused. Can a purchase notice be served? In applying the first test, it would probably be conceded that growing roses was a reasonably beneficial use of the land, and the fact that it was less profitable than a petrol filling station is not relevant. It would be unnecessary to apply the second test; a purchase notice would be unsuccessful.

2. A rambling old building in a conservation area and in a very bad state of repair has, until recently, been used for offices. The low rental value of this building for office purposes renders it uneconomic to carry out repairs and improvements to the present building. An application to demolish and redevelop the site is refused. In considering whether a successful purchase notice could be served, the first test requires us to decide whether the existing building, in its existing state, is incapable of reasonably beneficial use. Although unoccupied, the present use is offices, but in its existing state of age and dereliction, that use is not reasonably beneficial because rental income would not cover outgoings. The second test is then applied. Does the building, in its existing state, have a reasonably beneficial use for a purpose other than offices which does not involve new development? The answer is probably no, as a change of use will almost certainly involve new development: a purchase notice is likely to succeed in this example.

17.4 The Procedure

The procedure for the service of a purchase notice is found in sections 181–183 of the 1971 Act. The purchase notice is served on the district council (or London borough) within twelve months of the decision. Within three months of the service of the purchase notice, the council must serve a counter notice stating:

(a) that the council is willing to comply and to purchase the land; or
(b) that another specified authority is willing to purchase; or
(c) that neither the council nor any other authority are willing to accept the purchase notice, and that a copy has been sent to the Secretary of State together with a copy of the notice expressing unwillingness.

If (c) applies, the Secretary of State invites representations from the owner, the council and the county planning authority. And if he has in mind substituting any other authority for the council as being required to comply with the purchase notice, he seeks their views as well. If required, the Secretary of State holds a hearing or public local inquiry.

The Secretary of State may take the following courses of action (section 183). He may confirm the purchase notice where he is satisfied the various requirements have been met. He may substitute another authority for the council upon whom the notice was served. In lieu of confirming the purchase notice, he may grant planning permission for the development originally applied for, or vary or revoke any conditions attached to a planning permission, with the object of enabling the land to be rendered capable of reasonably beneficial use. If the Secretary of State considers the land, or part of the land, could be rendered capable of reasonably beneficial use, he may, in lieu of confirming the purchase notice, direct that planning permission should be granted for any development he thinks would achieve this.

Unless the Secretary of State has before him an appeal against the planning decision, in which case the time-table is suspended, a purchase notice is deemed to be confirmed if the Secretary of State fails to make a decision before the expiration of the time limit in section 186. That time limit is the earlier of:

nine months from the date of the service of the purchase notice; or

six months from the date on which a copy of the purchase notice was transmitted to the Secretary of State.

If a purchase notice is accepted by the council or some other authority, or confirmed by the Secretary of State, the authority acquiring are deemed to have served a notice to treat. The procedure from then on, and the compensation to be paid for the land, are the same as any compulsory purchase.

Chapter 18

Compensation

Introduction	217
Interference to property rights: is there a right to compensation?	218
Compensation for refusal of planning permission	219
Compensation for revocation, modification or discontinuance orders	227
Compensation in connection with Listed Buildings and Ancient Monuments	229
Compensation in connection with tree preservation orders, control of advertisements and stop notices	231

18.1 Introduction

There are two views about planning and the right to compensation if development control decisions affect the aspirations of landowners. The first is that planning and development control is an interference with property rights, and affected landowners should be entitled to compensation in accordance with the principles of the common law. The second view is that as the right to develop was in effect nationalised in 1948, planning and development control does not interfere with property rights but is akin to any other regulatory legislation which has social, welfare, economic or other objectives for the benefit of the wider community: all landowners suffer the losses for the greater benefit of all.

In fact, as this chapter describes, the statutory rights to compensation are today a bit of a compromise. The present legislation appears to recognise the theory that development rights, with some exceptions, were nationalised in 1948, and so provides no compensation for the ordinary denial of planning permission. As a recognition that the rights to develop were in effect nationalised in 1948, the 1947 Act made provision for a compensation claim for the loss of those rights. For the reasons explained below, that compensation was not, in general, paid out. It may now be claimed only where planning permission is refused for "new" development on the land in question, the claim having remained unsatisfied since 1948.

However, certain decisions are regarded by the legislation as taking away more than was nationalised in 1948; it is in respect of these matters that compensation may be available.

If the theory is correct that development rights were nationalised in 1948, it seems illogical that the value of those development rights may be retained by the fortuitous landowner who obtains planning permission. Some argue that this benefit belongs to the State. Again we had a sort of compromise in the form of development land tax on this benefit until its abolition in 1985.

18.2   Interference to property rights: is there a right to compensation?

There is said to be a principle which was restated by Viscount Simonds in *Belfast Corpn* v. *O.D. Cars Ltd.* [1960] HL:

> "It is no doubt the law that the intention to take away property without compensation is not to be imputed to the legislature unless expressed in unequivocal terms."

In that case the House of Lords decided that the Northern Ireland planning legislation was a regulatory measure and did not amount to the taking of "any property without compensation" contrary to the constitutional protection in the Government of Ireland Act 1920. Although the principle, that it is presumed that property is not taken without compensation, has been repeated in many cases, doubt was expressed by Viscount Radcliffe in *Burmah Oil Co.* v. *Lord Advocate* [1964] HL as to whether it was a right known to the common law:

> "There is not in our history any known case in which a court of law has declared such compensation to be due as of right."

After reviewing the cases involving the exercise of the royal prerogative to take property, he concluded there was no common law right to compensation where property was taken by the Crown, rather the so-called principle was ordinary public sentiment; the expectation that a government would not take property in a civilised society without compensation. There is, however, a substantial body of jurists and philosophers who have argued that property cannot be taken without compensation. Their views had a profound influence on the constitution of the United States of America, as the Fifth Amendment provides that private property cannot be taken without fair compensation.

The question that has arisen in the United States, and also arises in our experience in this country, is whether planning and development control decisions that restrict development rights are a taking of property that may invoke the principle. Clearly every restriction imposed by authorities deprives an owner of rights that he previously enjoyed, and if those rights are restricted to prevent some use or development harmful or dangerous to public interest, the non-payment of compensation is probably justified. But in an American case, *Pennsylvania Coal Co.* v. *Mahon* [1922] and cited in the *Belfast* case, Holmes J. said:

> "The general rule at least is, that while property may be regulated to a certain extent, if regulation goes too far it will be recognised as a taking."

More recently the United States Supreme Court decided that a planning restriction imposed to protect a famous building did not amount to a 'taking of private property' as it did not restrict the owner's existing use of the building, nor did it prevent the owner from transferring its development rights to another building: *Penn Central Transport Co.* v. *New York City* [1977].

In England, there is no written constitutional limit on Parliament's powers to authorise restrictions on property rights, and so any Act of Parliament imposing restrictions without compensation is perfectly valid in English law: but that is not to say it may not be contrary to the European Convention on Human Rights. A person who is affected by a law which imposes such restrictions on his property as to amount to a breach of the articles or protocols of the Convention may lodge a complaint with the European Commission on Human Rights. But as a State may enforce laws which control the use of property in the public interest, it can probably justify most planning restrictions. If the State enforced a law which denied any use of a person's property without compensation, that would be going too far. Under the planning Acts, the purchase notice procedure (see chapter 17) provides a suitable remedy for such a situation. For further reading: *Compensation for compulsory acquisition and remedies for planning restrictions:* Justice Report 1969.

18.3   Compensation for refusal of planning permission

1.   Background

If the rights to develop or use land without restriction are considered as part of the rights of a property owner, then these rights were taken away on the 1st July, 1948 by the provisions of the Town and Country Planning Act 1947. The Act provided that planning permission was required for the development of land (this included buildings, mining and engineering operations, and the making of a material change of use of land or buildings) and that if planning permission was refused for any development, other than some minor classes of development called "existing use development", no compensation was payable.

The Act also provided that if planning permission was granted for any development, other than existing use development, 100% of the development value was to be paid, as a development charge, to a body called the Central Land Board.

A landowner, in 1948, who considered he had been deprived of development value by the loss of the rights to develop, either because planning permission would be refused or, if granted, he would have had to pay the development charge, was entitled to make a claim, under Part VI of the Act, for compensation from a fund of £300 million set up for the purpose.

Although the development charge has long been abolished, this short historical sketch explains two claims that may be made today if planning permission is refused. Firstly, a claim may be made upon a refusal of planning permission if the Part VI claim, made in 1948 for the loss of development value, has not yet been paid out: see 2 below. Secondly, a claim may be made if planning permission is refused for some of the classes of existing use development; such development was, and still is, regarded as the landowner's right, it was not taken away in 1948, and although it needs planning permission, if that is refused, compensation is available: see 3 below.

A development order may grant planning permission for development (for example, the General Development Order 1977). If that planning permission is withdrawn from the order (such as by an Article 4 Direction under the 1977 Order), and a subsequent application for permission is refused, compensation may be payable. See 4 below.

2. Compensation for the "nationalisation" of development rights in 1948

This compensation only becomes payable today if planning permission is refused for "new" development, a Part VI claim was made in 1948 for the loss of development value, and there remains an "unexpended balance of established development value" in respect of the affected land. "New" development means any development other than the classes of existing use development specified in the

Eighth Schedule to the 1971 Act (section 22(5)). These classes
are more fully described in Appendix C of the author's companion volume, *Compulsory Purchase and Compensation*. The
Government made a proposal (1986) to abolish this compensation
claim.

In a consultation paper (1986) the government proposed that
the whole of Part VII of the 1971 Act should be repealed. After
a transitional period, claims for a refusal of planning permission for 'new development' on land registered with an unexpended balance of established development value would be abolished.

(a) Unexpended balance of established development value

Part VII of the 1971 Act provides for the payment of compensation for the refusal of planning permission, or a grant subject
to conditions, for the new development of land if at the time
of the decision the land has an "unexpended balance of established development value".

The "Part VI claims" under the 1947 Act were, in general,
never paid; this was due to a change of government in 1951
and the abolition of the development charge (but not the need
to obtain planning permission). The established claims are
adjusted to take into account any amounts actually paid out;
aggregated together if a lessee and the freehold reversioner of
the same land had both made claims in 1948; apportioned
if claims are made in respect of land in 1948 which is now
in divided ownership; and then increased by one-seventh in
lieu of interest lost between 1948 and 1955, the date the changes
were made. The resultant sum, which attached to the land,
is called the "unexpended balance of established development
value" (section 135–139).

It is relatively uncommon to come across land with an unexpended balance of established development value today; such
land would have been the land with development value in 1948;
if that land has been developed, the value of that development
is deducted from the unexpended balance, and a similar deduc-
tion is made if any compensation has been paid for a planning
permission refusal. The balance is extinguished if land is compulsorily acquired (because compensation for land taken
includes development value) and the balance is also extinguished or reduced by any payment of severance or injurious
affection compensation, in connection with the compulsory acquisition of other land, made in respect of the loss of development value (sections 140–144).

(b) The right to compensation

A person is entitled to compensation where a decision is made to refuse planning permission for new development, or to grant permission subject to conditions, the land has an unexpended balance of established development value (see (a) above) and the value of the person's interest in the land is depreciated by the decision (section 146 of the 1971 Act).

(c) Exceptions to the right to compensation: sections 147–148

Compensation is not payable if the decision was to refuse planning permission to make a material change of use of any buildings or other land, or was a decision made in respect of applications under the advertisement control regulations for consent to the display of advertisements.

Neither is compensation payable in respect of a decision granting planning permission, but including conditions as to the number or disposition of buildings, the dimensions, design, materials, layout, provision for vehicles, use of any buildings or other land and access to a highway; or in respect of any condition attached to planning permission to win and work minerals.

Compensation is not payable if the reason for the refusal of planning permission is that the development proposed is premature having regard to the development plan or there is any deficiency in the provision of water supplies or sewerage services. But this bar on the right to compensation does not apply if planning permission is refused in respect of the same land for the same reasons on an application made more than seven years after a similar decision.

If planning permission is refused on the grounds that the land is unsuitable for the proposed development because of its liability to flooding or subsidence, there is no right to compensation.

(d) The amount of compensation

If, despite all the hurdles so far considered, a person finds that he has a right to compensation, he may be disappointed to learn that he is only entitled to the depreciation in the value of his interest due to the decision *or* the amount of the unexpended balance relating to the affected land, whichever is the less (section 152).

(e) Procedure

A claim must be made to the Secretary of State within six months of the planning decision. The amount of compensation and any necessary apportionments are notified to the claimant and other persons with interests in the land; disputes are referred to the Lands Tribunal (sections 154–157).

If any new development is subsequently permitted on the land, it cannot be carried out until any compensation already paid in respect of that land has been recovered by the Secretary of State. Accordingly, where a payment of compensation exceeding £20 has been made, the amounts and details of any apportionment and the planning decision are registered on the local land charges register as a "compensation notice" (section 158–161). Failure to disclose a "compensation notice" to a subsequent purchaser conducting an official search of the local land charges register does not render the notice void against that purchaser. Such a purchaser may be compensated for his loss due to the failure to disclose the notice: section 10 of the Local Land Charges Act 1975.

3.   Compensation for a refusal of planning permission for "existing use development".

It will be recalled that certain classes of development, called "existing use development", were excepted from some of the provisions of the 1947 Act: the idea was that the right to carry out minor forms of development in respect of existing buildings, or existing uses of buildings and other land should not, in effect, be regarded as nationalised. Although planning permission was required for these classes of development, if it was refused, or an existing planning permission was revoked or modified, compensation for the loss of development value could be obtained as of right for some of these classes. Also, the value of the right to carry out development of any of these classes was taken into account in the assessment of compensation for a compulaory acquision of land. The development charge was not payable if planning permission was granted.

Today, the position is much the same, although the development charge has long been abolished. The classes of existing use development are found in the Eighth Schedule to the 1971 Act; upon a refusal of planning permission for development within Part II of this Schedule, compensation is payable; upon a compulsory acquisition of land, the value attributable to a right to carry out development of any of the classes in Part I and Part II of the Schedule must be paid (unless already paid out as compensation for a planning refusal).

Because of the unnecessary confusion between the classes of development in the Eighth Schedule and permitted development, the government (1986) has proposed that the right to compensation for a refusal of planning permission for existing use development should be repealed.

(a) The right to compensation: section 169
If planning permission is refused, or granted subject to conditions, in respect of development in Part II of the Eighth Schedule upon appeal to the Secretary of State or on an application referred to him, any person with an interest in the land may make a claim for compensation. The planning decision must be on an application for development that is within the tolerances set out in the classes of development in Part II, and compensation claims cannot be made where the application was for an increase above the tolerances: *Peaktop (Hampstead) Properties Ltd.* v. *Camden L.B.C.* [1983].

It should be pointed out that deemed planning permission is available under the general development order 1977 for the enlargement, improvement or other alteration of dwellinghouses, industrial, agricultural and forestry buildings and warehouses within specified tolerances. To that extent, planning refusals for such development will only occur where an Article 4 direction has withdrawn the deemed planning permission, or the G.D.O. is amended or revoked.

A claimant must show that the value of his interest is less than it would have been had the planning permission been granted. The amount of compensation, which is payable by the local planning authority, is the depreciation in value of the claimant's interest. In determining that depreciation, it must be assumed that any further applications for the same development would receive the same decision, but if the Secretary of State undertakes to grant some other development, the value of that must be taken into account.

The Secretary of State may decide that any condition imposed in a planning permission as to design, external appearance, size or height of buildings, which are reasonable in the local circumstances, shall be disregarded for the purpose of assessing any compensation.

If the owner of the land affected by an adverse planning decision serves a purchase notice, he cannot at the same time claim compensation under this provision of the Act. If he has been refused planning permission for development in Part I of the Eighth Schedule, essentially development consisting of the rebuilding of buildings, he cannot claim planning compensation; but if it is possible to serve a purchase notice the compulsory purchase compensation will include the value of the right to rebuild buildings and carry out other development within Part I of the Schedule.

(b) Summary of the classes of development in Part II ranking for compensation under section 169

Class 3. Alterations to buildings
Buildings in existence on 1 July 1948:
The enlargement, improvement or other alteration, as often as occasion may require so long as the cubic content of the original building is not increased or exceeded by more than one tenth (in the case of a dwellinghouse it is one tenth or 1,750 cu ft, whichever is the larger).

This class does not extend to the enlargement of a building in existence on 1 July 1948 if the building contains two or more separate dwellings divided horizontally from each other or from some other part of the building; and the enlargement would result in either an increase in the number of such dwellings contained in the building or an increase of more than one tenth in the cubic content of any such dwelling contained in the building: section 1, Town and Country Planning (Compensation) Act 1985 (to prevent compensation claims in relation to blocks of flats following *Peaktop (Hampstead) Properties Ltd. v. Camden L.B.C.* [1983]).

Buildings erected after 1 July 1948:
The improvement or other alteration, as often as occasion may require of any building in existence on the date when a claim for compensation is made. No increase in cubic content can be assumed in respect of any building erected after 1 July 1948.

For the purposes of assessing compensation, section 278 provides that any assumption of planning permission for this class is subject to the conditions in Schedule 18 to the 1971 Act. These conditions provide that in the case of an original building to the site the amount of gross floor space which may be used for any purpose shall not exceed by more than 10% the amount of gross floor space which was last used for that purpose in the original building. In the case of a building which is not original, for example because it replaced an earlier building, no increase in gross floor space can be assumed.

In *Church Cottage Investments v. Hillingdon L.B.C.* [1986], a series of five blocks of flats were regarded as one building for the purposes of this class because of the continuous bonding of the external brickwork.

Class 4. Certain building and other operations on agricultural or forestry land.

Class 5. Winning and working of minerals on and for agricultural land.

Class 6. Changes of uses within a class specified in the Town and Country Planning (Uses Classes for Third Schedule Purposes) Order 1948.

Class 7. Increases in existing uses

Part of a building or other land used for a purpose: an increase in the existing use of any building used for a particular purpose so long as the additional part of the building so used does not exceed 10% of the cubic content of the part of the building so used on 1 July 1948, or if first used after that date, on the date when the use first started. This class does not apply to buildings erected after 1 July 1948. In the case of other land, the limit is no more than 10% of the use on 1 July 1948.

Class 8. Deposit of waste materials or refuse on a site used for mineral workings on 1 July 1948.

4.   Compensation for refusal of planning permission for development specified in a Development Order.

This right to claim compensation for the refusal of planning permission, or its grant subject to conditions, seems at odds with the general philosophy of the 1971 Act that compensation is not generally payable for a planning refusal. However, section 165 provides that if planning permission has been granted by a development order, and the General Development Order of 1977 is a typical example, and that permission is withdrawn by revocation or amendment of the Order or by the issue of a direction (such as an Article 4 direction under the GDO 1977), then, if a person is subsequently refused planning permission for that development or it is granted subject to conditions, he is entitled to compensation. In the case of the revocation or amendment of the order, the planning application must have been made within twelve months of the revocation or amendment: section 1, Town and County Planning (Compensation) Act 1985. The amount of compensation and the procedure involved is the same as that for a revocation or modification of a planning permission granted following an express application; reference should be made to the section below. A person with a licence to use land may be a "person interested in land" and entitled to claim compensation: *Pennine Raceway Ltd.* v. *Kirklees M.D.C.* [1982].

If any application is made for planning permission for development that exceeds any of the tolerances in the definitions of development in the general development order, the whole of the development is outside the scope of the order: *Fayrewood Fish Farms* v. *Secretary of State for the Environment* [1984].

Permission for the development of operational land of statutory undertakers is often given in a development order (e.g. power stations); if such an order is withdrawn, compensation is not payable, however, under this section.

18.4 Compensation for revocation, modification and discontinuance orders

Under section 45 of the 1971 Act, a planning permission already granted may be revoked or modified by an order confirmed by the Secretary of State before the building or other operations to which it relates have been completed, or, if it permits a change of use, before that change has taken place.

Section 51 of the same Act enables a local planning authority to serve a discontinuance order, which must be confirmed by the Secretary of State, such an order can require the discontinuance of any use of land, or impose conditions as to its further use, or require the alteration or removal of any buildings or works.

The powers clearly interfere with rights already enjoyed by persons with interests in the land: the 1971 Act provides for compensation.

1. Compensation for the revocation or modification of a planning permission

Section 164 provides that a person, who has an interest in land affected by an order for the revocation or modification of a planning permission, may claim from the local planning authority compensation for the following matters: expenditure incurred on work rendered abortive by the order and other loss or damage directly attributable to that order. The preparation of plans and other similar preparatory matters can be included in the claim, if such work is also abortive; but any other work done before the grant of planning permission is disregarded. The claim must be made within six months of the order.

A person who has a licence to use land for motorcar and motorcycle racing is "a person interested in land" and entitled to claim compensation: *Pennine Raceway Ltd.* v. *Kirklees M.D.C.* [1982].

Apart from compensation for abortive work already carried out, a claimant, with an interest in the land, is entitled to compensation for the depreciation in the value of his interest by reason of the loss of development rights; but in this connection, it is assumed that planning permission would be granted for development of any class specified in the Eighth Schedule (see above). This presents a problem if the revocation order in fact concerns any such development. The claimant should immediately reapply for planning permission, and, when refused, claim compensation as described above; but if this proposed development is of one of the classes within Part I of the Eighth Schedule, he will be entitled to no compensation at all for the loss of development rights!

Compensation is not restricted to a depreciation in land value, it includes any loss or damage:

> *Hobbs (Quarries) Ltd.* v. *Somerset C.C.* [1975] LT
> A planning permission, granted in 1947, to work limestone in a quarry was revoked. At the time, the reserves of limestone amounted to 2 million tons and it was accepted as almost certain that the claimants, but for the revocation, would have obtained a sub-contract for the supply of material for the construction of the M5 motorway. Had that contract been obtained, they would have earned nearly £200,000 in profits; but without that contract they would have earned £84,000 supplying the general market.
>
> The depreciation in the market value of the quarry due to the revocation order was agreed to have been £72,000. The Tribunal decided that the loss of the motorway contract was not too remote; that, although £72,000 was the depreciation in the market value of the quarry, the claimant could not have purchased another quarry to earn the same profits; and, as the company did not claim for the depreciation in value of the land they could have loss of profits instead, suitably deferred.

Where it is proposed to move a business to a site, and planning permission for that site is revoked, compensation may be claimed for loss of profits to that business: *Cawoods Aggregates (Southeast) Ltd.* v. *Southwark B.C.* [1982]. In *Pennine Raceways Ltd.* v. *Kirklees M.D.C.* [1984], where a claim was made following an Article 4 direction under section 164 as applied by section 165, the compensation was awarded on the loss of profits. These were for a period of five years and adjusted to allow for corporation tax, but no allowance for deferment was made. Reinstatement work was disallowed as the licensee was obliged to do this under the terms of his licence.

There is no provision for the payment of interest from the date of the revocation order, although, if a reference is made to the Lands Tribunal, that body has discretion to award interest from the date of its award. In *Loromah Ltd.* v. *Haringay L.B.C.* [1978] LT, it was held that the payment of Development Land Tax on the compensation sum was not attributable directly to the revocation, accordingly any such liability could not be added.

Where compensation in excess of £20 is paid, it is registrable and repayable if development is subsequently allowed.

2. Compensation in respect of a discontinuance order: section 170

A claim for compensation can be made if any person has suffered damage, in consequence of a discontinuance order, by a depreciation of the value of his interest in the land; he is also entitled to be compensated for damage attributable to "being disturbed in his enjoyment of the land".

Additionally, the costs of carrying out any work to comply with the order which have been reasonably incurred for that purpose can also be recovered.

18.5 Compensation in connection with Listed Buildings and Ancient Monuments

A building of special architectural or historic interest may be listed under section 54 of the 1971 Act. It then becomes an offence if any works are carried out for the demolition of a listed building or for its alteration or extension in any manner which would affect its character as such a building, without obtaining a listed building consent. Compensation is not payable upon the listing of a building, although there are certain rights, detailed below, in connection with listed building consents and building preservation notices. There are similar provisions in the Ancient Monuments and Archaeological Areas Act 1979 in respect of scheduled monuments: these are considered below.

1. Compensation for the refusal of listed building consent: section 171

Compensation is payable if listed building consent is refused by the Secretary of State, or granted subject to conditions, for the alteration or extension of a listed building. The work proposed must not constitute development within the meaning of the Act, or, if it does, the development is permitted by a development order. There is no compensation for a refusal of consent to demolish a listed building.

Compensation shall equal the difference between the value of the claimant's interest had the consent been granted, and its value subject to the decision of the Secretary of State (including any alternative consent he may have granted or undertaken to grant).

2.   Compensation for the revocation or modification of a listed building consent: section 172

Compensation for the revocation or modification of a listed building consent is payable in the same circumstances as the revocation of a planning permission—see above.

3.   Compensation in respect of a building preservation notice: section 173

Under section 58 of the 1971 Act, a local planning authority may serve a "building preservation notice" on the owner and occupier of a building. They will do so where it is intended to seek the listing of the building and the building requires temporary protection because it is in danger of demolition or alteration.

If the Secretary of State decides not to list the building, the building preservation notice, and the temporary protection it afforded, lapses. Any person with an interest in the building at the time of the notice may then claim compensation in respect of any loss or damage directly attributable to the effect of the notice. The section permits the costs involved in terminating a contract to be claimed where the proposed work, say demolition, is prevented by the notice. However, such expenses cannot be claimed if the building is eventually listed. This can produce severe hardship: in *Amalgamated Investment and Property Co. Ltd.* v. *John Walker & Sons Ltd.* [1976] CA, a building sold for development was listed one day after the plaintiff signed a contract to purchase for nearly £1¾ million. The effect of listing was to reduce the value of the building to £200,000. *Amalgamated* were bound by their contract and could not seek a reduction in price: the 1971 Act provided no right to claim their loss of £1½ million.

4.   Compensation in respect of Ancient Monuments

Under the Ancient Monuments and Archaeological Areas Act 1979, the Secretary of State may compile a schedule of monuments; it then becomes an offence to carry out certain works to a "scheduled monument" without consent.

If scheduled monument consent is refused, or granted subject to conditions, compensation is payable to any person who has an interest in the monument and who "incurs expenditure or otherwise sustains any loss or damage in consequence" (section 2).

Compensation is only payable for a refusal of consent for the following works:

(a) works reasonably necessary for development for which planning permission was granted before the monument was scheduled;
(b) works which do not constitute development (or, for which permission is granted by a development order), other than works for the demolition or destruction of the monument;
(c) works which are reasonably necessary for the continuation of any use of the monument for any purpose for which it was in use immediately before the application for scheduled monument consent (section 7).

18.6   Compensation in connection with tree preservation orders, control of advertisements and stop notices

1.   Tree preservation orders: sections 174–175 of the 1971 Act

Section 60 of the 1971 Act empowers a local planning authority to make a tree preservation order for the preservation of specified trees, groups of trees or woodlands. The order may prohibit the cutting down, topping, lopping of trees without the authority's consent; it may also provide for replanting when any part of a woodland is felled in the course of permitted forestry operations.

If consent is refused for any matter prohibited by a tree preservation order, then compensation in respect of loss or damage as a result of that refusal is payable if the order itself permits of this. The standard form of order allows the payment of compensation for a refusal of consent, a grant subject to conditions and the revocation or modification of a consent to fell or lop trees, the subject of the order. However, any such decision which the authority certifies was made to ensure that the trees were preserved in the interest of good forestry or, in relation to individual trees, because they have outstanding or special amenity value, will not give rise to a liability to pay compensation.

When payable, compensation may equal the depreciation in the value of the trees: *Cardigan Timber Co.* v. *Cardiganshire C.C.* [1957] LT. It would seem that the capital value of the profits that could have been made from the land by growing Christmas trees had felling taken place cannot be recovered: *Bollans* v. *Surrey C.C.* [1968] LT. In *Bell* v. *Canterbury City Council* [1986], the Lands Tribunal allowed a claim based on the difference between the value of the land growing trees protected by a TPO, and the value of the land had the owner been able to convert the land to agricultural purposes.

A licence is required for the felling of timber, with some exceptions, under the Forestry Act 1967: there is provision in that Act for compensation if such a licence is refused.

In respect of a direction made under the provisions of a tree preservation order that replanting should take place, compensation for the loss or damage incurred complying with the direction is payable. However, such compensation is only payable where the Forestry Commission consider the replanting would not be in the interests of commercial forestry and the local planning authority require such replanting in the interest of amenity.

2.   Restriction on Advertisements

The Control of Advertisement Regulations 1984 provide for restricting and regulating the display of advertisements in the interests of amenity or public safety.

No compensation is payable for a refusal of consent to display an advertisement. But section 176 of the 1971 Act does provide for compensation to any person who carries out work to comply with the regulations in the following circumstances: he is entitled to any expenses reasonably incurred in complying with an order for removing an advertisement displayed on the 1st August, 1948; or for discontinuing the use of a site used for an advertisement displayed on that date. A claimant must submit his claim to the local planning authority within six months of completing the necessary work.

3.   Stop Notices

Section 90 of the 1971 Act (as amended by the Town and Country Planning (Amendment) Act 1977) empowers a local planning authority, who have served an enforcement notice requiring a breach of planning control to be remedied, to serve a further notice called a "stop notice". The stop notice may prevent the carrying out of the activity alleged to constitute the planning breach before the expiration of the period of compliance allowed in the enforcement notice.

If the enforcement notice takes effect, there is no compensation for loss or expense incurred in complying with such a notice, or a stop notice that may have been served with it. However, section 177 of the 1971 Act (as amended by the 1977 Act) does provide compensation for loss or damage directly attributable to a stop notice in the following cases: the enforcement notice is quashed on appeal; the enforcement notice is varied so that the matter covered by the stop notice is no longer part of the enforcement notice; and, either the enforcement notice or the stop notice is withdrawn. In such cases, any sum payable in respect of a breach of contract made necessary by compliance with a stop notice is considered to be loss or damage attributable to the prohibition in a stop notice.

A claim must be made within six months of the decision of the Secretary of State, and an informal letter may constitute such a claim: *Texas Home Care Ltd.* v. *Lewes D.C.* [1986]. The costs of the enforcement appeal cannot be recovered: *J. Sample (Warkworth) Ltd.* v. *Alnwick D.C.* [1981].

Although the Lands Tribunal may at its discretion allow interest on the sum awarded from the date of the award, there is no power to allow interest on the award between the date when the stop notice ceases to take effect and the date of the Tribunal's decision: *Robert Barnes & Co. Ltd.* v. *Malvern Hills D.C.* [1985]. Where actual interest charges have been incurred, and are attributable to the stop notice, these are recoverable: *J. Sample (Warkworth) Ltd.* v. *Alnwick D.C.* [1984].

Chapter 19

Judicial Supervision

Introduction   235
The Statutory Rights of Appeal to the Courts   236
Common Law Judicial Review   238
Grounds of Challenge   239
Private Law Remedies   242
Challenging the Validity of Enforcement Notices   243

19.1 Introduction

Most readers will have observed by now that the development control process has received a good deal of judicial interest. The purpose of this chapter is to describe how cases are brought before the courts, and the legal grounds upon which they are founded. The Town and Country Planning Act 1971 contains procedures for the judicial review of certain decisions and actions of local planning authorities and the Secretary of State. Apart from these statutory procedures, there is also a right to judicial review at common law. In many circumstances, this common law right is precluded by the statute, but where it is not precluded, it has provided a useful addition to the rights of aggrieved parties, as judicial review at common law may be available in circumstances outside the scope of the statutory right to review.

Although the scope of the statutory and common law rights to judicial review may differ, the principles upon which the courts have exercised these rights are similar. The Divisional Court of the Queen's Bench Division of the High Court is concerned with the judicial supervision of authorities or ministers to ensure that they act within the law; that their administrative and discretionary decisions are decisions that can properly be made under the law; and that they follow the statutory procedures as well as the rules of natural justice to ensure openness, fairness and impartiality where these are considered appropriate. The Court has developed a number of principles to test the legality of administrative decisions, they possess a mystery and meaning understandable only to the initiated!

The expectations of the Court are that administrative decisions are made in accordance with these principles, and that the decision-makers think appropriately. It is doubtful whether this really happens. Administrative decisions are made against a wide background of facts, policies and political views; the principles of this branch of the law, to be followed in decision-making, are rarely understood.

In any event these principles are often satisfied without in any way altering a decision. For example, the decision-maker must have regard to all the relevant considerations when making his decision (see below). If the Court later identifies a matter that was omitted from the decision-maker's consideration, then provided that matter is then considered, the original decision may still be made. It seems that often the right incantation in a written decision is all that is required.

These remarks may suggest a certain impatience with this aspect of the subject. That is not entirely the case as blatant unfairness, procedural irregularity or illegality should be remedied; although few cases seem to involve this. Also the large number of cases are extremely useful in determining the scope and meaning of the statutes and the legal boundaries of decisions.

19.2   The Statutory Rights of Appeal to the Courts

The right to challenge the validity of structure and local plans, certain orders, decisions and directions is precluded except in the circumstances outlined below (section 242 of the 1971 Act). The orders include revocation, discontinuance and tree preservation orders; and the decisions are those of the Secretary of State, either where some planning matter is referred to him, or following an appeal. The purpose of restricting the challenge of these matters is to ensure that action can only be taken within a limited period of six weeks so as to ensure that after that period there is no continuing legal uncertainty. Even if the grounds for challenging the legal validity of some plan, order, decision or direction is not apparent until after that period, the expiration of the six weeks will prevent any appeal to the High Court (*R. v. Secretary of State for the Environment ex p. Ostler* [1976]).

The right to question the validity of an enforcement notice or a listed building enforcement notice is separately considered below.

1.   Challenging development plans

A structure or local plan, or any alteration repeal or replacement of a plan, or any order made under the 1971 Act in respect of highways, may be challenged in the High Court within six weeks (section 244). The party making the application must be a "person aggrieved" and must either show that the development plan or order is outside the powers of the Act or that he has been "substantially prejudiced" by a failure to comply with the statutory procedures.

In *Edwin H. Bradley & Son* v. *Secretary of State for the Environment* [1982], the Court refused to quash a plan as the Secretary of State had sufficient information, and had given adequate reasons for excluding the applicant's land for development. A plan that makes express reference to guidelines that are not part of the plan may be quashed as not complying with the law to formulate "proposals for the development and other use of land in the area": *Great Portland Estates* v. *Westminster City Council* [1984]. The Court of Appeal doubted whether only part of a plan could be quashed in *Buckinghamshire C.C.* v. *Hall Aggregates Ltd.* [1985], and were also divided as to whether the right to challenge included all the preliminary stages in the preparation of a plan. But the local plan in *Fourth Investments Ltd.* v. *Bury B.C.* [1985] was quashed as the inspector could not have reached a conclusion on the adequacy of land for housing on the evidence before him.

2.   Challenging other orders and decisions

In respect of certain orders, and in respect of certain actions of the Secretary of State, a "person aggrieved" by the order or the action may question the validity of that matter in the High Court within six weeks on the ground that the order or action is outside the powers of the Act or there has been a non-compliance with some statutory procedure (section 245). The orders include those of revocation or modification, discontinuance or tree preservation; the actions include decisions of the Secretary of State on planning applications referred to him, decisions on a planning appeal, a decision to grant planning permission following an enforcement notice appeal, and other decisions in relation to such matters as tree preservation orders, advertisement control, listed building consents, and purchase notices (section 242(2)–(3)). The party making the application to the High Court must show that the order or action is outside the powers of the Act or that he has been "substantially prejudiced" by a failure to comply with statutory procedures.

It was held in *Co-operative Retail Services* v. *Secretary of State for the Environment* [1980] that a refusal to adjourn a local inquiry was not a decision within the scope of the statutory right of appeal.

3.   Person aggrieved

The statutory right of appeal to the High Court can only be brought by a "person aggrieved". Although a restricted meaning was once attached to this, so that adjoining landowners to a development, who had no legal right to have their representations considered by the Secretary of State, were held not to be entitled to appeal (*Buxton* v. *Ministry of Housing and Local Government* [1961]). A wider view of this is now taken by the Courts. In *Turner* v. *Secretary of State for the Environment* [1973], Ackner J. considered that persons who had been permitted to appear at the local inquiry could be "persons aggrieved".

4.   The Statutory Grounds of Appeal

The broad principles upon which the Courts are prepared to quash decisions and orders are really the same as where the common law judicial review applies, and are considered below. Although there is a specific statutory ground of a failure to comply with the relevant legislative requirements, and where substantial prejudice must be shown. This is also considered below.

5.   Decision of the Court

The power of the court is usually limited to quashing the decision. This would mean that the Secretary of State would have to remake his decision, avoiding the defects found by the Court.

19.3   Common Law Judicial Review

The jurisdiction of the Divisional Court of the Queen's Bench Division of the High Court goes back to the close association the original King's Bench had with the Council of the King, and the power the Court possessed over officials and other courts. The principles of judicial supervision, often referred to today as administrative law, have been substantially developed in the course of the last few decades.

The present procedure is known as an application for judicial review (Order 53 of the Rules of the Supreme Court) and the Court may make certain orders. *Certiorari* requires the official or authority to produce the record of the proceedings or the decision to the Court, and if it is bad, it is quashed. *Prohibition* is to prevent an official or authority doing something they have no power to do. *Mandamus* is an order commanding that a duty placed on an official or authority be carried out.

The procedure is for the applicant to seek leave of the Court, and if the Court accepts the matter as being arguable, there will be a full hearing. Application is usually required within three months of the decision to be reviewed.

In dealing with the statutory right of judicial review above, it was noted that certain plans, orders or actions could only be challenged in accordance with the provisions of the 1971 Act: in other words, after the particular decision has been made. The common law right to judicial supervision may be exercised before the decision has been made, or in respect of matters not covered or precluded by the statutory provisions.

Instead of seeking the orders described above, an application may be made for a declaration or an injunction. A declaration was used in *Pyx Granite Co.* v. *Ministry of Housing and Local Government* [1958] to determine the validity of certain planning conditions; and in *Heron Corporation* v. *Manchester City Council* [1978] to declare invalid the refusal of the authority to consider an application for the approval of reserved matters. In *Irlam Brick Co.* v. *Warrington B.C.* [1982], Woolf J. considered that judicial review under Order 53 was preferable to a declaration where the issues concerned the conduct of a public body, and persons beyond the immediate parties were affected. The interaction between public law and private law remedies is considered separately below.

Any person who has a sufficient interest in the matter may seek judicial review: an applicant must have *locus standi*. In *Covent Garden Community Association Ltd.* v. *Greater London Council* [1981], a local residents association were held to have *locus standi*, as representations of such bodies would be taken into account in planning appeals and inquiries; and in *Steeples* v. *Derbyshire County Council* [1981], a person was said to have *locus standi*, if he were a ratepayer or an adjoining owner as in *R.* v. *Castle Point U.D.C., ex parte Brooks* [1985].

19.4 Grounds of Challenge

The grounds upon which the High Court will accept a challenge to an administrative or policy decision, whether under the statutory appeals, or under the common law judicial review procedure, are broadly the same: the decision is *ultra vires*, or there has been some procedural irregularity. The role of the Court is to ensure that the process of decision-making is fair; it does not replace a decision with one of its own.

Three cases form the bedrock upon which all later developments in this branch of the law have evolved. In *Cooper* v. *Wandsworth Board of Works* [1863], the Court decided that the Board of Works could not pull down a house, of which no notice of construction had been received, without first giving the owner an opportunity of explaining his case. In *Associated Provincial Picture Houses* v. *Wednesbury Corpn.* [1948], Lord Green MR in the Court of Appeal said that an authority exercising some discretion must:

   (i) direct itself properly in law, and should not refuse to take into account matters that are relevant, nor take into account matters which ought not to be taken into account; and

  (ii) even if the first principle has been followed, the decision must not be so unreasonable that no reasonable authority would have made it.

Those principles, the *Wednesbury principles*, were enlarged on by Lord Denning MR in *Ashbridge Investments* v. *Minister of Housing and Local Government* [1965] C.A. He added that the Court could interfere with a decision if the decision-maker had acted on no evidence, or come to a conclusion to which on the evidence one could not reasonably come.

The grounds for judicial review of administrative decisions, and it is not always clear whether a planning decision is merely a policy matter or an administrative one, have been much developed in recent years. In *Council of Civil Service Unions* v. *Minister for the Civil Service* [1984] H.L. Lord Diplock said the grounds were:

  (a) *Illegality*—". . . I mean that the decision-maker must understand correctly the law that regulates his decision-making power and must give effect to it. . . ."

  (b) *Irrationality*—". . . I mean what can now be referred to as '*Wednesbury* unreasonableness'. It applies to a decision which is so outrageous in its defiance of logic or of accepted moral standards that no sensible person who had applied his mind to the question to be decided could have arrived at it."

  (c) *Procedural impropriety*. This covers a "failure to observe basic rules of natural justice or failure to act with procedural fairness towards the person who will be affected" as well as "failure . . . to observe procedural rules laid down in the legislative instrument by which . . . jurisdiction is conferred, even where such failure does not involve any denial of natural justice.

Examples of judicial supervision are as follows:

  R. v. *Hillingdon L.B.C. ex p. Royco Homes* [1974]
  Certiorari was granted to quash a planning decision containing conditions which were so unreasonable no reasonable authority could have imposed them.

The Covent Garden Case (see above)
A residents' association sought *certiorari* to quash a decision of the local planning authority to grant planning permission for office use contrary to a previous policy that favoured residential use of the property in Covent Garden. However, the order was not granted as there had not been a breach of statutory requirements: a modification to the local plan did not have to be made.

Fairmount Investments Ltd. v. *Secretary of State for the Environment* [1978]
Basing a decision on evidence obtained by an inspector on his site visit may involve a breach of the rules of natural justice, as a party is entitled to hear all the evidence against him. A breach of the rules may amount to *ultra vires*.

The Steeples Case (see above)
A member of the *Friends of Shipley Park* sought, and was granted, a declaration that planning permission granted by the County Council for the development of a "Wonder Park" in partnership with private developers was invalid as certain statutory procedures had not been properly complied with.

Co-operative Retail Services Ltd. v. *Taff-Ely B.C.* [1978]
A declaration and injunction was granted with the effect that a planning permission purported to have been granted for a supermarket site was invalid: the Borough Council had no power to grant, or to ratify the decision of their Clerk purporting to grant the planning permission that was issued.

Procedural irregularity and the Rules of natural justice
Where a decision is being appealed under the statutory right of appeal in the planning Act, rather than by common law judicial review, the statute requires proof of "substantial prejudice" if a procedural irregularity is being alleged. Although a serious procedural irregularity probably amounts to *ultra vires*. This separate ground is presumably to provide for the more trivial procedural irregularity. In *Performance Cars Ltd.* v. *Secretary of State for the Environment* [1977], the applicant failed to show that he had been substantially prejudiced by a refusal to give an adjournment of a length necessary to consider new evidence, the evidence made no difference to his case. Although, confusingly, that refusal was in breach of the rules of natural justice, and the decision was as a consequence *ultra vires* under the first ground.

In *Miller* v. *Weymouth and Melcombe Regis Corporation* [1974]. Kerr J. considered that if there was no substantial prejudice to the applicant as the result of a clerical error, the Court had a discretion not to quash the decision. The fact that the applicant did not make some early objection to a procedural irregularity may be accepted as showing he was not substantially prejudiced (*Davies* v. *Secretary of State for Wales* [1977]).

In *Reading B.C.* v. *Secretary of State for the Environment* [1986], it was said that even if the inquiry procedure rules have been satisfied, these did not exhaust the rules of natural justice. For Parliament could not have intended that statutory powers should be used in breach of the rules of natural justice. Secondly it was said there is no such thing as a technical breach of the rules of natural justice, and therefore substantial prejudice must be shown as in *George* v. *Secretary of State for the Environment* [1979].

Duty to give reasons
The duty to give reasons for a planning decision is imposed on the Secretary of State, or the inspector, by the inquiries procedure rules, and in practice reasons are always given. Woolf J. in *Grenfell-Baines* v. *Secretary of State for the Environment* [1985], inferring from the general duty under the *Wednesbury* principles, said it was implicit on a decision-maker to give reasons. Where the reasons are obscure, there will be a breach of this duty and the decision may be quashed: *Givaudan* v. *Minister of Housing and Local Government* [1967].

The increasing tendency in recent years to scan decisions of inspectors with the most precise scrutiny, seeking out minor issues which an inspector might not have dealt with fully, has been criticised by the Court of Appeal. In *Weitz* v. *Secretary of State for the Environment* [1987], Russell L.J. said that one must read a decision letter as a whole, and then ask whether the inspector did not or may not really have come to grips with the conflicts presented to him.

An inspector's decision letter will be regarded as disclosing inadequate reasons if it does explain the basis of the inspector's decision to the local planning authority: *Stephenson* v. *Secretary of State for the Environment* [1985].

19.5 Private Law Remedies

Examples of the use of the private law remedy of an injunction were given on an earlier page. In some circumstances there will be a cause of action in private law, such as an allegation of breach of contract, or a claim for damages for an alleged negligent statement. In *Avon C.C. v. Millard* [1985] it was said that where a landowner was in breach of a planning agreement, there was no obligation on the planning authority to exhaust the public law procedures before seeking an injunction to restrain the breach of what was a contract.

Confusion can arise where a party is seeking both to challenge an alleged unlawful decision, and to recover damages for any harm suffered. In the House of Lords case of *O'Reilly* v. *Mackman* [1983], it was said it would be an abuse of court procedures "... to permit a person seeking to establish that a decision of a public authority infringed rights to which he was entitled to protection under public law, to proceed by way of an ordinary action, and by this means evade the provision of Order 53 for the protection of such authorities". The provisions of the order filter out claims with little merit, or which do not substantial concern matters of wider public interest.

This check on private law actions did not prevent the House of Lords from allowing a claim based on negligence to be brought in *Davy* v. *Spelthorne B.C.* [1983]. The claimant alleged that he had foregone appealing an enforcement notice because of negligent advice he said he received from the planning department. His action for damages could be brought as he was not seeking to challenge the validity of the enforcement notice, and his private law claim did not really concern issues of wider public interest. It was also said that the privative clause in the planning Act (section 243(1)), that excluded a challenge of an enforcement notice otherwise than on the grounds provided by that section, did not prevent an action in private law.

19.6 Challenging the Validity of Enforcement Notices

The right to appeal to the Secretary of State against an enforcement notice, or a listed building enforcement notice, on the grounds in section 88 of the 1971 Act (or section 97 in the case of listed buildings), has already been dealt with in Chapter 14. Apart from this right of appeal, the validity of an enforcement notice cannot be challenged on any of the grounds in section 88 (see page 173) in any other legal proceedings (section 243). This would include any prosecution proceedings for failing to comply with an enforcement notice in the magistrates court. Where a person is prosecuted for breach of a stop notice, the defendant may challenge the validity of the stop notice in the magistrates court: *R.* v. *Jenner* [1983],

Section 243 does preclude an action for tort claiming damages in nuisance: *Davy Spelthorne B.C.* [1983].

In *Square Meals Frozen Foods* v. *Dunstable Corporation* [1974], a declaration was first sought to determine whether an intended user was lawful; an enforcement notice was then issued to stop the continuance of that user. It was held that as the application for a declaration was a proceeding in anticipation of enforcement, section 243 preventing that legal action from continuing.

However it was said in *Miller-Mead* v. *Minister of Housing and Local Government* [1963] that if an enforcement notice is *ultra vires* (see above) or is incurably bad in its content, it is a nullity and void. It may then be challenged by the ordinary common law right of judicial review (*Stringer* v. *Minister of Housing and Local Government* [1970]), either for *certiorari* to have the notice quashed, or for a declaration that the notice is a nullity, as confirmed in *Rhymney Valley D.C.* v. *Secretary of State for Wales* [1985].

The alternative to judicial review of an enforcement notice that is a nullity, is to await a prosecution for non-compliance, and then raise the validity of the notice as a defence to the prosecution.

If an enforcement notice is first appealed to the Secretary of State on one or more of the grounds in section 88, and the Secretary of State gives a decision in the proceedings, the appellant, the local planning authority or any other person served with a copy of an enforcement notice may appeal to the High Court on a point of law, or have a case stated for the opinion of the Court (section 246). This right must be exercised within 28 days of the decision.

The relationship between the statutory appeal and judicial review is summarised in the diagram on the opposite page.

For a fuller description of the right to appeal an enforcement, see chapter 14 above.

Summary

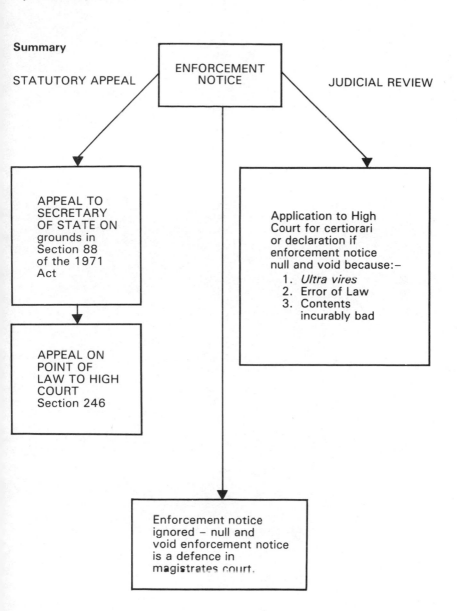

STATUTORY APPEAL

ENFORCEMENT NOTICE

JUDICIAL REVIEW

APPEAL TO SECRETARY OF STATE ON grounds in Section 88 of the 1971 Act

Application to High Court for certiorari or declaration if enforcement notice null and void because:–
1. *Ultra vires*
2. Error of Law
3. Contents incurably bad

APPEAL ON POINT OF LAW TO HIGH COURT Section 246

Enforcement notice ignored – null and void enforcement notice is a defence in magistrates court.

PART VI

SERVICES AND HIGHWAYS

Chapter 20

Provision and Adoption of Sewers

Introduction   249
Powers of Water Authorities to Provide Sewers and Works   251
Right to Requisition a Public Sewer   251
Adoption of Sewers   252
Right to connect to a Public Sewer   253

20.1 Introduction

Connection with a public sewer will be one of the objectives of a developer carrying out a development scheme. Doubtless he will be constructing sewers within the scheme and will want an assurance that such sewers can be adopted by the appropriate authority for the purposes of future maintenance. It may be possible to requisition the provision of a public sewer in certain cases; and the developer needs to know what right he has to connect to an existing sewer.

The inadequacies of a sewage system may be a reason for refusing planning permission. Arrangements concerning sewage disposal and sewers are often the subject of a planning agreement, provision being made for the commencement and rate of development to match the provision of sewers.

The authority concerned with sewers and sewage disposal is the water authority for the area under the Water Act 1973. There are also agency arrangements under which other local authorities may discharge certain functions of the water authority. The water authority is under a duty to provide such public sewers as may be necessary for effectually draining its area, and to make provision for the contents of sewers by sewage disposal works (section 14).

The Water Act provides no sanction if this duty is not carried out. Presumably if a water authority failed in its duty, a person with sufficient interest could seek *mandamus*, an order to compel the performance of a public duty.

What is a Public Sewer?

The duties and responsibilities of water authorities are in respect of public sewers, both as to provision and maintenance. A sewer is a public sewer if (Public Health Act 1936, section 20):

(a) constructed before 1 October 1937; or
(b) constructed or acquired by the local or water authority at any time (not just to drain their own property); or
(c) constructed under the private street works code for the draining of a street (see Part XI of the Highways Act 1980) and the sewers do not belong to a road maintainable at public expense by the highway authority; or
(d) adopted by the water authority following a vesting declaration.

In *Royco Homes* v. *Eatonwill Construction* [1978], a sewer was constructed by the defendant company in a lane which was subsequently adopted by the local highway authority; the intended adoption of the sewer as a public sewer was never effected as the authority never passed the necessary resolution. It was declared that by adopting the lane as a public highway maintainable at public expense, the authority had thereby "acquired" the sewer, which accordingly became a public sewer. It was assumed in this case that upon adoption, a highway, and the soil beneath it, is then owned by the highway authority. But this is not the position, and so this case must be considered as incorrect (only "the top two spits" will vest with the highway authority: per Denning L.J. in *Tithe Redemption Commission* v. *Runcorn R.D.C.* [1954]).

A sewer is a pipe for the drainage of more than one building or yard which are not in the same curtilage. Unless it is a public sewer, as defined above, it is a private responsibility. The private developer will usually take advantage of the adoption procedure as a way of relieving himself of future maintenance responsibilities. A pipe that drains only one building or buildings and yards in the same curtilage is a drain, and a drain is always a private responsibility.

In many areas there are separate pipe systems for foul drainage and surface water drainage. Both such pipe systems may be public sewers.

Maps of Public Sewers

There is a duty on local authorities to maintain a map of public sewers and of sewers to be adopted as public sewers, within their district (section 32 of the Public Health Act 1936). The map should distinguish between foul water only and surface water only public sewers where appropriate. As the *Royco* case showed, the indication on the map of a sewer is not conclusive as to the legal status of the sewer.

A developer can make use of this map in several ways: he may have a right to connect to a public sewer; he will need consent to construct anything over a public sewer; he can plan his own sewers to enable connection to the public sewer; or, if necessary, to make a requisition for a public sewer if the proposed development is domestic.

20.2 Powers of Water Authorities to Provide Sewers and Works

Section 15 of the Public Health Act 1936 provides the water authority with the necessary powers to construct public sewers and sewage disposal works. Under this power, a public sewer may be constructed in on or over any land upon giving the owner reasonable notice. The owner has no right of appeal but is entitled to compensation. Land has been widely construed to include a building (*Hutton* v. *Esher U.D.C.* [1973], where the owner's bungalow had to be demolished).

This power cannot be used by a private developer to lay a sewer through land not owned by him. If he cannot secure the necessary easements, he may persuade the water authority to exercise their powers to secure a right to lay a public sewer. The developer may be able to show that this exercise of their powers is necessary to fulfil their statutory duty to provide public sewers under section 14 of the Water Act 1973.

Or he may be able to requisition a public sewer in the circumstances next described.

20.3 Right to Requisition a Public Sewer

Section 16 of the Water Act 1973 enables landowners and local authorities to require the water authority to provide a public sewer for *domestic purposes* for the drainage of existing or new buildings.

In the case of existing buildings, a public sewer may be requisitioned if the reckonable charge attributable to the premises for the use of the sewer will be not less than one-eighth of the cost of the sewer, and the owner agrees to pay the reckonable charge for three years. The reckonable charge is the charge for the use of the sewer.

In the case of new buildings, a public sewer may be requisitioned for the drainage of buildings yet to be erected, if the public sewer will connect with a private sewer to be provided by the owners, and the owners agree to pay for 12 years the deficit between the one-eighth of the cost of the sewer and the reckonable charges paid each year for the use of the sewer.

The local authority may requisition a public sewer for existing or proposed buildings if they agree to meet the deficit between the one-eighth of the cost of the sewer and the reckonable charges for the use of the sewer.

The water authority may agree to accept a capital sum in place of the annual payments. This will usually be the most convenient arrangement for a private developer.

The water authority will be liable to a fine if they do not lay a public sewer that has been properly requisitioned within six months. Their general duty to provide public sewers is subject to the conditions in section 16 in the case of sewers required for domestic purposes. The wording of section 16 makes it clear that the water authority must provide the public sewer so that it may "communicate" with the private sewer. In *William Leech Ltd.* v. *Severn Trent Water Authority* [1981] this was held to mean that the authority must provide the public sewer to the point requisitioned by the owner to connect with his sewer, not to such part of the boundary of the owner's land as the authority may decide.

20.4   Adoption of Sewers

1.   Vesting Declaration

Section 17 of the Public Health Act 1936 makes provision for the adoption of a sewer. A water authority may make a declaration that a sewer shall vest in them: it is then a public sewer and maintainable by the authority.

An owner or owners of any sewer may request that a water authority make the vesting declaration. If any owner is aggrieved by the decision of the authority to adopt the sewer (unlikely), he may appeal to the Secretary of State.

The section specifies a number of matters to be considered by the authority before deciding to adopt: whether the sewer is adapted to or required for the general system of sewerage of the authority; whether it is constructed under a highway; the number of buildings it may serve; the method of construction and state of repair; and whether the adoption would be seriously detrimental to any objecting owner.

If the sewer is adopted, any person previously using it may continue to do so to the same extent. Otherwise the effect of vesting is to give the authority such rights as are necessary to enable them to discharge their responsibilities. This is a fee simple in the sewer determinable when the sewer ceases to exist: *Radstock Co-operative & Industrial Society* v. *North Radstock U.D.C.* [1968].

2.   Adoption Agreement

Section 18 of the Public Health Act 1936 enables an agreement to be made between a developer and the water authority under which sewers or sewage disposal works to be constructed by the developer will be adopted as public sewers by the authority. The terms of the agreement may specify the standard of construction; the obligation on the authority will be to make a vesting declaration when the works are completed.

3.   Powers of Water Authority in relation to proposed sewer

A developer proposing to construct a sewer will need planning permission as the work is regarded as an engineering operation. He may also be seeking an adoption agreement. In relation to the proposed construction of a sewer the water authority may require the developer to construct it to their stipulated specification if the proposed sewer is needed to form part of a general sewage system (section 19 of the Public Health Act 1936). The developer may appeal to the Secretary of State if he is aggrieved by these requirements.

The developer is entitled to be repaid by the water authority his reasonable extra expenses incurred to comply with these requirements, including extra maintenance costs until the sewer is adopted as a public sewer.

20.5   Right to Connect to a Public Sewer

Section 34 of the Public Health Act 1936 contains the important right of the owner or occupier of any premises or of any private sewer to connect to a public sewer. The person exercising the right may then discharge foul water or surface water through his private drain or sewer into the public sewer.

1.   Exceptions

The right of connection may not be exercised:

   (a)   to discharge liquids from a factory or a manufacturing process (domestic sewage or surface or storm water is permissible); or
   (b)   to discharge liquids or other matter which is prohibited from being discharged into a public sewer in any event i.e., certain chemicals or petroleum spirits; or
   (c)   to discharge foul water into a surface water sewer or, unless permitted, surface water into a foul water sewer; or
   (d)   to drain directly into a storm-water overflow sewer.

In *Thames Water Authority* v. *Blue and White Launderettes Ltd.* [1980] the Court of Appeal decided that the discharges from a launderette were not domestic sewage; the discharges were trade effluent produced in the course of a trade or business.

2. Procedure

Any person who wishes to exercise the right of connection must give the water authority 21 days notice of his intention. The authority may object if the proposed construction or the condition of the private drain or sewer would affect prejudicially their sewerage system. Disputes are settled in the magistrates court.

The person exercising this right may break open the street to effect the connection. However, this section gives no power to lay a drain or sewer through land not owned by the developer; he must first acquire the necessary easements or other rights. He may be able to requisition a public sewer, if required for domestic purposes, or persuade the authority to exercise their powers under section 15 (see above) at his expense, where he lacks the necessary legal rights.

The authority may respond to a notice under this section by stating that they intend to effect the necessary communication with the public sewer (section 36). The cost of this connection is paid for by the developer, and may have to be provided before the work is carried out. Although the water authority have a discretion to bear the cost or part of it themselves (section 13, Local Government (Miscellaneous Provisions) Act 1953).

Chapter 21

Water, Gas and Electricity

Supply of Water   255
Supply of Gas   257
Supply of Electricity   258

21.1 Supply of Water

1. The General Duty

The principal authority responsible for the supply of water is the regional water authority. In certain areas statutory water companies supply water as agents for the water authorities. The water authority has a duty to supply water within their area; and the local authority has a duty "to take such steps from time to time as may be necessary for ascertaining the sufficiency and wholesomeness of water supplies within their area and to notify the water authority of any insufficiency or unwholesomeness in those supplies" (section 11, Water Act 1973). The Secretary of State may hold an inquiry into a complaint that this duty has not been discharged, and may make an order following that inquiry (section 13).

2. Right to Water supply for domestic purposes

Where there is an existing mains to which a service pipe can be connected, the owner or occupier of premises is entitled to demand a connection and to receive a supply of water for domestic purposes, if he agrees to pay the water rate (Schedule 3, Water Act 1945). The water undertaker make the connection and take a communication pipe to the boundary of property: they are entitled to recover their costs for this work.

The water undertaker may insist that the water fittings in the premises comply with its requirements. They may also insist on a separate service pipe to each individual dwelling-house (Water Act 1981).

If the existing mains has insufficient capacity to supply premises with water at the prescribed pressure, the cost of replacing the mains, or of providing other works, cannot be recovered from the owners.

255

Water supply for domestic purposes means "a sufficient supply
for drinking, washing, cooking and sanitary purposes", it will
include the purposes of a profession carried on in a dwelling if
the greater part is used as a house, and for watering a garden or
washing vehicles (section 31, Water Act 1945). Sometimes higher
water rates are charged for these extra purposes.

3.   Right to Requisition a Water Supply for existing Premises

Where there is no existing mains, the owners or occupiers of premises may require the Water undertaker to provide the necessary
mains. That requirement must be satisfied if the aggregate annual
water rates of the requisitioners exceed one-eighth of the cost of
laying the necessary mains (Schedule 3, Water Act 1945). If the
aggregate annual water rates of the owners and occupiers requiring
a water supply are insufficient, the local authority may agree to
meet the deficit for a period of twelve years; the water undertaker
must then comply with the requisition (section 36).

This right to requisition a water supply only applies to a supply
for domestic purposes.

4.   Right to Requisition a Water Supply for Proposed Buildings

Section 37 of the Water Act 1945 provides for a useful requisition
procedure for developers proposing to erect buildings for which
a water supply for domestic purposes will be needed. The developer
may require the water authority "to construct any necessary service
reservoirs, [and] to lay the necessary mains to such point or points
as will enable the buildings to be connected thereto at a reasonable
cost".

The developer may be required to bear part of the cost of constructing the necessary service reservoirs and providing and laying
the necessary mains. The developers contribution is one-eighth of
the cost until the aggregate water rates payable annually in respect
of the buildings to be erected, or other premises connected, exceeds
that amount, or a period of twelve years elapses, whichever first
occurs. A deposit as security for this contribution can be demanded.

If the existing mains and reservoirs are insufficient in capacity
to meet the requirements of the buildings proposed to be erected,
and these require replacement or enlargement, the cost of this work
cannot be recovered from the developer requisitioning the water
supply. "Necessary mains" was held in *Cherwell D.C.* v. *Thames
Water* [1975] H.L. to mean those new mains to be laid between

an existing water supply and the boundaries of the proposed buildings, and necessary only for the purpose of meeting the requirements of the requisition. In the case, the local authority which requisitioned a water supply to two new housing sites, could not therefore be required to contribute to the cost of an enlarged 27" trunk main which would supply the whole of the borough of Banbury.

In *Royco Homes v. Southern Water Authority* [1980] H.L., the developer had requisitioned a water supply and necessary mains under this section, but objected to the length of the necessary mains and consequent cost. Royco contended that there was a point on the existing distribution mains which was closer to its site; but to supply water from this point would require the enlargement of the distribution mains, the cost of which the authority could not recover. They had therefore chosen a different point on the distribution main which had a sufficient capacity. The House of Lords decided in favour of the water authority, Lord Keith giving his opinion that the starting point for the necessary mains was to be determined in the light of sound water engineering practice. This is perhaps an unfortunate case for developers because a water undertaker is not obliged to lay a necessary mains along the shortest route, but may choose a point dictated by the engineering practice.

5. Water Supply for non-domestic purposes

A water supply for non-domestic purposes may be requested by the owner or occupier of any premises. Provided the request can be met without impairing the water undertakers existing obligations, or its probable future obligations to supply water for domestic purposes, water can be supplied for non-domestic purposes on reasonable terms and conditions (section 27, Water Act 1945).

21.2 Supply of Gas

The Gas Act 1986 made provision for the privatisation of British Gas. The principal company is British Gas; there are local area organisations which are part of the company responsible for distribution of gas throughout their areas.

The obligation of a public gas supplier to supply gas is detailed in sections 10–11 of the Gas Act 1986. The owner or occupier of premises requiring a supply of gas may serve a notice on the public gas supplier. The public gas supplier must comply with the request, if the premises are domestic and they are within 25 yards of the gas main. The public gas supplier is entitled to recover the costs of laying a pipe within the property to be supplied, and of the cost of any distribution pipe in excess of 30 feet between the property and the mains. A deposit as security for these costs may be demanded. A public gas supplier cannot be required to supply gas to premises in excess of 25,000 therms per year.

If a request has been made for a supply of gas for purposes other than lighting or domestic use and that supply cannot be given without a new main, or the enlarging of an existing main, or the constructing or enlarging of other works, the public gas supplier is not required to comply with the request unless certain matters can be satisfied. The first of these is that the person requesting the supply enters into a written contract to take and pay for minimum quantities of gas for a minimum period having regard to the expenditure necessary on the part of the public gas supplier and to make any payment towards that expenditure as may be reasonably required. A deposit as security may be demanded.

The developer will have to secure any necessary easements to lay pipes through any land not in his ownership. The public gas suppliers have power to acquire land or rights over land for the purpose of discharging their functions (Schedule 3 to the Gas Act 1986). It may be possible to persuade the public gas supplier to exercise this power if legal rights cannot be obtained over land not owned by a person requiring a gas supply, and the public gas supplier are under a duty to provide the supply as described above.

21.3 Supply of Electricity

The Central Electricity Generating Board are responsible for making electricity, and the electricity boards are responsible for its local distribution throughout their respective areas (section 1, Electricity Act 1947, and section 2, Electricity Act 1957).

Any person requiring a supply of electricity must serve a notice on the area board specifying the premises and power required (including the appropriate phase). The area board must then provide a supply of electricity if the premises are within 50 yards of a distribution mains providing a supply to private consumers. The area board is entitled to recover the costs of lines or cables provided on the property of the person requiring the supply, and of the cost of any line or cable in excess of 60 feet between the property and the mains supply (Electric Lighting (Clauses) Act 1899).

The person requiring a supply may be required to agree to use the supply of electricity for at least two years, and at an annual payment of at least 20% of the cost to the area board of providing the supply. As with the supply of gas, the developer may have to secure any necessary easements to place lines or cables through any land not in his ownership. The area boards have power to acquire rights over land to discharge their functions.

Under the 1899 Act, as applied by the Electricity Act 1947, a distributing mains can be requisitioned for a street, part of a street or along any other route. The requisition can be made by any six or more owners or occupiers of premises along the street or in the proximity of the route. The requisitioners may have to agree to take a supply of power for at least three years sufficient for the area board to recover 20% of their expenditure annually. There is a right of appeal by either of the parties to the Secretary of State.

Chapter 22

Highways

Introduction   261
Obstruction and Interference to highways   263
Adoption of highways   265
Making up private streets   266
Stopping up and diversion of highways   268

22.1 Introduction

A highway is a strip of land over which the public at large have the right to pass and repass. There are various categories of public rights over highways; on carriage ways there is the right to pass and repass on foot, horse or by vehicle; on bridleways, foot, horse or by bicycle; on footpaths, on foot only. There are in addition, special types of highways such as motorways, walkways and cycle paths.

The land over which the highway passes may be privately owned by the adjoining frontagers. Subject to any evidence to the contrary, ownership extends to the centre of the highway. This may mean that if a person on a highway conducts an activity that is not simply the exercise of his legal right to pass or repass, and matters incidental and ancillary thereto, he may be trespassing. Causing a disturbance to the landowner's grouse shooting (*Harrison* v. *Duke of Rutland* [1893]), or picketing outside premises which exceeds the immunity normally applicable in connection with a trade dispute (*Hubbard* v. *Pitt* [1975]), would amount to a trespass.

When land is privately owned, the highway over it is only maintainable at public expense if it was created before 1836, or, if created after 1835, has been adopted by the local highway authority. The interest of the highway authority in a highway maintainable at public expense is in "the top two spits of the road": *Tithe Redemption Commission* v. *Runcorn U.D.C.* [1954]. It is a fee simple determinable when the highway ceases to exist, and extends between the adjoining fences, hedges or ditches.

Where a highway passes over private land, and is not maintainable at public expense, it may be privately repairable, or there may be no private liability for repairs. A private liability to repair may arise

261

by prescription, either *ratione tenurae*, or *ratione clausurae*. Prescription under *ratione tenurae* occurs where it has been a condition of landownership to keep a highway in repair: *Esher and Dittons U.D.C.* v. *Marks* [1902]. An owner is liable to repair *ratione clausurae* where the owner fences open land over which the public had rights of passage to avoid a highway when it becomes impassable, and confines the public to the highway. If a highway passes over private land, and is not maintainable at public expense, the responsibility of the owner is limited to any liability he may owe under the law of public nuisance—he must not interfere with or obstruct the rights of the public.

The highway authorities are the Department of Transport for motorways and trunk roads, and the county councils for all other highways. In practice many of the functions of a highway authority are delegated to district and borough councils. The highway authorities will only own the land over which a highway passes if the land was acquired and used for the purpose of constructing and creating a new or improved highway.

Highways are created at common law or by statute. At common law, a highway may be created if the landowner "dedicates" the right for the benefit of the public at large, and the public "accept" this right by use of the highway. Dedication and acceptance are the two essentials. Dedication, must be intended, expressly or impliedly. If the public use a strip of land without consent or hindrance for a sufficient period of time (20 years), dedication will be implied on the part of the landowner.

Highways may also be created by statute. The Highways Act 1980 contains the principal powers enabling highway authorities to construct new highways or to make private roads into high ways.

Although there is a common law right of access onto a highway by adjoining landowners, the making of such an access may involve development and require planning permission, or may be restricted by the provisions of the Highways Act 1980 on the grounds of danger to traffic.

Certain features of highway law are dealt with in this chapter. The development of land may involve obstruction or interference to a highway. The developer may be constructing new streets and roads and may expect that these become highways maintainable at public expense. Although the common law rule "once a highway, always a highway", means that a highway can never cease to exist, there are several statutory provisions concerning the stopping up and diversion of highways to facilitate development or other purposes.

22.2 Obstructions and interferences to highways

1. Public nuisance

If in the course of the development of land, the developer obstructs the highway or carries out his activities so as to endanger the use of the highway, that will be a public nuisance. If a vehicle is parked on a highway for long enough, that removes that part of the highway from public use and will be an obstruction: *Dymond* v. *Pearce* [1972]. The erection of a fence, hoarding or scaffolding would similarly constitute an obstruction: *Harper* v. *Haden and Sons* [1933]. Unguarded excavations on land immediately adjoining the highway may endanger users of the highway (*Jacobs* v. *L.C.C.* [1950]); the same point would also apply to excavations in the highway (*Haley* v. *L.E.B.* [1965]).

If an obstruction or danger constitutes a public nuisance, either the Attorney General or the local authority may seek an injunction to remove the cause of the nuisance. It is also a criminal offence [section 137 Highways Act 1980].

A private individual may bring a civil action in respect of a public nuisance if he can show special and particular damage over and above that suffered by the public at large. This will include loss of business due to the obstruction: see the *Harper* case.

However any owner of land is entitled to erect hoarding or scaffolding in the highway to effect repairs or improvements to his premises: a temporary obstruction would not constitute a public nuisance provided it was reasonable in extent and duration (*Herring* v. *Metropolitan Board of Works* [1865])—six months obstruction of a business by hoardings). If the highway authority has given a licence to erect scaffolding or hoarding in the highway (see below), this will not make legal an obstruction that is otherwise illegal because it is a public nuisance by reason of its extent or duration.

2. Lawful and unlawful interference: Highways Act 1980

This Act makes provision for the protection of public rights on the highway by penalties. It also provides for precautions to be taken in connection with building works including the issue of licences for some activities.

(a) Builders skips: sections 139–140
These may only be deposited on the highway with the permission of the highway authority. Permission may be granted subject to

conditions as to siting, dimensions, visible colouring, care of contents, lighting and removal. A skip must be properly lit during darkness and must be marked with the owner's name and telephone number or an address. The Builders' Skip (Markings) Regulations 1984 (SI 1933) requires the marking of skips with the owner's details. Where a skip is placed in the road with the permission of the highway authority, an offence is committed if the skip is not lit, and the fact that lights are vandalised will only be a defence if all reasonable steps are taken to prevent the loss of the lights: *P.G.M. Building Ltd.* v. *Kensington Chelsea L.B.C.* [1982].

(b) Building operations affecting public safety: section 168
It is an offence to carry out building operations which give rise to the risk of serious injury to persons on a highway or would have given rise to such a risk if the local authority had not used its powers to remove the risk.

(c) Control of scaffolding on highways: section 169
It is an offence to erect scaffolding or other structure in a highway without permission of the highway authority. A licence to erect the scaffolding must be granted by the authority unless the scaffolding will cause an unreasonable obstruction or there is some other way of arranging the scaffolding than that proposed by the applicant. The person to whom the licence is granted must ensure that the scaffolding or other structure is properly lit during darkness; he must also comply with any directions given concerning the erection of traffic signs.

(d) Materials on the highway: sections 170–171
It is an offence to damage a highway by mixing mortar which will stick to the surface or enter drains or sewers. Consent may be given for the temporary deposit of building materials on a highway. Consent may be subject to conditions, and the materials must be properly lit and guarded.

(e) Hoardings: sections 172–173
Unless this requirement is dispensed with by the highway authority, hoardings must be erected between the highway and land where the erection or demolition of a building is to take place. If necessary, a covered platform and handrail must be provided for pedestrians. The hoarding must be properly secured and lit.

(f) Bridges and Cellars: sections 176 and 179
If a landowner owns the subsoil under a highway, or owns land on both sides of a highway as well as the subsoil, he may build a cellar under the highway, or a bridge over it if he obtains the

consent of the highway authority. That consent or licence may contain conditions. There is an appeal to the Crown Court against a refusal of a licence for a bridge, and to the magistrates court for a refusal of *consent* for a cellar.

(g) Buildings over highways: section 177
A licence is required to construct a building over a highway. The licence may contain conditions relating to headway, maintenance, lighting and use of the building. There is an appeal to the Crown Court against a refusal of consent. No appeal can be brought if the land on which the highway lies is owned by the highway authority.

22.3   Adoption of highways

Although any highway created before 1836 is maintainable at public expense, highways created since that date are only so maintainable if they have been adopted by the highway authority under the statutory provisions now found in the Highways Act 1980 (section 36). A developer laying out new roads and streets will usually comply with the appropriate procedures to ensure that these are adopted.

1.   Adoption following notice: section 37

Where a person proposes to dedicate a way over land as a highway, he may give three months notice of his intention to the local highway authority. The authority may complain to the magistrates court that the way will not be of sufficient utility to justify its being maintained at public expense. If the way has been properly made up in a satisfactory manner (to a standard specified by the authority), the highway authority will issue a certificate to that effect. Then, provided the way is kept in repair for twelve months from the date of that certificate, and the magistrates court do not make an order that the way will have insufficient utility, the highway will thereafter become maintainable at public expense.

2.   Adoption by agreement: section 38

This procedure is usually more satisfactory to a developer proposing to construct new roads. An agreement is made between the local highway authority and a person who either proposes to dedicate an existing private carriage or occupation road, or who proposes to construct new roads and then dedicate them as highways. The agreement will contain the specifications of the new highway, the date on which it will become a highway maintainable at public expense; it may contain a bond and surety to pay the costs of making up the road if the developer defaults; it may also contain a financial contribution from the developer to the authority.

A walkway is a special type of highway over through or under buildings or structures. They are created by an agreement, under section 35 of the 1980 Act, which will make particular provision for maintenance, lighting, support, making of payments, and the termination of the public rights of way in specified circumstances. By-laws may be made for the proper regulation and use of walkways.

3.   Adoption under the Advance Payments Code

This is dealt with below at 22.4.

4.   The duty to maintain: section 41

The 1980 Act imposes a duty on highway authorities to maintain a highway maintainable at public expense. The authority may be liable in damages to any user of the highway if they fail to discharge this duty. There are some special defences (section 58).

22.4   Making up private streets

The purpose of the two codes briefly described here is to ensure that existing private streets can be made up to a satisfactory standard and, that certain proposed private streets will be constructed to a proper standard, and then adopted (part XI of the Highways Act 1980).

1.   Private Street works code

If the highway authority is satisfied that a private street is not properly sewered, levelled, paved, metalled, flagged, channelled, made good and lighted, it may resolve that the necessary street works are carried out by the authority at the expense of the frontagers (section 205(1)).

A specification, estimates and provisional apportionment of the costs are prepared, and if approved by the authority, notice to frontagers and publicity will be given. Any frontager may object to the magistrates court (section 209) on the grounds that the road is not a private street, there has been some procedural irregularity, the proposed works are insufficient or unreasonable, the estimated cost is excessive, that certain premises ought to be excluded from the apportionment, or that the provisional apportionment is incorrect (section 208).

When the street works have been executed, the authority will make a final apportionment of the costs. Any frontager may then appeal within one month to the magistrates court if there has been an unreasonable departure from the specification, the actual expenses have without sufficient reason exceeded the estimated expenses by more than 15% or the apportionment has not been properly made (section 211).

The sums due from the frontagers under the final apportionment are a charge on their frontage land until paid off. There is power to allow the sums to be paid by way of annual instalments within a period not exceeding thirty years (section 212).

2. Advance Payments Code

This code ensures that a sum of money is deposited with the local authority as security for the proper construction of private streets; it also ensures that the frontagers can require that the private street be adopted as a highway maintainable at public expense.

Where it is proposed to erect a building or buildings for which plans must be deposited with the local authority in accordance with building regulations and the buildings will front a private street (existing or proposed), no building work may commence until a sum of money is deposited with the local authority (section 219(1)). The sum of money represents security for the costs of the necessary street works.

There are exemptions to this requirement of an advance payment, of which the following are the more important (section 219(4)):

(a) the proposed building will be in the curtilage of, or appurtenant to, an existing building;

(b) the advance payments code does not apply to the particular parish or community council area (it is extended to any such area by the county council, if not already an area to which the code applies);

(c) the developer has made an adoption agreement with the local highway under section 38 (see above); and

(d) the local highway authority are satisfied that more than three quarters of the aggregate length of the frontages, are or will consist of the frontages of industrial premises, or the proposed building will be industrial and has a frontage of at least 100 yards.

Unless any of the exemptions apply, the highway authority will serve a notice, within six weeks of the passing of the plans by the district council under the building regulations, specifying the sum to be deposited (section 220).

If the developer makes up the private street, the sum deposited will be refunded to that person, subject to any representation of the frontagers (section 221). If the highway authority make up the street, they may recover any excess cost above the advance payment deposited and held by them, and must refund any excess if the advance payment exceeds the cost of the works (section 222). There is provision for a return of the advance payment if the proposed building work is abandoned (section 223). Interest is paid on the sum deposited at rates stipulated from time to time (section 225).

When the street works have been carried out, the highway authority may, by notice, declare that the highway shall be maintainable at public expense. Any objections are considered by the magistrates court (section 228).

A majority of the frontagers, or those owning more than half the aggregate length of the street, may by notice require the highway authority to carry out the necessary street works and declare the highway to be maintainable at public expense (section 229). This right may only be exercised if more than half of the length of the street on both sides has been built up and the length of the street concerned is not less than 100 yards long.

22.5   Stopping up and diversion of highways

A highway may only be diverted or stopped up under statutory powers. Powers are available under the Highways Act 1980, the Town and Country Planning Act 1971, the Acquisition of Land Act 1981, and the Housing Act 1985.

1.   Stopping up and diversion of highways: Highways Act 1980

The highway authority may apply to the magistrates court for an order to stop up or divert a highway where the highway is unnecessary or it can be diverted so as to make it nearer or more commodious to the public (section 116(1)). In *Gravesham B.C.* v. *Watson* [1983], it was said that the word "commodious" had the dictionary meaning of being larger or roomier. A developer may request the highway authority to make such application (because only the authority may apply), and the authority are entitled, as a condition of granting such a request, to be reimbursed their costs (section 117).

The consent of the district council and parish or community council is required before an application can be made by the highway authority in respect of an unclassified highway (section 116(3)).

At the court hearing, the highway authority, frontagers to the highway, users of the highway, and, where the highway is classified, the Minister and the district council, parish or community council, are entitled to be heard (section 116(7)).

2. Stopping up footpaths and bridleways: Highways Act 1980

A public path extinguishment order may be made by the county council or a district council where a path or way is not needed for public use. If opposed, the order must be confirmed by the Secretary of State (section 118). An order should not usually be made on the ground that some obstruction made the highway impossible to use (*R.* v. *Secretary of State for the Environment ex p. Stewart* [1980]). There are provisions for compensating parties with interests harmed by the closure.

3. Diversion of footpaths and bridleways: Highways Act 1980

An owner, lessee or occupier of land crossed by a footpath or bridleway may request the county or district council to make a public path diversion order on the ground that it is expedient to do so in the interests of the owner, lessee or of the public. The order must be confirmed by the Secretary of State if opposed (section 119). The applicant may have to agree to reimburse the council making the order any costs it incurs, or any compensation it may have to pay to those with interests harmed by the diversion.

A footpath within 300 yards of Chequers was diverted under this power on the ground that there was an assassination risk to the Prime Minister: *Roberton* v. *Secretary of State for the Environment* [1976].

4. Stopping up and diversion of highways: Town and Country Planning Act 1971

Where planning permission has been granted for development, the Secretary of State may make an order to stop up or divert a highway to enable the development to be carried out (section 209(1)). The important point here is that the order is necessary to enable the development to proceed in accordance with planning permission.

The order may be made retrospectively where the development has already been carried out (*Ashby* v. *Secretary of State* [1980]). The order may make provision for a new highway as replacement or improvement of an existing one; and for a financial contribution towards the costs of this from any authority or developer.

A highway may be converted into a footpath or bridleway (e.g. a pedestrian policy) by an order made by the local planning authority and confirmed by the Secretary of State (section 212). The order may allow service vehicles at specified times, and compensation may be payable to frontagers affected. In *Saleem* v. *Bradford M.B.C.* [1984], the Lands Tribunal did not accept that the order closing the highway to vehicular traffic as the direct cause of the claimant's loss.

5.   Footpaths and bridleways affected by development: Town and Country Planning Act 1971

The local planning authority may make an order to stop up or divert a footpath or bridleway to enable development to be carried out in accordance with planning permission granted under the Act (section 210). The order may make provision for alternative routes, and for a contribution towards the costs of work in connection therewith. An order may be made retrospectively to the development (see the *Ashby* case above).

6.   Extinguishment of right of way

There is, finally, a general power in section 214 of the 1971 Act to extinguish any rights of way over land held by a local planning authority for planning purposes. There is also a power in section 32 of the Acquisition of Land Act 1981 to extinguish footpaths and bridleways in connection with the compulsory purchase of land, and there is power for a local authority to extinguish rights of way under Part IX of the Housing Act 1985 where land is acquired for clearance purposes; the approval of the Secretary of State is required.

7.   Stopping up or interfering with private rights

Where land has been acquired or appropriated by the local planning authority, for planning purposes and development is carried out in accordance with planning permission, private rights, such as easements, may lawfully be interfered with: section 127 of the Town and Country Planning Act 1971. It matters not whether the development is carried out by the local planning authority or a person deriving title under them. There is a right to compensation (section 127(3)), but the claimant must prove that the interference with his private right will cause depreciation in value to his interest (*Ward* v. *Wychavon D.C.* [1986].

PART VII

THE BETTERMENT PROBLEM

Chapter 23

Betterment

The Betterment Problem   273

23.1 The Betterment Problem

The Uthwatt Report of 1942 (Final Report of the Expert Committee on Compensation and Betterment, Cmnd 6386) recognised that a system of comprehensive planning and development control would have a significant effect on land values. The Report identified the principle of betterment "which is that, if property is enhanced in value by reason of some action, whether positive or negative, by the state or a local authority, the state or the local authority should be entitled to recover the whole or some part of the increase in value". Betterment has been recovered in the past by a direct charge on the owner of the property bettered (London County Council (Tower Bridge Southern Approach) Act 1895); by a set-off in respect of the betterment against compensation payable for the acquisition of or injurious affection of other land of the same owner (Land Compensation Act 1961); and by recoupment—that is the purchase of the land to be bettered at a price that ignores this effect, and then its resale at a price reflecting betterment (see the 1895 Act above).

The Report considered that the principle of betterment commanded general acceptance although there were great difficulties in its practical application. It recommended that local authorities should have wide general powers to buy land compulsorily to recoup betterment. Set-off and a direct charge were not favoured; the former because of its casual effect and historically unproductive nature, the latter because of the then known difficulties in collecting betterment by direct charge under the Town and Country Planning Act 1932. The Report also recommended that betterment should be collected by a scheme for a periodic levy on increases in annual site values.

These recommendations of the Uthwatt Committee were not wholly accepted by the Labour Government after World War II; the Town and Country Planning Act 1947, in nationalising development rights, and providing a claim for compensation for the loss of those rights (see page 219) provided that betterment would be collected by a development charge. This charge was 100% of the betterment: the difference between the value of the land with planning permission, and its existing use value.

It was said at the time that the development charge discouraged development, because it denied any financial incentive to release land for that purpose, and, where development took place, it was an additional cost borne by the developer and passed on to the ultimate user of developed land. Strictly speaking the charge only represented the betterment derived from planning permission, and the higher cost to the ultimate user was not the charge, but the land value consequence of a comprehensive system of planning and development control: if only specified land is to be released for development, that land will increase in value to a greater extent than if there was no planning and development control.

The Conservative government abolished the development charge from November 1952 by the Town and Country Planning Act 1953. But made no further or alternative provision for the collection of betterment. With another change of government, a further attempt to collect betterment was made with the Land Commission Act 1967: a 40% betterment levy was charged on net development value. The Act also set up the Land Commission, a body that was given wide powers of compulsory purchase of land suitable for development; this was a recognition of one of the recommendations of the Uthwatt Report. The Land Commission Act 1967 was repealed with yet another change of government in 1970—too early for any real conclusions to be made about the effectiveness of the policy it represented.

The Community Land Act 1975 represented another attempt by the next Labour Government to deal with the betterment problem and "to enable the community to control the development of land in accordance with its needs and priorities" (White Paper—Land— Cmnd 57307–1974). The Act contained not only wide powers for local planning authorities to acquire land needed for development, but enabled the Secretary of State, by order, to impose a duty on authorities to acquire certain development land. Betterment was to be collected for an interim period as a development land tax under the Development Land Tax Act 1976; eventually acquisition of development land under the 1975 Act would be on a compensation basis that excluded development value. This solution to the problem was fairly close to the original recommendation of the Uthwatt Committee that betterment should be collected by recoupment, i.e., purchase of development and its resale.

The present Conservative government repealed the Community Land Act 1975 but did not repeal the measure concerned with the collection of betterment: the Development Land Tax Act 1976 until 1985.

It seems doubtful whether a consensus has been reached over the problem of betterment; certainly the main political parties are as far from agreement over a solution as they were in 1947. At local government level the parties have probably never been further apart, with considerable evidence that the whole planning process is no longer regarded as an objective exercise in the administration of a regulatory device upon development where the initiative lies with the landowner and developer. Planning and development control is regarded by many local councillors as a political process which should be initiated and controlled through local government.

The United Kingdom enjoys the most comprehensive and restrictive planning and development control legislation of the free democratic countries of the world. Undoubtedly it has brought great benefits, but we have paid a high price for it.

Appendix A

Use Classes Order

1987 No. 764

TOWN AND COUNTRY PLANNING
ENGLAND AND WALES

The Town and Country Planning (Use Classes) Order 1987

Made	*28th April 1987*
Coming into force	*1st June 1987*

The Secretary of State for the Environment, in exercise of the powers conferred on him by sections 22(2) (f) and 287(3) of the Town and Country Planning Act 1971(a) and of all other powers enabling him in that behalf, hereby makes the following Order:—

Citation and commencement
1. This Order may be cited as the Town and Country Planning (Use Classes) Order 1987 and shall come into force on 1st June 1987.

Interpretation
2. In this Order, unless the context otherwise requires:—
   "care" means personal care for people in need of such care by reason of old age, disablement, past or present dependence on alcohol or drugs or past or present mental disorder, and in class C2 also includes the personal care of children and medical care and treatment;
   "day centre" means premises which are visited during the day for social or recreational purposes or for the purposes of rehabilitation or occupational training, at which care is also provided;
   "hazardous substance" and "notifiable quantity" have the meanings assigned to those terms by the Notification of Installations Handling Hazardous Substances Regulations 1982(b);
   "industrial process" means a process for or incidental to any of the following purposes:—
   (*a*) the making of any article or part of any article (including a ship or vessel, or a film, video or sound recording);

(a) 1971 c.78; section 22(2)(f) was amended by paragraph 1 of Schedule 11 to the Housing and Planning Act 1986 (c.63).
(b) S.I. 1982/1357.

(b) the altering, repairing, maintaining, ornamenting, finishing, cleaning, washing, packing, canning, adapting for sale, breaking up or demolition of any article; or

(c) the getting, dressing or treatment of minerals;

in the course of any trade or business other than agriculture, and other than a use carried out in or adjacent to a mine or quarry;

"Schedule" means the Schedule to this Order;

"site" means the whole area of land within a single unit of occupation.

Use Classes

3.—(1) Subject to the provisions of this Order, where a building or other land is used for a purpose of any class specified in the Schedule, the use of that building or that other land for any other purpose of the same class shall not be taken to involve development of the land.

(2) References in paragraph (1) to a building include references to land occupied with the building and used for the same purposes.

(3) A use which is included in and ordinarily incidental to any use in a class specified in the Schedule is not excluded from the use to which it is incidental merely because it is specified in the Schedule as a separate use.

(4) Where land on a single site or on adjacent sites used as parts of a single undertaking is used for purposes consisting of or including purposes falling within any two or more of classes B1 to B7 in the Schedule, those classes may be treated as a single class in considering the use of that land for the purposes of this Order, so long as the area used for a purpose falling either within class B2 or within classes B3 to B7 is not substantially increased as a result.

(5) No class specified in the Schedule includes any use for a purpose which involves the manufacture, processing, keeping or use of a hazardous substance in such circumstances as will result in the presence at one time of a notifiable quantity of that substance in, on, over or under that building or land or any site of which that building or land forms part.

(6) No class specified in the Schedule includes use:—

(a) as a theatre,

(b) as an amusement arcade or centre, or a funfair,

(c) for the washing or cleaning of clothes or fabrics in coin-operated machines or on premises at which the goods to be cleaned are received direct from the visiting public,

(d) for the sale of fuel for motor vehicles.

(e) for the sale or display for sale of motor vehicles,

(f) for a taxi business or business for the hire of motor vehicles,

(g) as a scrapyard, or a yard for the storage or distribution of minerals or the breaking of motor vehicles.

Change of use of part of building or land

4. In the case of a building used for a purpose within class C3 (dwellinghouses) in the Schedule, the use as a separate dwellinghouse of any part of the building or of any land occupied with and used for the same purposes as the building is not, by virtue of this Order, to be taken as not amounting to development.

Revocation
5. The Town and Country Planning (Use Classes) Order 1972(a) and the Town and Country Planning (Use Classes) (Amendment) Order 1983(b) are hereby revoked.

SCHEDULE

PART A

Class A1. *Shops*
Use for all or any of the following purposes:—
  (*a*) for the retail sale of goods other than hot food,
  (*b*) as a post office,
  (*c*) for the sale of tickets or as a travel agency,
  (*d*) for the sale of sandwiches or other cold food for consumption off the premises,
  (*e*) for hairdressing,
  (*f*) for the direction of funerals,
  (*g*) for the display of goods for sale,
  (*h*) for the hiring out of domestic or personal goods or articles,
  (*i*) for the reception of goods to be washed, cleaned or repaired,
     where the sale, display or service is to visiting members of the public.

Class A2. *Financial and professional services*
Use for the provision of:—
  (*a*) financial services, or
  (*b*) professional services (other than health or medical services), or
  (*c*) any other services (including use as a betting office) which it is appropriate to provide in a shopping area,
where the services are provided principally to visiting members of the public.

Class A3. *Food and drink*
Use for the sale of food or drink for consumption on the premises or of hot food for consumption off the premises.

PART B

Class B1. *Business*
Use for all or any of the following purposes:—
  (*a*) as an office other than a use within class A2 (financial and professional services),
  (*b*) for research and development of products or processes, or
  (*c*) for any industrial process,
being a use which can be carried out in any residential area without detriment to the amenity of that area by reason of noise, vibration, smell, fumes, smoke, soot, ash, dust or grit.

(a) S.I. 1972/1385.   (b) S.I. 1983/1614.

Class B2. *General industrial*
Use for the carrying on of an industrial process other than one falling within class B1 above or within classes B3 to B7 below.

Class B3. *Special Industrial Group A*
Use for any work registrable under the Alkali, etc. Works Regulation Act 1906(a) and which is not included in any of classes B4 to B7 below.

Class B4. *Special Industrial Group B*
Use for any of the following processes, except where the process is ancillary to the getting, dressing or treatment of minerals and is carried on in or adjacent to a quarry or mine:—
(a) smelting, calcining, sintering or reducing ores, minerals, concentrates or mattes;
(b) converting, refining, re-heating, annealing, hardening, melting, carburising, forging or casting metals or alloys other than pressure die-casting;
(c) recovering metal from scrap or drosses or ashes;
(d) galvanizing;
(e) pickling or treating metal in acid;
(f) chromium plating.

Class B5. *Special Industrial Group C*
Use for any of the following processes, except where the process is ancillary to the getting, dressing or treatment or minerals and is carried on in or adjacent to a quarry or mine:—
(a) burning bricks or pipes;
(b) burning lime or dolomite;
(c) producing zinc oxide, cement or alumina;
(d) foaming, crushing, screening or heating minerals or slag;
(e) processing pulverized fuel ash by heat;
(f) producing carbonate of lime or hydrated lime;
(g) producing inorganic pigments by calcining, roasting or grinding.

Class B6. *Special Industrial Group D*
Use for any of the following processes:—
(a) distilling, refining or blending oils (other than petroleum or petroleum products);
(b) producing or using cellulose or using other pressure sprayed metal finishes (other than in vehicle repair workshops in connection with minor repairs, or the application of plastic powder by the use of fluidised bed and electrostatic spray techniques);
(c) boiling linseed oil or running gum;
(d) processes involving the use of hot pitch or bitumen (except the use of bitumen in the manufacture of roofing felt at temperatures not exceeding 220°C and also the manufacture of coated roadstone);
(e) stoving enamelled ware;
(f) producing aliphatic esters of the lower fatty acids, butyric acid,

(a) 1906 c.14.

caramel, hexamine, iodoform, napthols, resin products (excluding plastic moulding or extrusion operations and producing plastic sheets, rods, tubes, filaments, fibres or optical components produced by casting, calendering, moulding, shaping or extrusion), salicylic acid or sulphonated organic compounds;

(g) producing rubber from scrap;
(h) chemical processes in which chlorphenols or chlorcresols are used as intermediates;
(i) manufacturing acetylene from calcium carbide;
(j) manufacturing, recovering or using pyridine or picolines, any methyl or ethylamine or acrylates.

Class B7. *Special Industrial Group E*
Use for carrying on any of the following industries, businesses or trades:—
Boiling blood, chitterlings, nettlings or soap.
Boiling, burning, grinding or steaming bones.
Boiling or cleaning tripe.
Breeding maggots from putrescible animal matter.
Cleaning, adapting or treating animal hair.
Curing fish.
Dealing in rags and bones (including receiving, storing, sorting or manipulating rags in, or likely to become in, an offensive condition, or any bones, rabbit skins, fat or putrescible animal products of a similar nature).
Dressing or scraping fish skins.
Drying skins.
Making manure from bones, fish, offal, blood, spent hops, beans or other putrescible animal or vegetable matter.
Making or scraping guts.
Manufacturing animal charcoal, blood albumen, candles, catgut, glue, fish oil, size or feeding stuff for animals or poultry from meat, fish, blood, bone, feathers, fat or animal offal either in an offensive condition or subjected to any process causing noxious or injurious effluvia.
Melting, refining or extracting fat or tallow.
Preparing skins for working.

Class B8. *Storage or distribution*
Use for storage or as a distribution centre.

PART C

Class C1. *Hotels and hostels*
Use as a hotel, boarding or guest house or as a hostel where, in each case, no significant element of care is provided.

Class C2. *Residential institutions*
Use for the provision of residential accommodation and care to people in need of care (other than a use within class C3 (dwelling houses)).
Use as a hospital or nursing home.
Use as a residential school, college or training centre.

Class C3. *Dwellinghouses*
Use as a dwellinghouse (whether or not as a sole or main residence):—
  (*a*) by a single person or by people living together as a family, or
  (*b*) by not more than 6 residents living together as a single household (including a household where care is provided for residents).

PART D

Class D1. Non-residential institutions
Any use not including a residential use:—
  (*a*) for the provision of any medical or health services except the use of premises attached to the residence of the consultant or practitioner,
  (*b*) as a crêche, day nursery or day centre,
  (*c*) for the provision of education,
  (*d*) for the display of works of art (otherwise than for sale or hire),
  (*e*) as a museum,
  (*f*) as a public library or public reading room,
  (*g*) as a public hall or exhibition hall,
  (*h*) for, or in connection with, public worship or religious instruction.

Class D2. *Assembly and leisure*
Use as:—
  (*a*) a cinema,
  (*b*) a concert hall,
  (*c*) a bingo hall or casino,
  (*d*) a dance hall,
  (*e*) a swimming bath, skating rink, gymnasium or area for other indoor or outdoor sports or recreations, not involving motorised vehicles or firearms.

28th April 1987

Nicholas Ridley
Secretary of State for the Environment

EXPLANATORY NOTE

(This note is not part of the Order)

This Order revokes and replaces the Town and Country Planning (Use Classes) Order 1972 as amended by the Town and Country Planning (Use Classes) (Amendment) Order 1983.

This Order specifies classes of use of buildings or other land for the purposes of section 22(2)(f) of the Town and Country Planning Act 1971. Section 22(2) specifies operations or uses which are not to be taken for the purposes of the Act as involving development, and which therefore do not require planning permission. Paragraph (f) provides that a change of use is not to be regarded as involving development where the former use and the new use are both within the same class specified in an order made under that paragraph.

Various changes are made in this Order to the classes of use specified in the Schedule to the 1972 Order.

Class I of the 1972 Order specified use as a shop (which expression was defined in the Order) subject to specific exclusions. The specific exclusions of tripe shops, cats-meat shops and pet shops are no longer to be found in the new shops class A1. Use for the sale of hot food is now to be found in the new class A3 (food and drink) and is excluded specifically from class A1. The former exclusion of use for the sale of motor vehicles is now in article 3(6)(e).

Class A2 is a new class of use for financial, professional and other services. This combines some of the office uses formerly in Class II, and some uses formerly within the definition of "shop" as being uses of buildings for a purpose appropriate to a shopping area. The test of appropriateness to a shopping area governs the whole of class A2.

Class A3 (food and drink) is a new class. It combines use for the sale of hot food, which was formerly excluded from Class I, with use as a restaurant or for the sale of drink.

Class B1 combines some of the office uses formerly within Class II with uses for light industrial purposes formerly within Class III into a business class. It also includes use for the research and development of products or processes. A test similar to that which formerly applied to Class III—that is a use which could be carried out in any residential area without detriment to the amenity of that area—now governs all the purposes in this class.

Class B2 (general industrial) reflects the old Class IV.

Classes B3 to B7 reflect old Classes V to IX (Special Industrial Groups (A) to (E)). Although there has been some reorganisation, the content of these classes is the same.

Class B8 (storage and distribution) is based on former Class X but extends additionally to use of open land and to use as a centre for distribution.

Class C1 (hotels and hostels) largely reflects the former Class XI but makes it clear that this class does not cover any residential establishment where a significant element of care (defined in article 2) is provided.

Class C2 (residential institutions) combines the former Classes XII and XIV.

Class C3 (dwellinghouses) is a new class which comprises use as a dwellinghouse by an individual, by people living together as a family or by not more than six residents living together as a single household. In the case of people living together as a household rather than as a family, the use will continue to be within the class notwithstanding that an element of care (as defined in article 2) is provided for residents. The intention of this class is to include, for example, use as a dwellinghouse by individuals living together in the community who have formerly been in an institution of some kind.

Class D1 includes the uses formerly contained in Classes XIII, XV and XVI. Dispensaries are no longer included, and these will be either within class A1 (shops) or, where ancillary to a hospital, within class C2 residential institutions.

Class D2 (assembly and leisure) includes uses formerly in Classes XVII and XVIII. It has been extended to include use for all indoor or outdoor sports with the exception of motor sports and sports involving firearms. Theatres which were formerly in Class XVII are no longer included in any of the classes (see article 3(6)).

One difference between this Order and the 1972 Order is that in Parts A and B of the Schedule to this Order the uses specified are uses of buildings or land whereas their equivalents in the 1972 Order specified uses of buildings. There are also more uses specifically excluded from the classes, and these are listed in article 3(6) of the Order.

Paragraph 1 of Schedule 11 to the Housing and Planning Act 1986 amended section 22(2)(f) of the 1971 Act by providing that a change of use of part of any building or land is not a material change of use where the former use and the latter use of the part are within the same class, subject to the provisions of an order made under that paragraph. Article 4 of the Order provides that use as a separate dwellinghouse of any part of a building or of land used for the purposes of class C3 (dwellinghouses) is not by virtue of this Order to be taken as not amounting to development.

Appendix B

Classes of permitted development extracted from Schedule 1 to the Town and Country Planning (General Development) Order 1977 (SI 1977/289) as amended.

Column (1) Description of Development	Column (2) Conditions

Class I.—Development within the curtilage of a dwellinghouse

1. The enlargement, improvement or other alteration of a dwellinghouse [(other than by the carrying out of operations within paragraph 2A of this class)] so long as:

(a) the cubic content of the original dwellinghouse (as ascertained by external measurement) is not exceeded by more than—

    (i) in the case of a terrace house, 50 cubic metres or ten per cent, whichever is the greater; or

    (ii) in any other case, 70 cubic metres or fifteen per cent, whichever is the greater,

subject (in either case) to a maximum of 115 cubic metres;

(b) the height of the building as so enlarged, improved or altered does not exceed the height of the highest part of the roof of the original dwellinghouse;

(c) no part of the building as so enlarged, improved or altered projects beyond the forwardmost part of any wall of the original dwellinghouse which fronts on a highway;

(d) no part of the building (as so enlarged, improved or altered) which lies within a distance of two metres from any boundary of the curtilage of the dwellinghouse has, as a result of the development, a height exceeding four metres;

(e) the area of ground covered by buildings within the curtilage (other than the original dwellinghouse) does not thereby exceed fifty per cent of the total area of the curtilage excluding the ground area of the original dwellinghouse:

Provided that:—

(a) the erection of a garage or coachhouse within the curtilage of the dwellinghouse shall be treated as the enlargement of the dwellinghouse for all purposes of this permission

Column (1) Description of Development	Column (2) Conditions

(including the calculation of cubic content) if any part of that building lies within a distance of five metres from any part of the dwelling-house;

(b) the erection of a stable or loose-box anywhere within the curtilage of the dwellinghouse shall be treated as the enlargement of the dwelling-house for all purposes of this permission (including the calculation of cubic content);

(c) for the purposes of this permission the extent to which the cubic content of the original dwellinghouse is exceeded shall be ascertained by deducting the amount of the cubic content of the original dwellinghouse from the amount of the cubic content of the dwelling-house as enlarged, improved or altered (whether such enlargement, improvement or alteration was carried out in pursuance of this permission or otherwise);

(d) where any part of the dwellinghouse will, as a result of the development, lie within a distance of five metres from an existing garage or coach-house, that building shall (for the purpose of the calculation of cubic content) be treated as forming part of the dwellinghouse as en-larged, improved or altered; and

(e) the limitation contained in subparagraph (d) above shall not apply to development consist-ing of:—

   (i) the insertion of a window (including a dor-mer window) into a wall or the roof of the original dwellinghouse, or the alteration or enlargement of an existing window; or

   (ii) any other alterations to any part of the roof of the original dwellinghouse.]

2. The erection or construction of a porch outside any external door of a dwellinghouse so long as:

(a) the floor area does not exceed 2 square metres;

(b) no part of the structure is more than 3 metres above the level of the ground;

(c) no part of the structure is less than 2 metres from any boundary of the curtilage which fronts on a highway.

[2A. The installation, alteration or replacement of a satellite antenna on a dwellinghouse or within the curtilage of a dwellinghouse, so long as:—

(a) the size of the antenna (excluding any projec-ting feed element) does not, when measured in any dimension, exceed 90 centimetres;

Column (1) Description of Development	Column (2) Conditions

(*b*) there is no other satellite antenna installed on the dwellinghouse or anywhere else within the curtilage of the dwellinghouse;

(*c*) in the case of an antenna installed on a dwelling-house the highest part of the antenna is not higher than the highest part of the roof of the building on which it is installed.]

[3. The erection, construction or placing, and the maintenance, improvement or other alteration, within the curtilage of a dwellinghouse, of any building or enclosure (other than a dwelling, stable, [satellite antenna] or loose-box) required for a purpose incidental to the enjoyment of the dwellinghouse as such, including the keeping of poultry, bees, pet animals, birds or other livestock for the domestic needs or personal enjoyment of the occupants of the dwellinghouse, so long as:

(*a*) no part of such building or enclosure projects beyond the forwardmost part of any wall of the original dwellinghouse which fronts on a highway;

(*b*) in the case of a garage or coachhouse, no part of the building is within a distance of five metres from any part of the dwellinghouse;

(*c*) the height does not exceed, in the case of a building with a ridged roof, four metres or, in any other case, three metres;

(*d*) the area of ground covered by buildings within the curtilage (other than the original dwellinghouse) does not thereby exceed fifty per cent of the total area of the curtilage excluding the ground area of the original dwellinghouse.]

4. The construction within the curtilage of a dwellinghouse of a hardstanding for vehicles for a purpose incidental to the enjoyment of the dwellinghouse as such.

5. The erection or placing within the curtilage of a dwellinghouse of a tank for the storage of oil for domestic heating so long as:

(*a*) the capacity of the tank does not exceed 3,500 litres;

(*b*) no part of the tank is more than 3 metres above the level of the ground;

(*c*) no part of the tank projects beyond the forwardmost part of any wall of the original dwellinghouse which fronts on a highway.

Class II.—Sundry minor operations
1. The erection or construction of gates, fences,

Column (1) Description of Development	Column (2) Conditions

walls or other means of enclosure not exceeding 1 metre in height where abutting on a highway used by vehicular traffic or 2 metres in height in any other case, and the maintenance, improvement or other alteration of any gates, fences, walls or other means of enclosure: so long as such improvement or alteration does not increase the height above the height appropriate for a new means of enclosure.

2. The formation, laying out and construction of a means of access to a highway not being a trunk or classified road, where required in connection with development permitted by article 3 of and Schedule 1 to this order (other than under this class).

3. The painting of the exterior of any building or work otherwise than for the purpose of advertisement, announcement or direction.

Class III.—Changes of use

1. Development consisting of a change of the use of a building to a use falling within class A1 (shops) of the Schedule to the Town and Country Planning (Use Classes) Order 1987(c) from a use falling within class A3 (food and drink) of the Schedule to that Order, or from a use for the sale (or display for sale) of motor vehicles.

2. Development consisting of a change of the use of a building:—

    (a) to a use for any purpose falling within class B1 (business) of the Schedule to that Order from any use falling within class B2 (general industrial) or B8 (storage and distribution) of that Schedule;

    (b) to a use for any purpose within class B8 (storage and distribution) from any use within class B1 (business) or B2 (general industrial);

where the total amount of floorspace in the building used for the purposes of the undertaking does not exceed 235 square metres.

Class IV.—Temporary buildings and uses

1. The erection or construction on land in, on, over or under which operations other than mining operations are being or are about to be carried out (being operations for which planning permission has been granted or is deemed to have been granted under Part III of the Act, or for which planning permission is not required), or on land adjoining such land, of buildings, works, plant or machinery needed temporarily in connection with the said operations, for the period of such operations.

Column (2) for Class IV.1: Such buildings, works, plant or machinery shall be removed at the expiration of the period of such operations and where they were sited on any such adjoining land, that land shall be forthwith reinstated.

Column (1) Description of Development	Column (2) Conditions
2. The use of land (other than a building or the curtilage of a building) for any purpose or purposes except as a caravan site on not more than 28 days in total in any calendar year (of which not more than 14 days in total may be devoted to use for the purpose of motor car or motor-cycle racing or for the purpose of the holding of markets), and the erection or placing of moveable structures on the land for the purposes of that use: Provided that for the purpose of the limitation imposed on the number of days on which land may be used for motor car or motor-cycle racing, account shall be taken only of those days on which races are held or practising takes place.	

Class V.—*Uses by members of recreational organisations*
The use of land, other than buildings and not within the curtilage of a dwellinghouse, for the purposes of recreation or instruction by members of an organisation which holds a certificate of exemption granted under section 269 of the Public Health Act 1936, and the erection or placing of tents on the land for the purposes of that use.

Class VI.—*Agricultural buildings, works and uses* 1. The carrying out on agricultural land having an area of more than one acre and comprised in an agricultural unit of building or engineering operations [(other than engineering operations to which paragraph 4 below applies)] requisite for the use of that land for the purposes of agriculture (other than the placing on land of structures not designed for those purposes or the provision and alteration of dwellings), so long as:—	[1. In the case of operations which involve the deposit on or under the land of refuse or waste materials no such material shall be brought onto the land from elsewhere.
(*a*) the ground area covered by a building erected pursuant to this permission does not, either by itself or after the addition thereto of the ground area covered by any existing building or buildings (other than a dwellinghouse) within the same unit erected or in course of erection within the preceding two years and wholly or partly within 90 metres of the nearest part of the said building, exceed 465 square metres;	2. Where an operation involves the extraction of any mineral from the land, or from any disused railway embankment on the land, or the removal of any mineral from a mineral-working deposit on the land, and no planning permission has been granted (on an application made to the local planning authority under Part III of the Act) for the winning and working of that mineral, the mineral shall not be moved off the land.]
(*b*) the height of any buildings or works does not exceed 3 metres in the case of a building or works within 3 kilometres of the perimeter of an aerodrome, nor 12 metres in any other case;	
(*c*) no part of any buildings (other than moveable	

Column (1) Description of Development	Column (2) Conditions

structures) or works is within 25 metres of the metalled portion of a trunk or classified road.
2. The erection or construction and the maintenance, improvement or other alteration of roadside stands for milk churns, except where they would abut on any trunk or classified road.
3. The winning and working, on land held or occupied with land used for the purposes of agriculture, of any minerals reasonably required for the purposes of that use, including—
  (i) the fertilisation of the land so used; and
  (ii) the maintenance, improvement or alteration of buildings or works thereon which are occupied or used for the purposes aforesaid,
so long as no excavation is made within 25 metres of the metalled portion of a trunk or classified road.	

	[No minerals extracted during the course of the operations shall be moved to any place outside the land from which they were extracted, except to the land which is held or occupied with that land and is used for agricultural purposes.]

[4. The carrying out of operations for the construction of fishponds (including the excavation of land and the winning and working of minerals) and other engineering operations on agricultural land used for the purposes of any business of fish farming or of shellfish farming which is registered in a register kept by the Minister of Agriculture Fisheries and Food or the Secretary of State (as the case may be) for the purposes of an order made under section 7 of the Diseases of Fish Act 1983 where—

(a) the area of the site within which the operations are carried out does not exceed 2 hectares;

(b) no operations are carried out within 25 metres of the metalled portion of a trunk or classified road;

(c) in a case where the operations involve the winning or working of minerals, they comply with both of the following limitations:—
  (i) that no excavation exceeds a depth of 2.5 metres; and
  (ii) that the area of excavation (taken together with any other excavations carried out on the land within the preceding two years) does not exceed 0.2 hectares.]

Class VII.—Forestry buildings and works
The carrying out on land used for the purposes of forestry (including afforestation) of building and other operations (other than the provision or alteration of dwellings) requisite for the carrying on of

Column (1) Description of Development	Column (2) Conditions

those purposes, and the formation, alteration and maintenance of private ways on such land, so long as:—

 (a) the height of any buildings or works within 3 kilometres of the perimeter of an aerodrome does not exceed 3 metres;

 (b) no part of any buildings (other than moveable structures) or works is within 25 metres of the metalled portion of a trunk or classified road.

Class VIII.—Development for industrial purposes
[1. Development of the following descriptions, carried out by an industrial undertaker on land used (otherwise than (i) in contravention of previous planning control or (ii) without planning permission granted or deemed to be granted under Part III of the Act) for the carrying out of any industrial process, and for the purposes of such process, or on land used (otherwise than as aforesaid) as a dock, harbour or quay for the purposes of an industrial undertaking:—

 (i) the provision, rearrangement or replacement of private ways or private railways, sidings or conveyors;

 (ii) the provision or rearrangement of sewers, mains, pipes, cables or other apparatus;

 (iii) the installation or erection, by way of addition or replacement, of plant or machinery, or structures or erections of the nature of plant or machinery, not exceeding 15 metres in height or the height of the plant, machinery, structure or erection so replaced, whichever is the greater;

 [(iv) the extension or alteration of buildings (whether erected before or after 1st July 1948), so long as the height of the original building is not exceeded, the cubic content of the original building (as ascertained by external measurement) is not increased by more than 25%, and its aggregate floor space is not increased by more than 1,000 square metres.]

so long as:—

 (a) in the case of operations carried out under subparagraph (iii) or (iv), the external appearance of the premises of the undertaking is not materially affected;

 (b) in the case of operations carried out under subparagraph (iv), no part of the building is, as

Column (1) Description of Development	Column (2) Conditions
a result of the development, within a distance of five metres from any boundary of the curtilage of the premises; and (c) in the case of operations carried out under subparagraph (iv), no certificate would be required under section 67 of the Act if an application for planning permission for the development in question were made: Provided that the erection on land within the curtilage of any such building of an additional building to be used in connection with the original building shall be treated as an extension of the original building, and where any two or more original buildings comprised in the same curtilage are used as one unit for the purposes of the undertaking, the reference in this permission to the cubic content shall be construed as a reference to the aggregate cubic content of those buildings, and the reference to the aggregate floor space as a reference to the total floor space of those buildings.] 2. The deposit by an industrial undertaker of waste material or refuse resulting from an industrial process on any land comprised in a site which was used for such deposit on 1st July 1948, whether or not the superficial area or the height of the deposit is thereby extended. *Class IX.—Repairs to unadopted streets and private ways* The carrying out of works required for the maintenance or improvement of an unadopted street or private way, being works carried out on land within the boundaries of the street or way. *Class X.—Repairs to services* The carrying out of any works for the purpose of inspecting, repairing or renewing sewers, mains, pipes, cables, or other apparatus, including the breaking open of any land for that purpose. *Class XI.—War damaged buildings, works and plant* The rebuilding, restoration or replacement of buildings, works or plant which have sustained war damage, so long as:— (a) the cubic content of the building or of the works or plant immediately before the occurrence of such damage is not increased by more than such amount (if any) as is permitted under Class I or Class VIII;	

Column (1) Description of Development	Column (2) Conditions

(*b*) there is no material alteration from the external appearance immediately before the occurrence of such damage except with the approval of the local planning authority.

Class XII.—Development under local or private Acts, or orders

Development authorised (i) by any local or private Act of Parliament or (ii) by any order approved by both Houses of Parliament or (iii) by any order made under section 14 or section 16 of the Harbours Act 1964 being, in any such case, a local or private Act, or an order, which designates specifically both the nature of the development thereby authorised and the land upon which it may be carried out:

Provided that where the development consists of or includes the erection, construction, alteration or extension of any building (which expression shall include any bridge, aqueduct, pier or dam, but not any other structure or erection), or the formation laying out or alteration of a means of access to any highway used by vehicular traffic this permission shall be exercisable in respect of such building or access as the case may be only if the prior approval of (*a*) the district planning authority (except in Greater London, [a metropolitan county] or a National Park); (*b*) in Greater London [or a metropolitan county], the local planning authority, or (*c*) in a National Park [outside a metropolitan county], the county planning authority is obtained for the detailed plans and specifications thereof; but that authority shall not refuse to grant approval, or impose conditions on the grant thereof, unless they are satisfied that it is expedient so to do on the ground that:—

(*a*) the design, or external appearance of such building, bridge, aqueduct, pier or dam would injure the amenity of the neighbourhood and is reasonably capable of modification so as to conform with such amenity; or

(*b*) in the case of a building, bridge, aqueduct, pier or means of access, the erection, construction, formation, laying out, alteration or extension, ought to be and could reasonably be carried out elsewhere on the land.

Class XIII.—Development by local authorities

1. The erection or construction and the main-

Column (1) Description of Development	Column (2) Conditions
tenance, improvement or other alteration by a local authority [or by an urban development corporation] of:— (i) such small ancillary buildings, works and equipment as are required on land belonging to or maintained by them, for the purposes of any functions exercised by them on that land otherwise than as statutory undertakers; (ii) lamp standards, information kiosks, passenger shelters, public shelters and seats, telephone boxes, fire alarms, public drinking fountains, horse-troughs, refuse bins or baskets, barriers for the control of persons waiting to enter public vehicles, and such similar structures or works as may be required in connection with the operation of any public service administered by them. 2. The deposit by a local authority of waste material or refuse on any land comprised in a site which was used for that purpose on 1st July 1948, whether or not the superficial area or the height of the deposit is thereby extended.	

Class XIV.—Development by local highway authorities ...

The carrying out by a local highway authority ... of any works required for or incidental to the maintenance or improvement of existing highways being works carried out on land outside but abutting on the boundary of the highway.

Class XV.—Development by drainage authorities

Any development by a drainage authority within the meaning of the Land Drainage Act 1930, in, on or under any watercourse or drainage works, in connection with the improvement or maintenance of such watercourse or drainage works.

Class XVI.—Development by water authorities

Development of any of the following descriptions by a water authority established under the Water Act 1973:—

(a) the laying underground of mains, pipes or other apparatus;

(b) the improvement, maintenance or repair of watercourses or land drainage works;

Column (1) Description of Development	Column (2) Conditions
(c) the erection, construction or placing of buildings, plants, or apparatus on land or the carrying out of engineering operations in, on, over or under land, for the purpose of surveys or investigations.	On completion of the survey or investigation, or at the end of 6 months from the commencement of the development permitted by this class, whichever is the sooner, all such operations shall cease and all such buildings, plant or apparatus shall be removed and the land restored to its former condition.

Class XVII.—Development for sewerage and sewage disposal

Any development by or on behalf of a water authority (established under the Water Act 1973), or by a Development Corporation authorised under section 34 of the New Towns Act 1965 to exercise powers relating to sewerage or sewage disposal, being development not above ground level required in connection with the provision, improvement or maintenance of sewers.

Class XVIII.—Development by statutory undertakers

A. Railway or light railway undertakings.

Development by the undertakers of operational land of the undertaking, being development which is required in connection with the movement of traffic by rail, other than:

(i) the construction of railways;
(ii) the construction or erection, or the reconstruction or alteration so as materially to affect the design or external appearance thereof, of—

(a) any railway station or bridge;
(b) any hotel;
(c) any residential or educational building, office, or building to be used for manufacturing or repairing work which is not situate wholly within the interior of a railway station;
(d) any car park, shop, restaurant, garage, petrol filling station or other building or structure provided in pursuance of the powers contained in section 14(1)(d) of the Transport Act 1962 or section 10(1)(x) of the Transport Act 1968 which is not situate wholly within the interior of a railway station.

Column (1) Description of Development	Column (2) Conditions

B. Dock, pier, harbour, water transport, canal or inland navigation undertakings.

1. Development by the undertakers or their lessees of operational land of the undertaking, being development which is required for the purpose or shipping, or in connection with the embarking, disembarking, loading, discharging or transport of passengers, livestock or goods at a dock, pier or harbour, or the movement of traffic by canal or inland navigation, or by any railway forming part of the undertaking, other than the construction or erection, or the reconstruction or alteration so as materially to affect the design or external appearance thereof, of:—

   (a) any bridge or other building not required in connection with the handling of traffic;
   (b) any hotel;
   (c) any educational building not situate wholly within the limits of a dock, pier or harbour;
   (d) any car park, shop, restaurant, garage, petrol filling station or other building not situate wholly within the limits of a dock, pier or harbour, provided in pursuance of the powers contained in any of the following enactments:—

the Transport Act 1962 section 14(1)(d);
the Transport Act 1968 section 10(1)(x);
the Transport Act 1968 section 50(6).

2. The improvement, maintenance or repair of any inland waterway to which section 104 of the Transport Act 1968 applies which is not a commercial waterway or a cruising waterway, and the repair or maintenance of culverts, weirs, locks, aqueducts, sluices, reservoirs, let-off valves or other works used in connection with the control and operation of such waterways.

3. The use of any land for the spreading of dredgings.

C. Water or hydraulic power undertakings.

Development required for the purposes of the undertakings of any of the following descriptions, that is to say:—

   (i) the laying underground of mains, pipes, or other apparatus;
   (ii) the improvement, maintenance or repair of watercourses or land drainage works;
   (iii) the maintenance or repair of works for measuring the flow in any watercourse or channel or the improvement of any such works (otherwise than by the erection or installation, by

Column (1) Description of Development	Column (2) Conditions
way of addition or replacement, of any structures of the nature of buildings or of any plant or machinery); (iv) the installation in a water distribution system of booster stations, meter or switch gear houses, not exceeding (except where constructed underground elsewhere than under a highway) 29 cubic meters in capacity; (v) the erection, construction or placing of buildings, plant or apparatus on land, or the carrying out of engineering operations, in, on, over or under land, for the purpose of surveys or investigations.	On completion of the survey or investigation or at the expiration of six months from the commencement of the development the subject of this permission, whichever is the sooner, all such operations shall cease and all such buildings, plant or apparatus shall be removed and the land restored to its former condition.
(vi) any other development carried out in, on, over or under the operational land of the undertaking except:— (*a*) the erection, or the reconstruction or alteration so as materially to affect the design or external appearance thereof, of buildings; (*b*) the installation or erection, by way of addition or replacement, of any plant or machinery, or structure or erections of the nature of plant or machinery, exceeding 15 metres in height or the height of the plant, machinery, structure or erection so replaced, whichever is the greater. D. Gas undertakings. Development required for the purposes of the undertaking of any of the following descriptions, that is to say:— (i) the laying underground of mains, pipes or other apparatus;	Not less than 8 weeks before the commencement of operations for the laying of a notifiable pipeline, the undertaker shall give notice in writing to the local planning authority of the intention to carry out such development, identifying the land under which the pipeline is to be laid.

Column (1) Description of Development	Column (2) Conditions
(ii) the installation in a gas distribution system of apparatus for measuring, recording, controlling or varying the pressure flow or volume of gas, and structures for housing such apparatus not exceeding (except where constructed underground elsewhere than under a highway) 29 cubic metres in capacity;	
(iii) the construction, in any storage area or protective area specified in an order made under section 4 of the Gas Act 1965 of boreholes, other than those shown in the order as approved by the Secretary of State for Energy for the purpose of subsection (6) of the said section 4, and the erection or construction, in any such area, of any plant or machinery, or structure or erections in the nature of plant or machinery, not exceeding 6 metres in height which is required in connection with the construction of any such borehole;	
(iv) the placing and storage on land of pipes and other apparatus needed for inclusion in a main or pipe which is being or is about to be laid or constructed in pursuance of a planning permission granted or deemed to be granted under Part III of the Act;	On completion of the laying or construction of the relevant main or pipe, or at the expiration of nine months from the date of commencement of those operations, whichever is the sooner, such pipes and apparatus shall be removed and the land shall be restored to its condition before the development took place.
(v) the erection on operational land of the undertaking, solely for the protection of plant or machinery, or structures or erections of the nature of plant or machinery, of buildings not exceeding 15 metres in height;	Approval of the details of the design and external appearance of the buildings shall be obtained from (a) the district planning authority (except in Greater London, [a metropolitan county] or a National Park), (b) in Greater London [or a metropolitan county], the local planning authority, or (c) in a National Park [outside a metropolitan county], the county planning authority, before the erection of the building is begun.

Column (1) Description of Development	Column (2) Conditions
(vi) any other development carried out in, on, over or under operational land of the undertaking except:—	

(a) the erection, or the reconstruction or alteration so as materially to affect the design or external appearance thereof, of buildings;

(b) the installation of any plant or machinery, or structures or erections of the nature of plant or machinery, exceeding 15 metres in height, or capable, without addition, of being extended to a height exceeding 15 metres;

(c) the replacement of any plant or machinery, or structures or erections of the nature of plant or machinery, to a height exceeding 15 metres or the height of the plant, machinery, structure or erection so replaced, whichever is the greater.]

E. Electricity undertakings.

Development required for the purpose of the undertaking of any of the following descriptions, that is to say:—

(i) the laying underground of pipes, cables of any other apparatus, and the construction of such shafts and tunnels as may be necessary in connection therewith;

(ii) the installation in an electric line of feeder or service pillars, or transforming or switching stations or chambers not exceeding (except when constructed underground elsewhere than under a highway [used by vehicular traffic]) 29 cubic metres in capacity;

(iii) the installation of service lines to individual consumers from an electric line;

[(iv) the extension or alteration of buildings on operational land, so long as the height of the original building is not exceeded, the cubic content of the original building (as ascertained by external measurement) is not increased by more than 25%, and its aggregate floor space is not increased by more than 1,000 square metres.]

(v) the sinking of any boreholes for the purpose of ascertaining the nature of the sub-soil, and the installation of any plant or machinery, or structures or erections of the nature of plant or machinery, as may be necessary in connection therewith;

    On completion of the development or at the expiration of six months from the commencement of the development the subject of this permission, whichever is the sooner, such plant or machinery or structures or

Column (1) Description of Development	Column (2) Conditions
	erections shall be removed and the land shall be restored to its condition before the development took place.
(vi) the erection on operational land of the undertaking, solely for the protection of plant or machinery, or structures or erections, of the nature of plant or machinery, of buildings not exceeding 15 metres in height;	Approval of the details of the design and external appearance of the buildings shall be obtained from (a) the district planning authority (except in Greater London, [a metropolitan county] or a National Park), (b) in Greater London [or a metropolitan county], the local planning authority, or (c) in a National Park [outside a metropolitan county], the county planning authority, before the erection of the building has begun.

(vii) any other development carried out on, in or under the operational land of the undertaking except:—

(*a*) the erection, or the reconstruction so as materially to affect the design or external appearance thereof, of buildings; or

(*b*) the installation or erection, by way of addition or replacement, of any plant or machinery, or structures or erections of the nature of plant or machinery, exceeding 15 metres in height or the height of the plant, machinery, structure or erection so replaced, whichever is the greater.

F. Tramway or road transport undertakings.

Development required for the purposes of the undertaking of any of the following descriptions, that is to say:—

(i) the installation of posts, overhead wires, underground cables, feeder pillars, or transformer boxes not exceeding 17 cubic metres in capacity in, on, over or adjacent to a highway for the purpose of supplying current to public vehicles;

(ii) the installation of tramway tracks; conduits and drains and pipes in connection therewith for the working of tramways;

(iii) the installation of telephone cables and apparatus, huts, step posts and signs required in connection with the operation of public vehicles;

Column (1) Description of Development	Column (2) Conditions

(iv) the erection or construction, and the maintenance, improvement or other alteration of passenger shelters and barriers for the control of persons waiting to enter public vehicles;

(v) any other development of operational land of the undertaking, other than:—

(a) the erection, or the reconstruction or alteration so as materially to affect the design or external appearance thereof, of buildings;

(b) the installation or erection, by way of addition or replacement, of any plant or machinery, or structures or erections of the nature of plant or machinery, exceeding 15 metres in height, or the height of the plant, machinery, structure or erection so replaced, whichever is the greater;

(c) development, not wholly within the interior of an omnibus or tramway station, in pursuance of the powers contained in section 14(1)(i)(d) of the Transport Act 1962 or section 10(1)(x) of the Transport Act 1968.

G. Lighthouse Undertakings.

Development required for the purposes of the functions of a general or local lighthouse authority under the Merchant Shipping Act 1894 and any other statutory provisions made with respect to a local lighthouse authority, or in the exercise by a local lighthouse authority of rights, powers or duties acquired by usage prior to the Merchant Shipping Act 1894, except the erection, or the reconstruction or alternation so as materially to affect the design or external appearance thereof, of offices.

H. The British Airports Authority.

Development by the Authority of operational land of the undertaking, being development which is required in connection with the provision by the Authority of services and facilities necessary or desirable for the operation of an aerodrome, other than:—

(i) the construction or erection, or the reconstruction or alteration so as materially to affect the design or external appearance thereof, of:—

(a) any hotel;

(b) any building (not being a building required in connection with the movement or maintenance of aircraft or with the embarking, disembarking, loading, discharge or transport of passengers, livestock or goods at an aerodrome); and

(ii) the construction or extension of runways.

Column (1) Description of Development	Column (2) Conditions
[I. Post Office. Development required for the purposes of the undertaking of any of the following descriptions: (1) the installation of posting boxes or self-service machines; (2) any other development carried out in, on, over or under the operational land of the undertaking except:— (a) the erection or reconstruction of buildings or the alteration of buildings so as materially to affect the design or external appearance thereof: (b) the installation or erection, by way of addition or replacement, of any plant or machinery, or structure or erection of the nature of plant or machinery, which exceeds 15 metres in height, or the height of the existing plant, machinery or structure or erection, whichever is the greater.] [J. Civil Aviation Authority. 1. The carrying out within the perimeter of an aerodrome at which the Civil Aviation Authority provide air traffic control services of development required in connection with the provision of services and facilities which are necessary or desirable either for providing air traffic control services or for assisting the navigation of aircraft using the aerodrome. 2. The carrying out, on any operational land of the Authority which is outside but within 8 kilometres of the perimeter of an aerodrome at which the Authority provide air traffic control services, of development required in connection with the provision of services and facilities which are necessary or desirable either for providing such air traffic control services or for assisting the navigation of aircraft using the aerodrome, with the exception of:— (a) the erection of buildings to be used for purposes other than housing equipment used in connection with the provision of air traffic control services or in connection with assisting the navigation of aircraft; (b) the erection of any building exceeding a height of 4 metres; (c) the installation or erection, by way of addition or replacement, of any radio mast, radar mast, antenna or other apparatus which exceeds the height of the mast, antenna or apparatus which is being replaced, or a height of 15 metres, whichever is the greater. 3. The carrying out, on land which was opera-	

Column (1) Description of Development	Column (2) Conditions
tional land of the Authority on 1st March 1986 and remains operational land, of development required in connection with the provision by the Authority of services and facilities necessary or desirable for assisting the navigation of aircraft, except—	

(a) the erection of buildings to be used for purposes other than housing equipment used in connection with assisting the navigation of aircraft;

(b) the erection of any building exceeding a height of 4 metres;

(c) the installation or erection of any radio mast, radar mast, antenna or other apparatus, save by way of replacement or substitution for an existing mast or antenna or existing apparatus by one which does not exceed the height of the mast, antenna or apparatus which is being replaced, or a height of 15 metres, whichever is the greater.

4. The use of land by or on behalf of the Civil Aviation Authority in case of emergency, for a period not exceeding six months, for the stationing of moveable apparatus required for the replacement of unserviceable apparatus.

5. The use of land by or on behalf of the Civil Aviation Authority, for a period not exceeding six months, for the purpose of providing services and facilities in connection with air traffic control services or assistance in the navigation of aircraft, and the erection or placing of moveable structures on the land for the purposes of such use.

6. The use of land by or on behalf of the Civil Aviation Authority, for a period not exceeding six months, for the stationing and operation of apparatus in connection with the carrying out of surveys or investigations.]

[On or before the expiry of any period of six months referred to in paragraphs 4 to 6, all such uses shall cease and any apparatus or structure shall be removed, and the land shall be restored to its condition before the development took place.]

Class XIX.—Development by mineral undertakers

1. Where mining operations have been carried out in any land at any time on or after 1st January 1946 and before 1st July 1948,

(a) in conformity with the provisions of a planning scheme or of permission granted thereunder or in accordance with permission granted at any time before 22nd July 1943 by or under

Column (1) Description of Development	Column (2) Conditions

an interim development order and in force immediately before 1st July 1948, or

(b) under article 4 of the Town and Country Planning (General Interim Development) Order 1946,

and an application for permission to continue those mining operations in adjoining land was made during the period of six months from 1st July 1948 or was treated by virtue of paragraph 1 of Schedule 10 to the Town and Country Planning Act 1947 as having been made under that Act, the continuation of those operations until the application (or any appeal in respect thereof) has been dealt with.

2. The erection, alteration or extension by mineral undertakers on land in or adjacent to and belonging to a quarry or mine comprised in their undertaking of any building, plant or machinery, or structure or erection of the nature of plant or machinery, which is required in connection with the winning or working of minerals, including coal won or worked by virtue of section 36(1) of the Coal Industry Nationalisation Act 1946, but not any other coal, in pursuance of permission granted or deemed to be granted under Part III of the Act, or which is required in connection with the treatment or disposal of such minerals:

Provided that where the development consists of or includes the erection, alteration or extension of a building, this permission shall be exercisable in respect of such building only if the prior approval of the [minerals planning authority] is obtained for the detailed plans and specifications of the building; but that authority shall not refuse to grant approval, or impose conditions on the grant thereof, unless they are satisfied that it is expedient so to do on the ground that:—

(a) the erection, alteration or extension of such building would injure the amenity of the neighbourhood and modifications can reasonably be made or conditions can reasonably be imposed in order to avoid or reduce the injury; or

(b) the proposed building or extension ought to be, and can reasonably be, sited elsewhere.

3. The deposit of refuse or waste materials by, or by licence of, a mineral undertaker in excavations made by such undertaker and already lawfully used for that purpose so long as the height of such

Column (1) Description of Development	Column (2) Conditions
deposit does not exceed the level of the land adjoining any such excavation. *Class XX.—Development by the National Coal Board* Development of any of the following descriptions carried out by the National Coal Board, or their lessees or licensees, that is to say:— (i) the winning and working underground, in a mine commenced before 1st July 1948, of coal or other minerals mentioned in paragraph 1 of Schedule 1 to the Coal Industry Nationalisation Act 1946, and any underground development incidental thereto; (ii) any development required in connection with coal industry activities as defined in section 63 of the Coal Industry Nationalisation Act 1946 and carried out in the immediate vicinity of a pithead: Provided that where the development consists of or includes the erection, alteration or extension of a building this permission shall be exercisable in respect of such building only if the prior approval of the [minerals planning authority] is obtained for the detailed plans and specifications of the building, but the [minerals planning authority] shall not refuse to grant approval, or impose conditions on the grant thereof unless they are satisfied that it is expedient so to do on the ground that:— (*a*) the erection, alteration or extension of such building would injure the amenity of the neighbourhood and modifications can reasonably be made or conditions can reasonably be imposed in order to avoid or reduce the injury; or (*b*) the proposed building or extension ought to be, and can reasonably be, sited elsewhere; (iii) the deposit of waste materials or refuse resulting from colliery production activities as defined by paragraph 2 of Schedule 1 to the Coal Industry Nationalisation Act 1946 on land comprised in a site used for the deposit of waste materials or refuse on 1st July 1948, whether or not the superficial or the height of the deposit is thereby extended;	1. If the [minerals planning authority] so require, the Board shall, within

Column (1) Description of Development	Column (2) Conditions
	such period as the authority may specify (not being less than three months from the date when the requirement is made) submit to them for approval a scheme making provision for the manner in which the depositing of waste materials or refuse is to be carried out and for the carrying out of operations in relation thereto (including, where appropriate, the stripping and storage of surface soil and the after-treatment of the deposit) for the preservation of amenity, such scheme to relate only to the depositing and after-treatment of waste materials or refuse deposited after 1st April 1974.
	2. Where a scheme submitted in accordance with condition 1 has been approved the depositing of waste materials or refuse and their after-treatment shall be carried out in accordance with the scheme, or in accordance with the scheme as modified by conditions imposed on the grant of approval, as the case may be.
(iv) development by the National Coal Board consisting of the temporary use of land for the purpose of prospecting for coal workable by opencast methods and carrying out of any operations requisite for that purpose.	1. No development shall be begun until after the expiration of 42 days from the date of service of notice in writing on the [minerals planning authority], indicating the nature, extent and probable duration of the prospecting.
	2. At the expiration of the period of prospecting, any buildings, plant or machinery and any waste

Column (1) Description of Development	Column (2) Conditions
	materials shall be removed and any boreholes shall be properly and sufficiently sealed and other excavations filled in and levelled, any topsoil removed being replaced as the uppermost layer.

Class XXI.—Uses of aerodrome buildings

The use of buildings on an aerodrome which is vested in or under the control of the British Airports Authority for purposes connected with the air transport services or other flying activities at such aerodrome.

Class XXII.—Use as a caravan site

The use of land, other than a building, as a caravan site in any of the circumstances specified in paragraph 2 to 9 (inclusive) of Schedule 1 to the Caravan Sites and Control of Development Act 1960 or in the circumstances (other than those relating to winter quarters) specified in paragraph 10 of the said Schedule.

The use shall be discontinued when the said circumstances cease to exist, and all caravans on the site shall then be removed.

Class XXIII.—Development on licensed caravan sites

Development required by the conditions of a site licence for the time being in force under Part I of the Caravan Sites and Control of Development Act 1960.

Class XXIV.—Development by Telecommunications Code System Operators

The carrying out of development by or on behalf of a telecommunications code system operator where the development is being carried out either—

(a) on land occupied by the operator in respect of which he is the estate owner in respect of the fee simple or he holds a lease granted for a term of not less than 10 years; or

(b) in pursuance of a right conferred on the operator under the telecommunications code, and in accordance with any conditions relating to the application of that code which have been imposed by the terms of his licence, and for the purposes of the operator's telecommunication system; and where the development is within any of the following descriptions:—

1. In the case of the installation, alteration or replacement on a building of an antenna the antenna of any kind, or any apparatus which is intended to support an antenna, the antenna or apparatus shall so far as practicable be sited so as to minimise its effect on the external appearance of that building.

2. Where development within paragraph (2) in column (1) has been carried out, then at the expiration

308 *Development and Planning Law*

Column (1) Description of Development	Column (2) Conditions
(1) the installation, alteration or replacement in, on, over or under land of any telecommunication apparatus where—	of the period of six months from commencement of the use, or when the need for the use of the land for the stationing and operation of moveable telecommunication apparatus ceases (whichever first occurs), all such apparatus, and all moveable structures erected or placed on the land for the purpose of the use, shall be removed and the land shall be restored to its condition before development took place.

(a) in the case of the installation of apparatus (other than on a building or other structure), the apparatus does not exceed a height of 15 metres above ground level;

(b) in the case of the alteration or replacement of apparatus already installed on a building or other structure), the apparatus does not when altered or replaced exceed the height of the existing apparatus or a height of 15 metres above ground level whichever is the greater;

(c) in the case of the installation, alteration or replacement of apparatus on a building or other structure, the height of the apparatus (taken by itself) does not exceed:—
  (i) 15 metres where it is installed, or is to be installed, on a building or other structure which has a height of 30 metres or more; or
  (ii) 10 metres in any other case;

(d) in the case of the installation, alteration or replacement of apparatus on a building or other structure, the highest part of the apparatus when installed, altered or replaced does not exceed the height of the highest part of the existing building or structure by more than—
  (i) 10 metres in the case of a building or structure which is 30 metres or more high;
  (ii) 8 metres in the case of a building or structure which is more than 15 metres but less than 30 metres high; or
  (iii) 6 metres in any other case;

(e) in the case of the installation, alteration or replacement of any apparatus other than a mast, any kind of antenna, a public call box or any apparatus which does not project above the level of the surface of the ground, the ground or base area of the structure does not exceed 1.5 square metres;

(f) in the case of the installation, alteration or replacement of any microwave antenna, or any apparatus which includes or is intended for the support of such an antenna, on a building or other structure—

Column (1) Description of Development	Column (2) Conditions
(i) the building or other structure on which the antenna is installed or is to be installed exceeds a height of 15 metres; (ii) the size of the antenna, when measured in any dimension, does not exceed 1.3 metres (excluding any projecting feed element); (iii) the development does not result in the presence on the building or structure of more than two microwave antennas; (2) the use of land in case of emergency, for a period not exceeding six months, for the stationing and operation of moveable telecommunication apparatus required for the replacement of unserviceable telecommunication apparatus, and the erection or placing of moveable structures on the land for the purposes of that use.	
Class XXV.—Other telecommunications development The installation, alteration or replacement on any building or other structure (except a dwellinghouse), in circumstances other than those set out in class XXIV of this Schedule, of a microwave antenna and any structures intended for the support of such an antenna where— (a) the building or other structure on which the antenna is installed or is to be installed exceeds a height of 15 metres; (b) in the case of a terrestrial microwave antenna— (i) the size of the antenna, when measured in any dimension, does not exceed 1.3 metres (excluding any projecting feed element); and (ii) the highest part of the antenna or its supporting structure is not more than 3 metres higher than the highest part of the existing building or structure on which it is installed; (c) in the case of a satellite antenna, the size of the antenna, taken together with its supporting structure (but excluding any projecting feed element), does not exceed 90 centimetres; (d) the development does not result in the presence on the building or structure of more than two microwave antennas.	1. The antenna shall, so far as practicable, be sited so as to minimise its effect on the external appearance of the building or other structure on which it is installed. 2. When an antenna is no longer needed for the reception or transmission of microwave radio energy it shall be removed from the building or structure.

310 — Development and Planning Law

Column (1) Description of Development	Column (2) Conditions

Class XXVI.—Mineral exploration
1. The carrying out of any of the following operations, namely:—
   (i) the drilling of boreholes for the purpose of ascertaining the presence, extent or quality of a deposit of a mineral with a view to the exploitation of that mineral;
  (ii) operations required for the carrying out of seismic surveys designed for the purpose of ascertaining the presence, extent or quality of a deposit of a mineral with a view to the exploitation of that mineral;
  (iii) the making of other excavations for the purpose of ascertaining the presence, extent or quality of a deposit of a mineral with a view to the exploitation of that mineral;
on any land during a period not exceeding 28 consecutive days, and the erection, assembly or construction on the land, or adjoining land, of buildings, plant or machinery, or other structures, which are required in connection with any of those operations, where:—
 (*a*) no operations are carried out in, on, over or under land which is within 50 metres of any part of an occupied residential building or a building which is occupied and used as a hospital or a school;
 (*b*) no operations are carried out on land which is within a National Park, an area of outstanding natural beauty or a site of archaeological interest or special scientific interest;
 (*c*) in the case of operations carried out under sub-paragraph (ii) above, no explosive charge of more than 1 kilogram is used;
 (*d*) in the case of operations carried out under sub-paragraph (iii) above—
   (i) no excavation made during the carrying out of the operations exceeds 10 metres in depth or 12 square metres in surface area; and
  (ii) the operations do not result in the making of more than 10 excavations over any period of 24 months within any area of 1 hectare within the land;
 (*e*) in the case of the erection, assembly or construction of buildings, plant or machinery or other structures—
   (i) no such building, plant or machinery or
	1. No operations shall be carried out between the hours of 6 pm and 7 am.
	2. No trees on the land shall be removed, felled, lopped or topped except insofar as the mineral planning authority may otherwise have agreed in writing and no operations shall be carried out (or any other thing done on the land) which is likely to have any detrimental effect on the trees.
	3. Before any operation consisting of an excavation is carried out the topsoil shall be removed from the area of land excavated and shall be stored separately from other excavated material; and the subsoil shall then be removed and stored separately from other excavated material (including the topsoil).
	4. Within a 28 day period following the cessation of the operations the following action shall be taken (unless, in any particular case, the mineral planning authority have otherwise agreed in writing):—
	 (*a*) all buildings, plant, machinery and other structures and any waste materials, shall be removed from the land;
	 (*b*) all boreholes shall be adequately sealed or (as the case may be) all other excavations shall be filled in with material from the site; the surface shall

Column (1) Description of Development	Column (2) Conditions
other structure exceeds a height of 12 metres; and (ii) no building, plant or machinery or other structure which exceeds a height of 3 metres is erected, assembled or constructed on any land which is within 3 kilometres of the perimeter of an aerodrome.	be levelled and the topsoil shall be replaced as the uppermost layer; and (c) the land shall (so far as it is practicable to do so) be restored to its condition before the development took place (with the carrying out of seeding and replanting so far as may be necessary).

2.—(1) The carrying out of any of the following operations, namely:—
  (i) the drilling of boreholes for the purpose of ascertaining the presence, extent or quality of a deposit of a mineral with a view to the exploitation of that mineral;
  (ii) operations required for the carrying out of seismic surveys designed for the purpose of ascertaining the presence, extent or quality of a deposit of a mineral with a view to the exploitation of that mineral;
  (iii) the making of other excavations for the purpose of ascertaining the presence, extent or quality of a deposit of a mineral with a view to the exploitation of that mineral;
on any land during a period not exceeding 4 months, and the erection, assembly or construction on that land, or on adjoining land, of buildings, plant or machinery or other structures, which are required in connection with any of those operations, where:—
  (a) in the case of operations carried out under subparagraph (ii) above, no explosive charge of more than 2 kilograms is used;
  (b) in the case of operations carried out under subparagraph (iii) above, no excavation made during the carrying out of the operations exceeds 10 metres in depth or 12 square metres in surface area; and
  (c) in the case of the erection assembly or construction of buildings, plant or machinery or other structures, no such building, plant or machinery or other structure exceeds a height of 12 metres,
so long as the developer has previously notified the
	1. The development shall be carried out in accordance with the details specified in the written notice given to the mineral planning authority, except insofar as the mineral planning authority have otherwise agreed in writing.
	2. No trees on the land shall be removed, felled, lopped or topped except insofar as the mineral planning authority may otherwise have agreed in writing, and no operations shall be carried out (or any other thing done on the land) which is likely to have any detrimental effect on the trees.
	3. Before any operation consisting of an excavation is carried out, the topsoil shall be removed from the area of land excavated and shall be stored separately from other excavated material; and the subsoil shall then be removed and stored separately from other excavated material (including the topsoil).
	4. Within a 28 day period following the cessation of the operations, the

Column (1) Description of Development	Column (2) Conditions

mineral planning authority in writing of his intention to carry out development under this paragraph (specifying the nature of the development), and the relevant period has elapsed.
(2) The relevant period elapses:—
(*a*) where the mineral planning authority do not issue a direction under article 4A:—
  (i) 28 days after the notification referred to in paragraph (1) above, or
  (ii) if earlier, on the date on which the mineral planning authority notify the developer in writing that they will not issue such a direction;
(*b*) where the mineral planning authority issue a direction under article 4A:—
  (i) 28 days from the date on which notice of it is sent to the Secretary of State, or
  (ii) if earlier, the date on which the mineral planning authority notify the developer in writing that the Secretary of State has disallowed the direction.
	following action shall be taken (unless in any particular case, the mineral planning authority have otherwise agreed in writing):—
	(*a*) all buildings, plant, machinery and other structures and any waste materials, shall be removed from the land;
	(*b*) all boreholes shall be adequately sealed or (as the case may be), all other excavations shall be filled in with other material from the site; the surface shall be levelled and the topsoil shall be replaced as the uppermost layer; and
	(*c*) the land shall (so far as it is practicable to do so) be restored to its condition before development took place (with the carrying out of seeding and replanting so far as may be necessary).

Class XXVII.—Removal of material from mineral-working deposits

1. The removal of material of any description from a mineral-working deposit, where material has been extracted from the deposit, otherwise than in breach of planning control, at any time during the period of 12 months immediately preceding the date of the coming into operation of section 1 of the 1981 Act: Provided that—

(1) this permission does not authorise the carrying out of development after the end of the period of six months from the date of the coming into operation of section 1 of the 1981 Act, unless an application has been made, before the end of that period, for planning permission to continue to remove material from the deposit;

(2) where an application for permission to con-

Column (1) Description of Development	Column (2) Conditions

tinue to remove material from the deposit has been made before the end of the period described in proviso (1), this permission does not authorise the carrying out of any development after the date when that application is determined by the mineral planning authority or, in the event of an appeal to the Secretary of State, the date when that appeal is finally determined;
   (3) where an application for permission to continue to remove material from the deposit has been made before the end of the period described in proviso (1), this permission does not authorise the carrying out of any development other than the development described in the application.
   2.—(1) The removal of material of any description from a stockpile or a mineral-working deposit other than a stockpile which either—
     (i) covers a ground area not exceeding 2 hectares; or
     (ii) contains no mineral or other material which was deposited on the land more than 5 years before the date of removal;
Provided that:
  (*a*) this permission does not authorise the removal of material from any stockpile or other mineral-working deposit which derives from the carrying out of any operations permitted under class VI; and
  (*b*) no material shall be removed from a mineral-working deposit which is not a stockpile unless the developer has notified the mineral planning authority in writing of his intention to carry out development within this class, specifying the nature of that development, the exact location of the mineral-working deposit from which material is to be removed, the proposed means of vehicular access to the site at which the development is to be carried out and the earliest date at which any material presently contained in the deposit was deposited on the land, and the relevant period has elapsed.
   (2) The relevant period elapses:—
  (*a*) where the mineral planning authority do not issue a direction under article 4A:—
     (i) 28 days after the notification referred to in paragraph (*b*) of the proviso above, or
     (ii) if earlier, on the date on which the mineral planning authority notify the developer in writing that they will not issue such a direction;
	Where the development consists of the removal of material from a mineral-working deposit which is not a stockpile—
	   (1) it shall be carried out in accordance with the details given in the notice sent to the mineral planning authority in accordance with proviso (*b*) in column (1) except where the authority have otherwise agreed in writing;
	   (2) if the mineral planning authority so require, the developer shall submit to them for approval a scheme making provision for the restoration and aftercare of the site, such scheme to be submitted within such period as the authority may specify (which shall not be less than 3 months from the date when the requirement is made); and
	   (3) where submission of a scheme of restoration and aftercare has been required, the site shall be restored and aftercare shall be carried out in accordance with the provisions of such scheme (as

Column (1) Description of Development	Column (2) Conditions

(*b*) where the mineral planning authority issue a direction under article 4A:—
  (i) 28 days from the date on which the notice of it is sent to the Secretary of State, or
  (ii) if earlier, on the date on which the mineral planning authority notify the developer in writing that the Secretary of State has disallowed the direction.
	those provisions are approved).

Class XXVIII.—Warehouses

The extension or alteration of a building (whether erected before or after 1st July 1948) which is lawfully used as a warehouse, and which is to be used for that purpose, so long as:—

(*a*) the height of the original building is not exceeded;

(*b*) the cubic content of the original building (as ascertained by external measurement) is not increased by more than 25%, and its aggregate floor space is not increased by more than 1,000 square metres;

(*c*) the external appearance of the premises is not materially affected;

(*d*) no part of the building is, as a result of the development, within a distance of 5 metres from any boundary of the curtilage of the premises; and

(*e*) the development does not result in a decrease in the extent of any existing vehicle parking area or area laid out for the turning of vehicles:

Provided that the erection on land within the curtilage of an existing warehouse of an additional building to be used in connection with that warehouse shall be treated as an extension of the existing warehouse and, where any two or more existing buildings in the same curtilage are used as one unit for warehouse purposes, the references in paragraph (*b*) above to the cubic content and to the aggregate floor space shall be construed as references to the aggregate cubic content and the total floor space (respectively) of those buildings.

Class XXIX.—Amusement Parks

The carrying out of any of the following operations on land (or on a seaside pier) which is lawfully used as an amusement park:—

(*a*) the erection of any booths, stalls, other similar buildings or structures, or the installation of any plant or machinery (which expression, in

Column (1) Description of Development	Column (2) Conditions

this class, includes structures or erections in the nature of plant or machinery) to be used for or in connection with the provision in the amusement park of entertainment or amusement for the public;
(*b*) the extension, alteration or replacement of any plant or machinery, building or other structure so used;
so long as—
   (i) no plant or machinery installed, extended, altered or replaced pursuant to this permission exceeds a height of 25 metres above ground level (or, if the land or pier is within 3 kilometres of the perimeter of an aerodrome, 25 metres or the height of the highest existing structure, whichever is the lesser), and
  (iii) no other building or structure erected pursuant to this permission exceeds the height of 5 metres above ground level (or, in the case of an extension to a building or structure, 5 metres or the height of the roof of the existing building or of the structure, whichever is the greater),
and so long as no such operation is carried out within 25 metres of the curtilage of a dwelling.
 	
Class XXX.—Development by the Historic Buildings and Monuments Commission for England
Development of the following descriptions, by or on behalf of the Historic Buildings and Monuments Commission for England, required for the purpose of securing the preservation of any building or monument in the ownership, or under the guardianship, or otherwise under the control or management of the Commission:—
(*a*) the maintenance, repair or restoration (but excluding the extension) of any such building or monument;
(*b*) (insofar as the development is not permitted by sub-paragraph (*a*) above) the erection of structures of the nature of screens or covers, designed or intended to protect or safeguard such buildings or monuments (including any fencing which may be necessary for that purpose);
 	
(*c*) the carrying out of works for stabilising ground conditions of any cliff, water-course or the coastline.
	
	Such structures as are referred to in (*b*) shall be removed at the expiration of 6 months (or such longer period as the local authority may agree in writing) from the date on which work was commenced to erect them.

Appendix C

Modifications to the General Development Order in the special areas

1985 No. 1012

TOWN AND COUNTRY PLANNING, ENGLAND AND WALES

The Town and Country Planning (National Parks, Areas of Outstanding Natural Beauty and Conservation Areas, etc.) Special Development Order 1985 (SI 1985/1012) (as amended by SI 1986/8) modifies the effect of the general development order in the special areas.

Made	*3rd July 1985*
Laid before Parliament	*12th July 1985*
Coming into Operation	*1st November 1985*

The Secretary of State for the Environment, in exercise of the powers conferred on him by sections 24 and 287 of the Town and Country Planning Act 1971 (a) and of all other powers enabling him in that behalf, hereby makes the following order:—

1.—(1) This order shall apply to the following descriptions of land:—

    (*a*) land which, on the date when it comes into operation, is within a National Park;

    (*b*) land which, on the date when it comes into operation, is within an area of outstanding natural beauty designated by an order made by the Countryside Commission under section 87 of the National Parks and Access to the Countryside Act 1949 (b) and confirmed by the Secretary of State;

    (*c*) land which, on the date when it comes into operation, is within an area designated by a local planning authority as a

---

(a) 1971 c.78; section 24 was amended by paragraph 1 of Schedule 15 to the Local Government, Planning and Land Act 1980 (c.65) and extended by paragraph 53(2) of Schedule 4 to the Telecommunications Act 1984 (c.12).

(b) 1949 c.97.

(c) 1981 c.69.

(d) S.I. 1977/289; relevant amending instruments are S.I. 1980/1946, 1981/245 and 1983/1615.

conservation area, under the powers conferred by section 277 of the Town and Country Planning Act 1971;

(d) land which, on the date when it comes into operation, is within an area which has been specified by the Secretary of State and the Minister of Agriculture, Fisheries and Food for the purposes of section 41(3) of the Wildlife and Country-side Act 1981 (c).

(2) This order may be cited as the Town and Country Planning (National Parks, Areas of Outstanding Natural Beauty and Conservation Areas, etc.) Special Development Order 1985 and shall come into operation on 1st November 1985.

2. In this order, "the General Development Order" means the Town and Country Planning General Development Order 1977 (d); and expressions used in this order shall have, unless the contrary intention appears, the meaning which they bear in the General Development Order.

3. The General Development Order shall apply to the descriptions of land to which this order applies, subject to the following modifications to Schedule 1 (permitted development):—

(a) class I.1 (the enlargement, improvement or other alteration of a dwellinghouse) shall be subject to the following limitations and provisos in place of those set out:—

"(a) the cubic content of the original dwellinghouse (as ascertained by external measurement) is not exceeded by more than 50 cubic metres or ten per cent, whichever is the greater, subject to a maximum of 115 cubic metres;

(b) the height of the building as so enlarged, improved or altered does not exceed the height of the highest part of the roof of the original dwellinghouse;

(c) no part of the building as so enlarged, improved or altered projects beyond the forwardmost part of any wall of the original dwellinghouse which fronts on a highway;

(d) no part of the building (as so enlarged, improved or altered) which lies within a distance of two metres from any boundary of the curtilage of the dwellinghouse has, as a result of the development, a height exceeding four metres;

(e) the area of ground covered by buildings within the curtilage of the dwellinghouse (other than the original dwellinghouse) does not thereby exceed fifty per cent of the total area of the curtilage excluding the ground area of the original dwellinghouse:

Provided that:—

(a) the erection of a garage, stable, loosebox or coachhouse within the curtilage of the dwellinghouse shall be treated as the enlargement of the dwellinghouse for all purposes of this permission (including calculation of cubic content);

(b) for the purposes of this permission the extent to which the cubic content of the original dwellinghouse is exceeded shall be ascertained by deducting the amount of the cubic content of the original dwellinghouse from the amount of the cubic content of the dwellinghouse as enlarged, improved or altered (whether such enlargement, improvement or alteration was carried out in pursuance of this permission or otherwise); and

(c) the limitation contained in subparagraph (d) above shall not apply to development consisting of:—

(i) the insertion of a window (including a dormer window) into a wall or the roof of the original dwellinghouse, or the alteration or enlargement of an existing window; or

(ii) any other alterations to any part of the roof of the original dwellinghouse.";

(aa) class I.2A (the installation of satellite antennas on dwellinghouses and in the curtilages of dwellinghouses) shall not include the installation of a satellite antenna in such a position that any part of it, when installed, will be beyond the forwardmost part of any wall of the original dwellinghouse which fronts on a highway;";

(b) class I.3 (the erection and alteration of buildings and enclosures in the curtilage of a dwellinghouse) shall not include development consisting of the erection, construction or placing, or the maintenance, improvement or other alteration, of garages and coachhouses;

(c) in class VIII.1 (the carrying out of certain operations by industrial undertakers) the limitations on the cubic content and the aggregate floor space of buildings extended or altered pursuant to subparagraph (iv) shall be that:—

(i) the cubic content of the original building (as ascertained by external measurement) is not exceeded by more than ten per cent; and

(ii) the aggregate floor space of the original building is not exceeded by more than 500 square metres;

(cc) in class XVIII.E (development by electricity undertakings) the limitations on the extension or alteration of buildings shall be as follows, in place of those specified in sub-paragraph (iv):—

(i) the height of the original building shall not be exceeded; and

(ii) the cubic content of the original building (as ascertained by external measurement) shall not be increased by more than 10%, nor its aggregate floor space by more than 500 square metres;";

(d) class XXIV (development by telecommunications code system operators) shall be subject to an additional condition and an additional limitation, as follows:—

(1) in the case of the installation of apparatus on or over land which is occupied by the operator and in respect of which either—

(a) he is the estate owner in respect of the fee simple; or

(b) he holds a lease granted for a term of not less than 10 years, the operator shall (except in a case of emergency) give notice in writing to the local planning authority, not less than 8 weeks before the development is begun, of his intention to carry out such development; and where the operator needs to install apparatus on such land as a matter of emergency, he shall give written notice of such installation as soon as possible after the emergency begins; and

(2) nothing in the permission is to be construed as authorising (except in a case of emergency)—

    (a) the installation or alteration of a microwave antenna or of any apparatus which includes or is intended for the support of such an antenna; or

    (b) the replacement of such an antenna or such apparatus by an antenna or apparatus which differs in size, design, appearance or siting from that which is being replaced;

(e) class XXV (other telecommunications development) shall not apply.

(f) in class XXVIII (the extension and alteration of warehouses), the following paragraph shall be substituted for paragraph (b):—

"(b) the cubic content of the original building (as ascertained by external measurement) is not increased by more than 10% and its aggregate floor space is not increased by more than 500 square metres.

Index

A

PAGE

ABANDONMENT 26
    cessation 27
    intention 27
    length of time 27
    planning permission 95
    seasonal resumptions 28
ACTION AREA 61, 64, 88, 186
ACQUISITION OF LAND 185
    see COMPULSORY PURCHASE
ADOPTION
    sewers 252
    highways 262
ADVANCED PAYMENTS CODE 266, 267
ADMINISTRATIVE DECISIONS 236
    grounds of challenge 239
    Wednesbury principles 240
ADVERTISEMENTS .... 72, 131 et seq
    areas of special control 131, 133, 134, 136
    business premises 134
    compensation for restriction 136, 232
    conservation areas 123
    deemed consent 133
    defined 132
    discontinuance notices 133, 135
    exclusions from control 132
    express consent 133, 136
    illuminated 132, 133, 135
    judicial control 238
    offence 132
    purchase notice 210
    regulations 131
    specified classes 134
    temporary 134
    time limits 134
AGRICULTURE 82, 289
    areas of outstanding natural beauty 127
    buildings 42
    environmentally sensitive areas 129
    green belt 128
    horses 16
    management agreements 128

minerals 43, 82, 83
mineral extraction 148
sites of special scientific interest 127
AGRICULTURAL TENANT 76
ALLOTMENTS 16
ANCIENT MONUMENTS 55, 125, 229, 231
APPEALS .... 197 et seq
see also JUDICIAL REVIEW
caravans 155
call-in procedure 86
challenging planning conditions 101
development plans 236
diagram 245
discontinuance orders 162
enforcement notices 173, 179
inspector's reports 203
listed buildings 118, 121
locus standii 239
person aggrieved 237
preservation notices 180
secretary of state 198
statutory rights 236
time limit 198, 237
written representations 204
ARCHAEOLOGICAL AREAS 125
AREAS OF OUTSTANDING NATURAL BEAUTY 127
AREAS OF SPECIAL CONTROL 136
AREAS OF SPECIAL SCIENTIFIC INTEREST 83, 127

B

BETTERMENT .... 273 et seq
BETTERMENT RECAPTURE 112, 237
BENEFICIAL USE
see REASONABLY BENEFICIAL USE
BLIGHT 67, 209
BREACH OF PLANNING CONTROL 163, 171
BRIDLEWAYS 261, 269, 270
BRIDGES 264
BUILDING OPERATIONS 9, 43
compensation 275
enforcement 120, 164
internal 9
listed buildings 12, 118
outline planning permission 73
permitted 38
planning permission 97
public safety 264
units 18, 21, 24
BUILDING PRESERVATION NOTICE 119
compensation 229
enforcement 122
exempted building 122

C

CABLES 44
CALL-IN PROCEDURE 86, 121
CAMPING 28, 42
CARAVANS 10, 22, 41, 45, 143, 153
CARAVAN SITES 153
    conditions 155
    definition 154
    exemptions 154
    offences 155
CELLARS 264
CENTRAL LAND BOARD 220
CERTIORARI 107, 198, 238
CHANGE OF USE .... 15 et seq 41, 288
    see also MATERIAL CHANGE OF USE
CHURCH 122
CIRCULARS
    development plans 60
    material considerations 66, 86
    planning gain 112
    public local inquiry 206
COMMON LAW JUDICIAL REVIEW 235, 238
    certiorari 238
    prohibition 238
    mandamus 238
COMPENSATION .... 217 et seq
    advertisements 232
    amount 222
    ancient monuments 229
    any loss 228
    constitutional provision 218
    development order 226
    discontinuance orders 227, 229
    enforcement notice 233
    exception to right to compensation 222
    existing use development 223
    general development order 226
    listed buildings 229
    minerals 151
    nationalisation of development rights 270
    permitted development 46
    refusal of planning permission 215
    revocation and modification 160, 227
    right to 217, 222, 224, 225, 228
    royal prerogative 218
    stop notices ,,,, ... 232
    time limits 233
    tree preservation orders 231
COMPLETION NOTICES 98
COMPULSORY PURCHASE 181, 185
    see also COMPENSATION
    blight 209
    costs 206

    Land Authority for Wales 191
    planning decisions 209
    procedure 187
    purchase by agreement 186
    purchase notice 209
CONSERVATION AREAS .... 12, 43, 54, 55, 78, 83, 91, 117 et seq, 123, 289
    advertisements 125
    designation 123
    dwellinghouses 124
    general development order 124, 125
    industrial buildings 124
    legal consequences 123, 188
    planning applications 78, 123
    preservation 180
    publicity 78
    trees 147
COSTS AT INQUIRY 206
COUNTRYSIDE 126
COUNTRYSIDE COMMISSION 126
COUNTY MATTER 53, 83, 95
CRANE 9
CROSS-EXAMINATION 201, 202
CROWN 187

D

DECLARATION 107, 112, 198, 239
DELEGATION 56
DEMOLITION 12
    conservation areas 123
    listed buildings 119, 121
DENMAN D. 60, 184
DETERMINATION 57
DEVELOPMENT 7
    abandonment 26
    acquisition 185
    agriculture 16
    ancillary and multiple uses 23, 25
    building operations 9
    change of use 15, 20, 35, 88, 171
    compensation 217
    conservation areas 78
    control 15
    demolition 12
    development plans 59, 66, 78
    division of a dwellinghouse 19
    engineering operations 10
    exclusions 8, 15, 17, 32, 285
    forestry 16
    general development order 285
    highways 84
    industrial purposes 44, 291
    intensification 18, 22
    listed buildings 28

local plans 61, 63
meaning of 7
minerals 149, 303
mining operations 10, 28
nationalisation 220
permitted development 37
planning application 69
planning conditions 93
planning unit 24, 31
public authorities 183
seasonal resumptions 28
simplified planning zones 47
special development orders 47
structure plans 60
tipping 11, 19
use classes order 17, 277
DEVELOPMENT CHARGE 223, 274
DEVELOPMENT CONTROL 15
development plans 59
exclusions 15
planning application 69
pre-1964 32
DEVELOPMENT CONTROL POLICY NOTES 86, 88
DEVELOPMENT LAND TAX 274
DEVELOPMENT PLANS 59, 85
action area plans 61
blight 67
challenging a plan 68, 236
compulsory purchase 67
county level 60
discontinuance orders 161
district level 61, 63
effect of 87
judicial review 238
legal consequences 66
legal requirements 61
local plans 63
meaning of 66
old type 60
public participation 62
role of 66
structural plan 60
survey 61
unitary 65
DIRECTIONS 85, 86
DISABLED PERSON 71
DISCONTINUANCE NOTICES 135, 210
DISCONTINUANCE ORDERS 161
compensation 229
judicial review 237
objections 162
purchase notice 210
DISPOSAL OF LAND 186, 192
DISTRICT PLANS 64

DWELLING HOUSES 16, 18
    ancillary 42
    building incidental to 46
    caravans 154
    divisions 19
    fees 70
    units 26
    use 21
    within curtilage of 38, 285

E

ECCLESIASTICAL BUILDINGS... 122, 124
ECONOMIC CONSIDERATIONS 89, 91
ELECTRICITY .... 255 et seq
    supply 258
EMPLOYMENT AGENCY 104
ENFORCEMENT .... 163 et seq
    building operations 166
    breach of planning control 163
    conditions 167
    enforcement notice 169
    engineering operations 166
    four-year rule 166
    injunction 178
    intensification 171
    listed buildings 179
    material change of use 171
    mining operations 169
    prosecution 176
    stop notice 177
    under enforcement 170
ENFORCEMENT NOTICE .... 163 et seq
    appeals 173
    challenging validity 107, 169, 179, 243
    clarity 171
    compensation 233
    contents 169
    continuing effect 179
    costs 207
    fees 71
    Mansi principle 171
    over enforcement 170
    stop notice 177
    time limit 170
ENGINEERING OPERATIONS
    meaning 10, 43
ENTERPRIZE ZONES 137
    adaption of 138
    challenge 138
    designation 139
    finance 140
    planning permission 139
    publicity 137

ENVIRONMENTALLY SENSITIVE AREAS 129
ERROR OF LAW 240
ESTABLISHED USE CERTIFICATES 33
    abolition of 35
    intensification 34
ESTOPPEL 56
EVIDENCE 203
EXCLUSIONS 8, 15, 17
EXISTING USE DEVELOPMENT 223
EXISTING USE RIGHTS 30
EXPERT WITNESS 201, 202

F

FEES 70
    calculation 73
    enforcement notices 173
    exceptions 70
    listed buildings 120
FENCES 40
FLOODLIGHTS 10
FOOTPATHS 261, 268, 269, 270
FORESTRY 16, 43, 291
    see trees, Tree Preservation Orders
FOUR YEAR RULE 165
FRANKS COMMITTEE 200

G

GARAGE 39
GAS .... 255 et seq
    supply 257
GREEN BELTS 128, 206
GENERAL DEVELOPMENT ORDER 17, 188, 285, 317
    agricultural buildings, works & uses 289
    appeals 198
    Article 4 Directions 46
    changes of use 40, 288
    conservation areas 124
    determination of planning application 81
    dwelling house 38, 285
    fees 71
    forestry buildings & works 43, 291
    garage 38, 285
    industrial purposes 44, 291
    mineral workings 149, 303
    miscellaneous 45, 292
    planning permission conditions 38, 41
    planning permission 93, 224
    porch 38, 285
    publicity for planning gain 76
    Secretary of State 56
    sundry minor operations 40
    time limit 198

H

HAWKE JN 110
HAZARDOUS MATERIALS 141
HIGHWAYS .... 261 et seq
    adoption 265
    diversion 268
    highway authority 84, 262
    obstructions & interferences 263
    private streets 266
    public nuisance 263
    statutory provisions 262
    stopping up 268
HIGHWAY AUTHORITY 82, 84, 191, 250
HISTORIC BUILDINGS & MONUMENTS COMMISSION 117
HOARDINGS 264
HORSES 18, 261

I

INDUSTRIAL BUILDINGS 17, 44
INDUSTRIAL PURPOSES 44, 291
INJUNCTION 178, 242
INQUIRIES .... 197 et seq
    see also public local inquiries
INSPECTOR 198
    see also public local inquiries
    decision 205
    reasons 205, 242
    site inspection 202
INTEREST 229

J

JUDICIAL REVIEW .... 86, 92, 235 et seq
    see also administrative decisions
    advertisements 237
    common law rights 238
    diagram 245
    discontinuance orders 237
    error of law 240
    listed buildings 237
    locus standi 237, 239
    person agrieved 237
    prerogative orders 238
    purchase notice 238
    revocation & modification orders 237
    statutory grounds 238
    tree preservation order 237
    ultra vives 237
JUDICIAL SUPERVISION 240
JUSTICE REPORT 219

L

LAND AUTHORITY FOR WALES 191
    function 191
    power of acquisition 192
    sewers 192
LANDS TRIBUNAL 111, 128, 228, 229
LAND VALUE 221, 228
LISTED BUILDINGS .... 8, 12, 55, 70, 78, 91, 117 et seq
    building preservation notice 119, 122
    certificate of immunity 118
    compensation 229
    compulsory purchase 181
    conditions & time limits 121
    demolition 119
    enforcement 122, 179
    listing 117
    meaning 118
    planning permission 120
    preservation 180
    purchase notice 210
    revocation & modification 230
LISTED BUILDING ENFORCEMENT NOTICE 179
LOCAL OMBUDSMAN 164
LOCAL PLANNING AUTHORITIES .... 51 et seq
    advertisements 136
    ancient monuments 125
    appeals 198
    circulars 87
    conservation areas 123
    compensation 224
    completion notice 98
    compulsory purchase 181
    delegation 56
    determinations 20, 97
    development 186
    development plan 60, 78, 85, 87
    discontinuance orders 161
    distribution of functions 52
    enforcement 163, 173
    Established Use Certificates 35
    estoppel 56, 57
    fees 70
    General Development Order 37, 188, 285
    hazardous materials 141
    highways 261
    injunction 178
    listed building consent 119
    listed building enforcement notice 179
    local plans 61, 63
    material considerations 67, 87
    mineral compensation 152
    ministerial policy 37
    national parks 126

negligence 57
outline planning permission 73
planning agreements 108
planning conditions 99
private interest in planning application 76
public local inquiry 197
public participation 62
purchase notice 209, 213
register of land 192
removal of powers 57
revocation & modification 159
scientific interest 127
Secretary of State 55
sewers 250
simplified planning zones 47
Special Development Order 47
stop notices 177
structure plans 60
survey 61
Tree Preservation Orders 143
LOCAL PLANS 61, 63, 83
    see also development plans
    adoption of 65
    Unitary Development Plans 65

M

MANAGEMENT AGREEMENTS 128, 129
MANDAMUS 238, 249
MANSI PRINCIPLE 171
MARKETS 41
MATERIAL CHANGE OF USE
    see change of use
    abandonment 26
    agriculture 16
    ancillary & multiple uses 23, 25
    determinations 20
    forestry 16
    itensification 18, 21, 22
    material considerations 87
    meaning of 20
    planning permission unnecessary 35
    planning unit 24
    substantial difference 21
    tipping 11, 19
    Use Classes Order 17, 277
MATERIAL CONSIDERATIONS
    circulars 86, 206
    development plans 66
    economic 89
    encouraging uses 90
    future decisions 90
    non-statutory policies 91
    other 87, 91

preserving uses 90
public local inquiry 205
MIDDLE TEMPLE 55
MINERALS 53, 143, 148
    discontinuance order 151
    mineral planning authority 148
    prohibition order 151
    restoration condition 151
    Stevens committee 148
    suspension order 151
MINERAL OPERATIONS 72
    see mining operations
    compensation 151
    conditions 149
    duration 150
    notification 149
    permitted development 149, 303
    positive planning powers 150
MINING OPERATIONS 11, 28
    see mineral operations
    definition 148
    Four Year rule 166
    modification 160
MINISTERIAL DECISIONS 11, 27, 44, 153, 207, 212
MINISTERIAL PLANNING AUTHORITY 148
MINISTERIAL POLICY
    permitted development 37
    Simplified Planning Zones 38
MODIFICATION
    see revocation order

N

NATIONAL PARKS 38, 55, 126, 136, 143
NATURAL JUSTICE 188, 199, 203, 206, 238, 241
NATURE CONSERVANCY COUNCIL 128
NEGLIGENCE 57
    estoppel 56
NEW DEVELOPMENT 220
NEW TOWNS 189
    see Urban Development Areas
NEW TOWN DEVELOPMENT CORPORATION 55
NON-COMPLIANCE 244
NOTICE TO TREAT 215
    see also purchase notice

O

OBJECTORS 204
OFFICES 17
OFFICE DEVELOPMENT PERMITS 131
OPERATIONS 8
    building 9, 43
    definition 9

    engineering 10, 43
    mining 10
    ministerial decision 11
    other 11
    tipping 11
OUTLINE PLANNING PERMISSION 73, 74

P

PAINTING 41
PARISH COUNCILS 52, 84, 201, 267, 268
PARTNERSHIP SCHEME 188
PERSON AGGRIEVED 237
PERMITTED DEVELOPMENT .... 37 et seq
    classes of 38
    compensation 46
    General Development Order 38, 285
    purchase notice 210
    Simplified Planning Zones 38
PETROL FILLING STATIONS 29, 106, 134
PLANNING ADVISORY GROUP 60
PLANNING AGREEMENTS 93, 108
    discharge/modification 111
    enforcement 110
    planning gain 112
    public planning 111
    scope 109
    statutory powers 109
PLANNING APPEALS
    see Appeals
PLANNING APPLICATION 69
    compensation 217
    determination of 81
    fees 70
    farm 69
    outline 73
    publicity 76
    purchase notice 210
PLANNING AUTHORITY
    see local planning authority
PLANNING CONDITIONS 93, 96, 99
    applicable 102, 105
    certainty 103
    challenging of planning conditions 107
    compensation 224
    existing rights 104
    legality 100, 106
    listed buildings 121
    negative 105
    planning purpose 103
    purchase notice 210
    statutory power 99
    unreasonableness 101
PLANNING DECISIONS 209

PLANNING GAIN 112
PLANNING OFFICER 57
PLANNING PERMISSION .... 93 et seq
    Article 4 Directions 37, 46
    buildings 97
    caravans 154
    certificate of immunity 118
    change of use 31, 35
    compensation 217
    conditions 99, 168
    consultation 82
    development 7
    development order 226
    discontinuance order 229
    effect of 95
    enforcement 164
    enterprize zones 138
    established use certificates 34
    exclusions 32
    extinguishing a use 25
    fees on applications 70
    general development order 31
    inconsistencies 95, 97
    listed buildings 120
    meaning 93
    nationalization of planning permission 220
    notice of decision 94
    notice to owners & tenants 75
    outline 73, 98
    previous lawful use 28, 36
    purpose 30
    refusal of planning permission 219, 226
    revocation and modification 227
    Secretary of State 55
    Simplified Planning Zones 47
    Special Development Orders 47
    temporary planning permission 34
    time limit 75, 98
PLANNING UNIT 24, 31
PLANT & MACHINERY 9, 41, 43, 54
POLICY
    see Ministerial Policy
    grounds of challenge 239
    inquiries 205, 206
POLLUTION 141
PRIVATE LAW ACTIONS 178, 242
PRIVATE STREETS 266
    advance payment code 267
PREROGATIVE ORDERS 238
PROHIBITION 238
PROOF OF EVIDENCE 202
PROPERTY ADVISORY GROUP 112
PROPERTY RIGHTS 217
    see compensation

PUBLIC AUTHORITIES .... 183 et seq
    local planning authority 188
    register of land 192
    statutory undertakers 188
    The Crown 187
PUBLIC LOCAL INQUIRY .... 65, 197 et seq
    conduct 199
    costs 206
    Franks Committee 200
    Inspector 198
    notification of decision 203
    procedure 200, 206
    representation 198, 201
    site inspection 202, 205
    written representations 204
PUBLIC PARTICIPATION 62, 138, 198
    see public local inquiry
PURCHASE NOTICE .... 209 et seq
    advertisements 210
    discontinuance order 210
    judicial review 214
    listed buildings 210
    modification 210
    planning applications 210
    procedure 214
    revocation 210
    trees 210

Q

QUESTION OF FACT 7, 8, 10, 18, 20, 203

R

REALISED DEVELOPMENT VALUE 274
REASONS 205, 242
REASONABLY BENEFICIAL USE 209
    examples 214
    meaning 211
    prospective use 213
RECOUPMENT 273
REPAIRS NOTICE 180
REPRESENTATION 62, 199, 201
REQUISITION
    electricity 259
    sewers 256
    water 256
RESERVED MATTERS 73
RESTAURANT 20
RESTRICTIVE COVENANTS 111, 128
REVOCATION & MODIFICATION ORDERS .... 159 et seq
    compensation 160, 223
    development order 226
    procedure 159

purchase notice 210
ROYAL PREROGATIVE 218

S

SCAFFOLDING 264
SECRETARY OF STATE
    advertisements 131, 135
    ancient monuments 125
    betterment 274
    building preservation notice 119, 180
    certificate of immunity 118
    challenging planning conditions 107
    circulars 56, 86
    compensation 222
    compulsory purchase 185
    decisions 205
    delegation 56
    determinations 81, 197
    development plans 59
    directions & policy guidance 85, 188
    discontinuance order 161
    enforcement notice 173, 243, 244
    enterprize zones 137
    fees 70
    highways 84
    listed building consent 121, 230
    local plans 64
    material considerations 67, 87
    new towns 189
    planning agreement 111
    powers of 193
    public local inquiries 200
    purchase notice 211, 212
    reasons 242
    register of land 192
    revocation & modification orders 160
    scientific interest 128
    structure plans 62
    urban development area 189
SEWERS .... 249 et seq
    adoption 252
    adoption agreement 253
    connection 253
    definition 249
    procedure 254
    requisition 192, 251
SHOP 17
SIMPLIFIED PLANNING ZONES 47
    objections to 48
SITE INSPECTION 202
SKIPS 263
SPECIAL DEVELOPMENT ORDERS 47, 56, 125, 127
STATEMENTS 200

STATUTORY UNDERTAKERS 188, 190
STEVENS COMMITTEE 148
STOP NOTICE 177
    compensation 232
STOPPING UP & DIVERSION OF HIGHWAYS 268
STRUCTURE PLANS 60
    see also development plans
    action areas 61
    preparation 61
    public participation 62
    unitary development plan 65
SUBMISSIONS 200
SUPERMARKET 75, 100

T

TIPPING 11, 19, 54, 167
TREE PRESERVATION ORDERS 143
    compensation 231
    confirmation 146
    contravention 144
    notification 145
    procedure 145
TREES 124, 143
    see Tree Preservation Orders
    conservation areas 147
    defined 144
    felling 147
    purchase notice 210
    replacement 147
    value for compensation 232

U

ULTRA VIRES 239
    illegality 240
    irrationality 240
    procedural impropriety 240
    reasons 242
    Wednesbury principles 240
UNITARY DEVELOPMENT PLANS 65
UNITED STATES CONSTITUTION 218
UNEXPENDED BALANCE OF ESTABLISHED DEVELOPMENT VALUE 220
URBAN DEVELOPMENT AREAS 189
    planning control 190
    urban development corporation 189
URBAN DEVELOPMENT CORPORATION
    see urban development areas 189
USE
    see material change at use
USE CLASSES ORDER .... 15, 17 et seq, 23, 277
UTHWATT REPORT 1942 273

V

VESTING DECLARATION 252

W

WALKWAY 265
WAREHOUSE 18, 73, 102, 118, 172
WASTE DISPOSAL 53, 77, 83, 84, 147
WATER .... 255 et seq
    non-domestic purposes 257
    requisition of 256
    supply 255
WATER AUTHORITY 249
    powers 251, 253
WATER SUPPLY 255
    communication pipe 255
    costs 256
    domestic purposes 255
    duty to supply 255
    necessary mains 256
    non-domestic purposes 257
    requisition rights 256
    service pipe 255
WRITTEN REPRESENTATIONS 204